MAYWOOD PUBLIC LIBRARY
459 Maywood Ave.
Maywood, NJ 07607

Nightwalkers

D1597072

Nightwalkers

Gothic Horror Movies

The Modern Era

BRUCE LANIER WRIGHT

TAYLOR PUBLISHING COMPANY

DALLAS, TEXAS

ALSO BY
BRUCE LANIER WRIGHT:

Yesterday's Tomorrows:
The Golden Age of Science Fiction Movie Posters

Copyright © 1995 Bruce Lanier Wright

All rights reserved.

No part of this book may be reproduced in any form or by any means—including photocopying and use of all electronic devices—without written permission from the publisher.

Published by Taylor Publishing Company
1550 West Mockingbird Lane
Dallas, Texas 75235

Photograph facing title page of Ingrid Pitt in *The Vampire Lovers*

Designed by David Timmons

Library of Congress Cataloging-in-Publication Data
Wright, Bruce Lanier
    Nightwalkers : gothic horror movies : the modern era / Bruce Lanier
Wright.
        p.   cm.
    Includes bibliographical references and index.
    ISBN 0-87833-979-9
    1. Horror films—History and criticism. I. Title.
  PN1995.9H6W73 1995
791.43'6116—dc20   95-4858
                                                          CIP

Printed in the United States of America
10 9 8 7 6 5 4 3 2 1

791.43
WRI

For Laura, who made it possible.

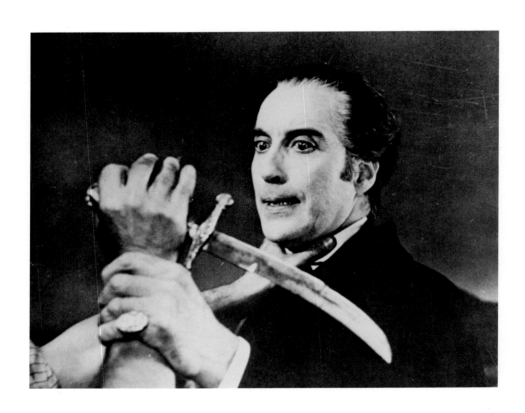

Contents

ACKNOWLEDGMENTS

As always, some very good people helped make this book possible. I would like to thank Dick Klemensen, Hammer expert number one, for sharing his valuable knowledge on the origins and endings of Hammer Film Productions, and his kindness in reviewing this manuscript; and Parker Riggs, the Vampire King of Houston, Texas, for allowing me to borrow rare resources from his mountainous collection. I also owe David Welling and Mark and Laura Shaw big-time for giving me access to other vital materials. Thanks to Russ Lanier, he knows why. Kudos again to Jeff Rowe of Austin Prints for Publication, for top-notch photographic assistance. And, of course, my deepest thanks to my wife, Laura, and adorable baby Samantha for tolerating my little obsessions.

"...IN THE EXCRUCIATINGLY EXCITING DARK SHADOWS OF SATURDAY NIGHT..."

—JACK KEROUAC, *Dr. Sax*

Nightwalkers

In

BEAMINSTER CHURCHYARD

o what *is* horror, anyway?
Mind you, I'm not much
more interested in semantic
questions than most people.
But the word could be defined
with more rigor, particularly in
connection with so-called horror movies.
Leafing through a few popular works on the
subject, I come across *Jaws* and *Psycho; Chopping
Mall, The Toolbox Murders,* and assorted slasher
movies; *Godzilla,* of all things, and *Night of the
Lepus,* a giant-bunny yarn. Clearly, any definition
broad enough to encompass all these titles must
be very nearly without meaning. (And if their
sole common feature, mayhem, is enough to
constitute a horror film, why don't we just put
The Dirty Dozen in there too?)

I think I define 'horror' a little differently
than most, and that definition may help justify

an apparently odd conviction of mine; that genuine horror movies are fairly rare today. To
explain, I'd like to begin by exercising the
author's privilege of telling a personal anecdote
in more detail than it may deserve.

I go to Britain fairly often, and I usually
travel by the back roads, dividing my time
between pubs and stone circles, sacred wells,
ruined fortresses, cobbled closes, and avoiding,
as best I can, Ye Olde tourist traps that the
British, curiously, do so very badly. I seem to be
looking for places with atmosphere, whatever we
mean by that overused word; some just-palpable
sense of other days and ways of life, of *deep* time
and vague menace, that lingers on in a few lonely spots.

One such place is in a village called
Beaminster, in the rolling hills of western
Dorset. The area is a peaceful, woody landscape

BEAMINSTER CHURCHYARD. (*PHOTOGRAPHY BY THE AUTHOR.*)

of copses, fields, and hedgerows, with greens brilliant enough to hurt your eyes on a sunny day. Beaminster itself is an intimate collection of gray and russet-colored stone, and in its center is the fifteenth-century parish church of St. Mary's, an attractively somber pile that is, I suppose, not greatly different from many another of its kind, in appearance or historical significance.

Still, it's haunted, some say, which is what brought me to Beaminster in the first place, some years back.

Most British haunts have an accompanying tale, and this one is sad if sketchy. Two centuries ago, more or less, a young boy from the village named John Daniel was murdered, and the crime only discovered after his specter appeared to various schoolmates and neighbors. His killer was never caught, and for this reason, presumably, his spirit is unable to rest. According to some versions of the story, he still appears in the church's vicinity each June 27. Not exactly a courtroom standard of proof, I agree.

Without putting much credence in the story, I do think there's something strange about the place. A man I know was working alone on the church's tower clock one evening some years ago, when footsteps came thudding quite loudly up the staircase—and, as you've already guessed, there was no one on the stairs, or anywhere else in the church. You mull over stories like these when you find yourself standing in Beaminster's small churchyard, listening to the crows grumble among half-toppled and weather-eaten headstones that lean this way and that, like broken teeth. Sounds from the village and nearby traffic always seem muted here, as if muffled by the place's damp antiquity.

I passed through Beaminster again just before I began this book; I was traveling with a friend, an avid photographer, and I'd wanted to show him the churchyard. We pondered the site for awhile, near dusk on a cloudy autumn day, then fortified ourselves against the evening chill, as it were, with Palmer's Ale (and hello to everyone at the Eight Bells). It was Real Country Dark when we strolled back to our car, bound for lodgings some miles away. We saw from a distance that the churchyard gate had not yet been locked, and thought we'd take one last turn through the grounds. We thought this all the way up to the gate. Beyond lay the cemetery, in absolute blackness. We hovered in the gateway for a minute; the night air was cool and electric.

Are you there, Johnnie boy? Are you there, now?

Then we both laughed and walked away. I felt elated, and energized in a peculiar way, and I knew as a cold fact that *bull elephants* could not have persuaded me to enter that churchyard just then.

✠   ✠   ✠

When you're afraid of a ghost, what is it you're afraid of?

The definition of *horror*, in the sense I mean, can begin with this question. I think it's safe to assume you are *not* worried the ghost will pull a knife. And even if you believe in ghosts, folklore gives us little reason to think they pose any threat to your immortal soul—assuming you believe in that, too. So, again: what are you afraid of?

I think there are *two* kinds of fear.

The first kind is the body-fear you've known since the first time you burned your fingers as a child—the fear of pain, of injury, when you become a bit more aware of dying. All our dark-alley shudders over violent accident, over the prospect of rape, assault, or murder, express the same fear animals know. It's mammalian instinct, written in our genes, intensely personal but older and deeper than personality. Let's call it *terror*. Terror can be a perfectly valid inspiration for entertainment, obviously. Danger at a safe distance forms the basis of most suspense stories, and was as much the driving impulse behind a classic like *Psycho* as it is for what Roger Ebert calls dead-teenager cinema.

Horror is something quite different, and far more rare. Again, it wasn't fear of injury that kept me out of Beaminster churchyard. (This was England, for God's sake. Their prisons are safer than our malls.) I wasn't thinking about my safety. I don't think I was thinking of myself at all. Horror is a fear unconnected to thoughts of your personal welfare. Horror has nothing to do with you, in that respect. Horror is *impersonal*.

You fear a madman because he might harm you. You fear a ghost, if you happen to find yourself doing so, simply because of its existence—which is a crucial distinction of horror, I think.

An element of awe is always present in true horror. Animals feel terror, but they can't experience horror; it's a human sensibility, a peculiarly intellectual fear. In effect, horror tells us that our maps of "reality" are incomplete, that some impossible thing can in fact happen. The inexplicable tends to awaken a nebulous sort of panic in us, a suspicion that the universe is even stranger and more uncertain than we had imagined it to be. Humans don't like that feeling much, not at first hand.

PETER CUSHING AS VICTOR FRANKENSTEIN, CREATING NEW LIFE IN HAMMER'S *THE EVIL OF FRANKENSTEIN* (1964).

a large and somewhat sluggish psychopath? Again, the horror doesn't spring from what these monsters *do*, but what they *are*—the dead moving among us, deadness made animate. Nightwalkers.

And the thought of these reliable standbys of traditional horror leads me to a final puzzle concerning Beaminster churchyard: that this ancient place, so utterly unlike anything in my everyday life, should seem *familiar* to me. *Real* crumbling tombs and brooding towers are fairly scarce today, at least in the world's more comfortable corners; but we still know them well as the props and stage settings for a specifically Western cultural phenomenon, the myth-pattern that we've come to call Gothic horror.

Our most common horrific thoughts, of course, revolve around that abrupt blackness that closes our little windows of consciousness, which are all we possess: Lights out, everybody. The first unthinkable and truly horrifying idea, for the reasonably sensitive mind, is that *all* thinking will stop for good, and our bodies will feed the grass. As a kid, coming to grips with the thought, I used to lie awake at night, trying to imagine not being. I couldn't do it. It's the thing that defines us as human: the human is the animal that knows he must die.

And yet this is only half of it, after all. There's another side to our dread of death, another midnight thought, that seemingly impossible idea behind nearly all earthly religion and folklore: Do the dead ever return?

An early lesson: fear of dying is terror. Fear of *being* dead, fear *of* the dead, of *deadness*, is horror. It's a great and fundamental irony, that we can fear the dead as much as death. The only thing that horrifies us as much as death is those who somehow escape it.

Like terror, horror can be transmuted into entertainment, and when it's done well, the result is something close to wonder. It's a much more difficult task, though. Horror as pleasure is a fragile mood, difficult to sustain, and one that requires our active sympathy. Do all the films in this book succeed in generating horror? Good Lord, no. But they *are* linked and defined by a specifically horrific intent. Absent the element of horror, after all, what is Dracula, but Ted Bundy in formal wear? Or Frankenstein's monster, but

⁜   ⁜   ⁜

And just what do we mean by "Gothic?"

While tales of terror are as old as the *Odyssey*—as old as man, I guess—horror as pleasure is a surprisingly recent innovation. Naturally, some horror enthusiasts like to give the tradition more of a pedigree, and certainly there are horrific episodes in Greek myth, Dante, and so forth. But the tale of horror intended to entertain, rather than to admonish or induce piety, is only a little more than two centuries old.

Horror entertainment emerged from a more general flowering of human imagination prompted by the invention and immediate popularity of the modern novel, beginning with the publication of Samuel Richardson's *Pamela* in 1740. The renegade philosopher Colin Wilson has called this event, with only a bit of hyperbole, "the dividing line between [the] world of the past and our own world"—by which he refers to the West's sudden discovery that works of imagination could be a source of amusement and wonder, a way to escape the dreariness of day-to-day reality. Before *Pamela*, "popular" writing consisted almost entirely of volumes of collected sermons and documentary accounts of crimes and disasters; a few years later, literally *hundreds* of novels were being written, all over the continent.

A byproduct of this ferment of emotion and imagination was a sudden, unprecedented fascination with picturesquely ancient things and places. The Renaissance had looked backward as well, but with an eye to reviving and *reproducing* the glories of the ancient world, not to revel in its broken remnants. Renaissance writers such as Vasari initially used the term Gothic as an insult, a generalized (and historically inaccurate) name for the medieval architecture they considered inferior to Greco-Roman styles. The eighteenth century turned this idea on its head by embracing antiquity as a positive quality, and enthusiastically slapping the Gothic label on any tumbledown abbey or faded tapestry that took its fancy. For the first time, antiques and ruins were appreciated and admired precisely *because* of, and not despite, their condition.

No one adopted this fashion for things ancient more exuberantly than England's Horace Walpole, an indefatigable collector of medieval bric-a-brac who helped spread the Gothic craze throughout English and continental society. Today, he's remembered primarily for taking the Gothic trend beyond decor and affectation and weaving it into imaginative literature, by writing history's first Gothic novel, *The Castle of Otranto* (1764). *Otranto* is nearly unreadable now, for all save the specialist, but even so it's obviously the progenitor of a great many of the someday-clichés of Gothic horror, including ancient prophecies, mouldering castles and crypts, eerie subterranean passages, and animated skeletons.

Within a few more decades, the Gothic novel would become an industry, producing hundreds of works filled with ghosts, mad dukes, violent sexual obsession and seduction, family curses, and barrel-loads of supernatural revenge. The peak years of the Gothic boom—roughly the two decades straddling the end of the eighteenth century and the beginning of the nineteenth—created essentially all the settings and furnishings of Gothic horror. All that was needed was a cast of durable characters to inhabit and use them.

This was largely accomplished in June 1816, during the celebrated party at Villa Diodati, on the shores of Lake Geneva in Switzerland. This unusually fruitful literary gathering included the poet Percy Bysshe Shelley; his mistress and soon-to-be wife, Mary Godwin, better known today as Mary Shelley; and the most infamous man in Europe, George Gordon, Lord Byron. Byron's famous suggestion that they each write a ghost story to while away a rainy week led directly to the creation of Mary Shelley's *Frankenstein*. Less generally known is the fact that it also spurred the first literary vampire tale in English, "The Vampyre," by Byron's personal physician, John Polidori. Both *Frankenstein* and "The Vampyre" proved wildly popular and spurred numerous stage adaptations in England and on the Continent. Byron's own attempt at a story went nowhere, but he still proved extremely important to the development of Gothic horror, as a role model for the all-purpose Gothic villain.

By this time, Byron was already a cause for gossip, scandal, and admiration throughout Europe. Born into threadbare gentility, he began life as a lonely, club-footed child and through talent and will transformed himself into his own most memorable character—the protean artist, gloomy and guilt-ridden; the irresistible seducer of women and boys; defier of heaven, breaker of taboos, self-dramatist par excellence; master of the grand and foolish gesture—history's first rock star, more or less. There is much of Byron in Victor Frankenstein's magnificently blasphemous ambition, and Polidori's vampire, Lord Ruthven, was explicitly modeled on the poet. When Bram Stoker created the most famous vampire of all, Count Dracula, some eighty years later, he consciously or unconsciously gave the count a full range of suitably Byronic traits.

Thus, well before the mid-nineteenth century, Gothic horror had coalesced into a definite art form (if one of only sporadic merit), and the prototypical characters conceived at Villa Diodati—the charming fiend with a remnant of humanity and the pitiable monster—would reappear repeatedly, in varying guises. Across the Atlantic, Edgar Allan Poe added his own distinctive obsessions, while remaining firmly within the basic parameters laid down by British goth-icists. From the "insufferable gloom" of the melancholy House of Usher, whose "principal feature seemed to be that of an excessive antiquity," crumbling and rotting with fungi, to the grim and excessive passion of the unnamed narrator of "Ligeia," Poe's palette is taken almost entirely from the language and imagery of an already vital Gothic tradition.

Nearly a century later, America's other great master of horror, H. P. Lovecraft, would take the Gothic deeper into time and farther into space than ever before. Lovecraft too, nonetheless, inhabited a familiar Gothic territory, in which "the massed mould and decay of centuries" holds its own secret horror, and human life itself is only an unimportant speck in an unimaginably malign universe—"a placid island of ignorance in the midst of the black seas of infinity."

Lovecraft brought the Gothic myth into the twentieth century, but in a form that, in its essentials, would have been easily recognizable to Horace Walpole. Indeed, perhaps the most interesting thing about Gothic horror is its remarkable consistency over more than two hundred years. The Gothic has become as formalized as religion, and its symbols have penetrated deeply enough into Western culture to produce a conditioned 'horrific' response in most of us, even though precious few still have any actual experience with the settings and character types behind its clichés. The Gothic survives as a separate mental landscape even as it disappears from the so-called real world.

✣   ✣   ✣

But the development of Gothic horror hasn't been smooth or uninterrupted. Horror may be eternal, but the public's fascination with Gothic seems to come and go in definite cycles. The initial boom in Gothic novels, around the turn of the nineteenth century, was certainly the first such cycle. The enormous popularity of the ghost story in America and Britain at the end of the Victorian period might constitute another.

The continuing vitality of Gothic horror in the twentieth century, however, is largely due to

BARON MEINSTER, THE CHARMING VAMPIRE OF HAMMER'S EXCELLENT *BRIDES OF DRACULA* (1960).

its popularity in film. The Gothic mood, so full of exaggeration and overheated passion, is difficult to sustain in cold print, but it's ideally suited for the hypnotic world of the darkened theater. Since Edison's day, the movies have never been entirely devoid of Gothic horror (with the possible exception of the bone-dry years immediately following World War II); nevertheless, in terms of both quantity and significance, the bulk of the century's output falls into two distinct waves. The first ran from the early 1920s through the mid-1940s, encompassing a handful of German silent classics such as *Nosferatu* and the prolific horror output of America's Universal studios and its imitators. The second began in 1957 and ran through 1976, a period more or less corresponding to the rise and fall of the era's greatest producer of Gothic horror movies, Britain's Hammer studios.

As for why this should be the case, it's fairly easy to see some striking similarities among the eras in which Gothic entertainment has been most popular. The first Gothic cycle peaked as the smug certainties of the Age of Reason were coming adrift amid revolution and continent-wide war; the ghost story reached its apogee near the chaotic conclusion of an equally self-satisfied period. The initial movie-based cycle was initiated largely by German filmmakers, as the Weimar Republic rotted around them. Many of these same talents, as exiles from their own land, helped to fertilize the horror industry in the United States, just as the nation sank into the Great Depression. The 1957–76 Gothic wave grew out of a whole familiar catalog of disillusionment—H-bombs, assassinations, Vietnam, the Day the Music Died; you know the drill.

It seems to me that, for each of these eras, the Gothic has expressed a sort of spiritual dissatisfaction with contemporary life, a longing for a wider, deeper reality. A characteristic of the Gothic mind-set seems to be an anxiety about the future, and a slightly perverse nostalgia for a time when mankind knew less and dreamed more. Gothic horror is timeless. It insists upon the reality of mysteries older and deeper than ourselves. It offers clearly defined and unambiguous representations of Good and Evil. These traits all can be oddly comforting in times when society's shared values seem to be unraveling, and the most common fears concern mundane human stupidities.

And that is, perhaps to your relief, about all the philosophizing I plan to do about What It All Means. Suffice it that many people obviously enjoy this sort of entertainment. I assume *you* do, or you'd be over browsing in the gardening section.

I believe the 1957–1976 wave of Gothic horror movies was superior to the prior cycle, all in all. Fans will realize just how controversial this statement is. The small world of Gothic horror has at times seemed divided between what we might call the Universal faction and the Hammer camp, although their mutual distaste for the butcher-knife epics of the seventies and eighties has helped to mute their differences. Even so, at least one fairly prolific writer of Universal and so-called poverty-row horrors of the thirties and forties still fairly curls his lip in print at the mere mention of Hammer films. Well, it's a matter of taste, I suppose. For me, those mad-doctor things Monogram and PRC used to churn out in the forties pack all the raw entertainment power of televised Sunday services.

Let's be clear about this. I think James Whale's two *Frankenstein* films and Karl Freund's *The Mummy* are among the best films of *any* kind ever made. These movies fully earn their formidable reputations with a dignity and painterly beauty of which modern filmmakers seem quite incapable. Many of their brethren, such as *The Wolfman* and the Fredric March version of *Doctor Jekyll and Mr. Hyde*, don't quite achieve this level of excellence, but remain interesting and entertaining. Beyond a handful of films such as these, however, it ought to be admitted that the "Golden Age" horrors are a mixed bag at best, with scattered bright spots and many deadly dull programmers.

Yet rather too much rosy nostalgia lingers around these older films as a group, obscuring their deficiencies. Also, until fairly recently, what we might call the Baby Boom horror cycle simply hasn't benefited from as much concerted praise and myth-making on the part of film critics, fans, and marketers. (Ironically, much of the reverence for the so-called Golden Age dates not from the era in which the movies were released, but from their critical and popular *rediscovery* during the grand monster-mania years that spawned the 1957–1976 cycle.)

It goes without saying that quite a few of the Baby Boom Gothics were as boring, inept, or cynically trite as anything made during the previous horror cycle. That's certainly to be expected, especially given the profligate nature of the second wave, which in sheer volume dwarfed its predecessor. Literally hundreds of Gothic horror films, good, bad, and indifferent, were released between 1957 and 1976, in a dozen or more countries; a filmography of the vampire movies *alone* fills more than a hundred pages in one reference I've seen. Moreover, many of the best Golden Age horrors were 'A' pictures, with reasonably generous budgets and shooting schedules, while the later movies with few exceptions were exploitation products, made as quickly and cheaply as possible.

But the rapid-fire nature of exploitation filmmaking proved to be a strength as well as a weakness of the 1957 cycle. While the later films may lack the sheer visual gorgeousness of Universal's best, many of them also have a vitality quite unprecedented in prior horror film, a brutal, sexy energy that keeps them fresh and interesting decades later. Then, too, the Boomer horrors display a remarkable off-the-cuff sort of inventiveness, a willingness to tinker and improvise freely with old formulas, characters, and conventions while remaining true to the essential Gothic spirit.

I don't mean to suggest that many movie buffs don't enjoy the movies of both generations. And as I mentioned earlier, the whole notion of a radical split between the two eras of horror film has come to seem increasingly irrelevant since the latter 1970s, when Gothic horror in *any* recognizable form almost vanished from the screen in favor of simpleminded sadism. Today, the films in *Nightwalkers* are beginning to acquire a fine patina of age themselves, settling into respectability despite their disreputable origins.

A good deal of the original controversy regarding these movies, as we shall see, concerned their alleged explicitness in matters violent and sexual. This is, of course, a relative judgment, and one that seems pretty laughable in the wake of the gory tide that followed *The Exorcist* and *Halloween*. The decorative little gouts of blood that stirred up such indignation against 1958's *Horror of Dracula* are negligible to the point of invisibility in an era that offers real-life surgery on cable television. It's also worth remembering that the original Universal films, which now seem so circumspect and restrained, prompted just as much furor in the days before they ossified into "classics"; the 1931 *Dracula*, which in 1994 tends to produce a sedative effect in all but the most hard-core devotee, was denounced by the PTA upon release, and slashed or rejected outright by censors around the world.

Leaving aside, however, the incredible changes in the sophistication or depravity (take your pick) of modern audiences, much of the disdain for post-1957 Gothic horror that lingers among a dwindling band of "purist" aficionados seems to spring from a critical dictum that subtle and understated horrors are *always* best. I have considerable sympathy for this position, which informs more than a few of my own opinions in *Nightwalkers*. But it's important to remember that understatement, at least in the mid-1930s Hays Office sense, played no part in the original Gothic tales, which stressed vivid, clammy, tactile frights, often with an open sexual content. At their best, the gaudy horror movies of Hammer and its contemporaries capture the ornate, breathless, and overwrought quality of the classic Gothic novels far better than did their timid Universal predecessors.

1

THE GOTHIC RENAISSANCE OF 1957

Although no one seems to have suspected it at the time, the world of the late 1950s was hungry for horror.

The embers of the horror cycle spurred by Universal Studios had sputtered and died nearly a decade before, their passing marked by the lame "horror comedies" of Abbot and Costello. By 1957, the Gothic icons of the thirties had been reduced to bad jokes—dying, unemployed Bela flashing the cape one last time for Ed Wood—or dim memories. In that pre-videotape world, an entire generation was growing up without any direct knowledge of classic horror.

There were still monsters abroad, of course. Radioactive lizards, flying saucer jockeys, and an impressive variety of giant insects stalked the screens of a thousand drive-ins. These were rubbery substitutes for atom-fear and the other half-disguised anxieties of an era locked in what

Walter Kendrick has perceptively called "history's grandest fit of paranoid dementia." And the look, the approach, the style of these films, what there was of it, was completely different from the horror work of twenty years before, in ways that went well beyond subject matter. The subtler possibilities of mood and atmosphere seemed largely forgotten in fifties monster flicks. Shadows and fog-machine mists fell out of style, in favor of a flat, monochrome, documentary-style approach that owed a lot to the era's crime films (and even more to inadequate budgets). A handful of these movies were genuinely well-made; most were hilariously inept. Many of them are still quite enjoyable, approached in the right spirit. They aren't *horror*, though.

But horror never dies. It only lies dormant awhile, transmuting itself to match the temper of the times. In 1957, two events suddenly set the stage for the greatest explosion of Gothic horror entertainment in history.

CHRISTOPHER LEE'S DRACULA RADIATES REPTILIAN MENACE IN 1970'S *TASTE THE BLOOD OF DRACULA*.

The first of these was the release to television of the Shock Theater syndicated package of fifty-two Universal films, essentially the entire corpus of the first great horror-movie age. Shock Theater, in all its various local guises, proved hugely popular with kids as well as adults, and made regional celebrities out of a number of "horror hosts." For years, these movies had been available to the public, if at all, only through limited and sporadic theatrical re-releases. (Television and the movie business were barely on speaking terms in the fifties, and movies were a long time in becoming a regular feature of television programming.) With Shock Theater, a whole new audience would become acquainted with the classic characters and situations of the Gothic genre.

But Shock Theater, as much fun as it was, was basically an exercise in nostalgia, mined as much for laughs as for chills by the horror hosts. In this, it was an early sign of the off-center, mocking amusements that would flourish as camp in the mid-1960s. A new film series was needed to revitalize the tired Gothic conventions and put some shudders back into Dracula, Frankenstein and the rest of their crowd. That effort began in 1957 as well, with a small and obscure English film studio called Hammer Film Productions.

HAMMER: THE HORROR OUT OF BRITAIN

For most of its active life, the company that would bring about the Gothic Renaissance was a family affair. Or, more precisely, a two-family affair.

Enrique Carreras was a Spaniard from tobacco money who immigrated to Britain in the years before the First World War, and in 1913 began building a chain of English movie houses. Will Hinds was a businessman with interests in jewelry stores, seaside music halls, and a theatrical agency. He was also a frustrated vaudevillian who liked to perform baggy-pants comedy at company picnics and in his own theaters, under the stage name Will "Hammer." In 1935,

Carreras formed a film distribution business, Exclusive Films Ltd., that dealt mainly in reissues and low-budget exploitation films, and soon persuaded Hinds to become his partner.

Will Hinds's love of show business, however, wasn't satisfied with the fairly dry work of film distribution. It was actually slightly before the foundation of Exclusive Films, in November 1934, that Hinds put together a film production company called Hammer Productions. This early effort held together only long enough to produce four films over about three years, all forgettable supporting features. (In view of what came later, it is interesting to note that the second and most ambitious 'proto-Hammer' production, a modestly entertaining suspenser called *The Mystery of the Marie Celeste*, starred Bela Lugosi.)

After World War II, management of Exclusive passed to Enrique Carreras's son James, while Hinds and the elder Carreras, both getting on in years, stepped back into executive directorships. Jimmy Carreras kick-started the unimpressive little empire he'd inherited, and has received universal credit for creating what became by many yardsticks Britain's most consistently successful movie company.

Carreras *fils* was by all accounts a formidable whirlwind of a man, a born salesman of limitless charm and poise. He began his career as an usher in one of his father's cinemas, and later worked as a theater manager and a car salesman—a successful one, I suspect. Carreras first demonstrated his ambition and his talent for self-promotion during his army service in the war. He entered the army as a thirty-year-old private but rose to the rank of lieutenant colonel by the war's end, ultimately commanding a coastal air defense unit whose success against Hitler's V-1 bombs put him in the newspapers and newsreels of the day. A handsome, dapper figure who looked the part of war hero, he took full advantage of his status to begin cultivating prominent contacts throughout English society, connections that ultimately would include members of Parliament and the royal family.

Upon assuming the managing directorship of Exclusive, Carreras soon decided that the company's best chances lay in returning to low-budget movie production. Hollywood releases dominated the British box office, then as today. To encourage native film companies, a government quota required a set portion of all films exhibited in Britain to be British-made. The Hammer name was resurrected in 1947 for a newly formed production subsidiary of Exclusive, and in the following year, Hammer began cranking out lowest-budget "quota quickies," which often played as second bills before Hollywood lead features. (Eventually, the subsidiary would swallow its parent, when Hammer Productions left the distribution business entirely in 1968.)

The quota, however, didn't help British filmmakers penetrate the vastly larger and more lucrative American market, and as British movies generally lacked the stars and production values Americans preferred, they had little success in doing so; again, this is still pretty much the situation today. In 1951, Carreras scored a coup by signing a coproduction deal with Robert Lippert, a prolific American producer of low-budget exploitation films (whose name, by the way, graces a good number of the most amusingly awful sci-fi movies of the fifties). The Lippert deal guaranteed Hammer movies would receive distribution in the United States, an arrangement no British film company had ever achieved before. In the years to come, Carreras would build on this toehold, forging personal friendships as well as business deals with some of Hollywood's most powerful men, including Columbia's Mike Francovich and Eliot Hyman, eventual owner of Warner. Hammer's American partnerships included long-term relationships with Columbia, Universal, and Seven Arts, another Hyman company. Such backers provided much of the financing for Hammer's activities and set up American distribution deals for its products. Throughout Hammer's best years, Jimmy Carreras acted as the company's highly effective salesman and ambassador to Hollywood money.

Another Hammer milestone, also in 1951, was the company's move to its long-term home at Down Place, an ancient if modest country manor in Berkshire, about an hour from central London. Hammer had already occupied three other country mansions, as such lodgings were relatively inexpensive and useful as backdrops for the costume pictures that would become a company specialty. Down Place became Hammer's primary base of operations until 1966. Initially, the house itself provided the company's only sets; photos exist showing entire film crews comically crammed into Down Place's rather small rooms. As Hammer grew, additional sets were built on the grounds, producing Bray Studios, a small but productive studio complex still in use today. A stretch of woodlands in an area ominously called Black Park often served for exteriors. The sets and locations were overused over the years, but fans have a good deal of warmth for these familiar settings, and hardest-core Hammerites seem to know and have an affectionate nickname for every doorknob, archway, and tree (and, by the way, Down Place itself is reputedly haunted).

While the Hammer name has become inextricably linked with Gothic horror, Jimmy Carreras had no particular interest in the topic, and precious little in film itself, for that matter. He once said to Kevin Francis, a Hammer employee who ultimately headed up his own short-lived production company, "If people liked Strauss waltzes we'd be in the Strauss waltz business." As long as there was room in a picture for some thrills and a few pretty girls, Carreras was generally happy. He had a knack for plucking exploitable topics out of the air. Hammer screenwriter Tudor Gates once told the seminal Hammer fanzine, *Little Shoppe of Horrors*, that "Jimmy Carreras has this marvellous thing where he'd come up with a title, and the title would go to an artist who would make up a poster. A couple of pages of story might help, but that was usually considered extraneous." Carreras would use the (suitably lurid) poster in making his fundraising pitches to American and English backers, often while the studio still had only the haziest idea of what the film would actually be about. In the course of more than 160 films released between 1948 and 1978, Hammer would tackle a bewildering variety of subjects, including mysteries (*Murder by Proxy*); swashbucklers (*Sword of Sherwood Forest*); Benny Hill-ish comedy (*Don't Panic Chaps!*); Psycho-clone thrillers (*Maniac*); prehistoric epics (*When Dinosaurs Ruled the Earth*); and a peculiar series of violent, sensationalist readings of historical events that I like to call Sadistic History, such as *Rasputin—the Mad Monk* and *Terror of the Tongs*.

Given science fiction's popularity during the fifties, Hammer was bound to test the field. Two early entries (*Four Sided Triangle* and *Spaceways*, both released in 1953) did unspectacular business, but Hammer's third attempt in 1955, *The Quatermass Xperiment* (called *The Creeping Unknown* in the United States.) was a critical and box-office success. *The Quatermass*

Xperiment—the cutesy name played on the "X" rating most Hammers received from Britain's squeamish censors—was the first in what would become a highly regarded trilogy of films based on a series of science-fiction teleplays by screenwriter Nigel Kneale. The first movie in some ways plays like a futuristic treatment of the *Frankenstein* story, as a returned astronaut slowly succumbs to a spaceborn infection that transforms him into a hideous yet pitiable menace. Despite its cheesy effects and often creaky plotting, *The Quatermass Xperiment* holds up remarkably well. With uniformly fine performances and a resolute seriousness of purpose, it helped set the tone for Hammer's Gothic cycle.

The success of *Xperiment* gave Hammer a boost at a crucial moment. The Lippert arrangement had ended, temporarily cutting the company off from the all-important United States market. Furthermore, on-the-cheap black and white features like Hammer's were losing popularity with exhibitors on both sides of the Atlantic, who were desperately fighting the audience erosion, caused by television with color and gimmicks like Cinemascope. The obvious need for a new strategy prompted Hammer to turn to horror.

Production of Hammer's *The Curse of Frankenstein* began in late November 1956. Initially, the company planned to hedge its bets with another quick black-and-white shoot. Early on, though, Jimmy Carreras decided to gamble on an expanded production in color, which seems like a fairly gutsy move. There's an oft-told story that *The Curse of Frankenstein* was screened for Warner executives in New York, who were enthusiastic enough to ship the print to Jack Warner himself within two hours. The Great Man liked it as well, and quickly sewed up worldwide distribution rights, setting up the first general American release for a British film since before the war. (Recent scholarship suggests that this story, while colorful, may be apocryphal, and that Carreras's friend Eliot Hyman helped arrange American distribution in advance.)

The Curse of Frankenstein proved to be a high-water mark in the history of 1950s exploitation cinema, and one of the most successful British films made up to that point. The movie earned $7 million worldwide, $3 million in the United States alone, on production costs variously reported at between $200,000 and $300,000—a fairly tidy profit in 1957. It snapped all box-office records in England and ran in unprecedented round-the-clock saturation bookings across America. Critical response to the film was violently mixed; some American reviews were fairly warm, but the *Hollywood Reporter* proclaimed itself "nauseated." English reviewers seemed positively offended. The London *Observer* critic called it one of "the half dozen most repulsive films I have ever encountered" (I'd love to see the rest of his list). This sort of press, naturally, was *pure gold* for Hammer, free publicity they couldn't purchase otherwise, and helped pack the teen crowd into movie houses all over the world. Of course, in terms of what the nineties mean by screen violence, *The Curse of Frankenstein* is mild as melba toast; nearly all of the movie's violent acts take place offscreen, including all the monster's attacks, and Baron Frankenstein's surgical procedures occur demurely below the frame. About all the "repulsiveness" on display consists of a few shots of body parts floating in jars in the baron's lab. (Note too that many of the reviewers who professed to be so shocked invoked the memory of the comparatively mild-mannered Universal classics, which were denounced in almost identical terms twenty years before.)

Nonetheless, Hammer's first Gothic does display a kind of verve, an exuberant glee in its own wickedness, which was quite unlike anything else in the cinema of the day. Part of the shock it delivered came simply from the film's obvious professionalism. This was no crude, torpid Grade Z flick, but a quite polished-looking production, with a star-quality performance from Peter Cushing. And yet, oh-my-oh-my how *utterly* different it was from the classic horrors of Shock Theater. *The Curse of Frankenstein* is fast-moving and ruthless, with nothing whatever stately or Germanic about it. And that sumptuous color! The ruby splashes of blood! Those sleek, improbably buxom women, in their flimsy bodices! There was a fleshy, sensual quality immediately apparent in the film that quickly became a Hammer trademark.

The film's incredible success may have caught Hammer by surprise, but Carreras was quick to begin capitalizing on it. Within four months of the movie's British premiere, the company had announced a production of *Dracula* for Universal and a three-picture-a-year contract with Columbia. *Dracula*, better known in America by its United States title, *Horror of*

Dracula, was shot in November and December 1957 and debuted in summer 1958 to a critical furor similar to that of *The Curse of Frankenstein*, and an even bigger box-office reception. *Dracula* cemented Hammer's financial success, and its ultimate reputation with fans. An infinitely better film than the first, *Dracula* is also more overtly sexual. Unlike Lugosi, Hammer's Dracula sported fangs and indulged in onscreen caresses and bites. His female victims go to their deaths with a specifically erotic enthusiasm.

HORROR ACTOR SUPREME: PETER CUSHING, IN A LATE PORTRAIT.

After *Dracula*, Hammer settled into a long period of prosperity, producing an admirably consistent series of low-budget but well-made and highly entertaining yarns. (It's worth noting that, unlike the bulk of fifties exploitation cinema, Hammer's "camp factor" remains low; while some of the company's movies are mediocre, very few are bad enough to be perversely amusing.) The flow of product that Jimmy Carreras was selling so ably was sustained by a talented team of actors, artists, and technicians who worked together on feature after feature.

Among the notables of this team, during its best years, were the studio's heirs apparent, Jimmy Carreras's son Michael and Will Hinds's son Anthony. After hitches in the military, both men joined Exclusive/Hammer and learned a variety of jobs; the company was, as Michael Carreras put it, "a kindergarten with all the toys available to play with and experiment with as we wished." Michael worked awhile in casting and story editing, and soon he and Tony Hinds moved into production. For a time, the two traded off the line producer and executive producer jobs. Beginning in 1961, Michael left the company for a decade to run his own production company, but continued to write, direct, and produce projects for Hammer. Hinds remained active in production and, with *Curse of the Werewolf* in 1960, moved into screenwriting as well, ultimately becoming one of Hammer's most productive scripters under the pen-name John Elder. Carreras's and Hinds's resumés highlight another factor in Hammer's success; the way in which this lean little company blurred the boundaries between traditional job descriptions and, to the extent permitted under Britain's strict union rules, encouraged its principals to shuttle freely between roles. Kevin Francis has remembered that at Hammer, "you did everything, otherwise you didn't stay working for the company."

The twin kings of the Hammer repertory company were Peter Cushing and Christopher Lee, who by now have won comfortable places next to Karloff and Lugosi in the horror fans' pantheon. Peter Cushing, in particular, seems to me simply the finest actor ever to grace the horror cinema. He seems to have been capable of anything; an accomplished stage performer who comfortably shared the boards with Olivier, he had already become Britain's first television star before joining Hammer. In his glory years at Hammer, Cushing proved to be that rarest of combinations, a fine actor who could submerge himself in very different roles, *and* a true movie star, who brought to his every project a compulsively watchable blend of charm, self-assurance, and strength. And Cushing *never* gave his second best. Even in a fairly hopeless piece of trash like *The Satanic Rites of Dracula*, he delivers an unforgettable performance, making you believe in the surrounding tackiness as long as his face is on screen.

Christopher Lee was a very different but

equally interesting performer. Lee won the role of the monster in *The Curse of Frankenstein* largely on the basis of his six-foot-four height and his imposing physical presence. (He was reportedly happy for the work. His career as a supporting player had been foundering, since leading men felt overshadowed by this handsome giant.) But Lee won lasting fame, and became something of an international sex symbol, with his unforgettable Dracula, whom he invests with a leonine, dangerous sexuality and the icy charm of a born aristocrat. Unfortunately, Lee found himself more typecast than Cushing, and much relatively unrewarding villainy lay ahead for him—a great pity, since (among other things) he makes a fine hero.

TERENCE FISHER (IN SPECTACLES), HAMMER'S BEST DIRECTOR, ON THE SET OF THE STUDIO'S *PHANTOM OF THE OPERA*.

It's tempting to define virtually all of Hammer's Gothic style in terms of the direction of Terence Fisher; probably an inaccurate idea, but tempting nonetheless. Fisher helmed both *The Curse of Frankenstein* and *Horror of Dracula*, and went on to direct many other of Hammer's best horror projects. Once dismissed by many as a hack, Fisher's reputation has skyrocketed since his death in 1980. Today, he's often mentioned as a worthy successor to the likes of Universal's James Whale and Karl Freund. A lot of film-crit blather has been written about Fisher, which is ironic considering the director repeatedly denied such inflated claims. In truth, Fisher's work displays few of the attributes associated with the so-called *auteur*. "I'm only a working director," he remarked more than once—one who was never able to pick his projects, scripts, or actors. His directorial style is rather bland, with little intercutting and a minimum of fluid or flashy camera movement. What Fisher *did* excel at was crisp, understated story-telling, with careful attention to mood and atmosphere. (In this, he's reminiscent of Jack Arnold, arguably the best American

director of fantasy film during the 1950s.) Moreover, he was a sensitive actors' director, who worked closely with his casts and was much beloved because of it. Fisher had a sincere love for period settings, and was at his most effective in evoking Hammer's favored nineteenth-century European dreamscape of castles, coaches, and taverns, of comic cockneys and busty barmaids.

Building this "Hammerland" was the responsibility of the studio's production designer, Bernard Robinson, who proved to be positively brilliant at hiding Hammer's budgetary limitations and stretching the company's pounds as far as they could go. Under Robinson's direction, Hammer artists conjured up marble floors from painted paper, crafted ancient Egypt from papier-mâché, and it all looked *great*. He regularly designed the studio's large sets—castles, villages, and whatnot—to be reused for a whole series of productions, and a major part of his job was carefully disguising that fact. Robinson's contribution to the studio really can't be overstated. His flamboyant yet finely detailed sets, so reflective of his precision and perfectionism, were the largest single visual element separating Hammer from its low-budget competitors. Dick Klemensen, writing in *Little Shoppe of Horrors*, has with perfect accuracy called Robinson the "backbone and heart of the Hammer success story."

Another contributor to the Hammer look was cinematographer Jack Asher, who pioneered the studio's distinctive use of color in his relatively brief tenure at Hammer—"only" a dozen films over about six years, including the first two Frankenstein and Dracula movies. In an era of detergent-bright, flatly lit Technicolor, Asher devised shadowy palettes of cool, saturated blues and greens, carefully contrasted with Hammer's favorite color, blood red. Hammer used other competent directors of photography after Asher's departure, but none of them rivaled him in the sheer richness of his imagery.

There were many others, of course: producer Anthony Nelson-Keys, whom Jack Asher credited with convincing the studio to film *Curse* in color; screenwriter-directors John Gilling and Jimmy Sangster; makeup artists Phil Leakey and Roy Ashton; character actors like Michael Ripper and George Woodbridge, who served as familiar background furniture in many of the Hammer horrors. In all, they constituted an unusually competent and dedicated filmmaking machine, "a highly efficient factory," in the words of one critic. It was a situation almost unheard of today, and rare even then, given the fractious state of Britain's union politics. And Hammer's survivors still fondly refer to themselves as a family. In *Little Shoppe of Horrors*, Jack Asher once recalled that "everybody knew everybody else…It was like being with close friends every day."

By the mid-sixties, Hammer was profitable beyond its founders' dreams. Most astonishing of all, the little film company at Bray became respectable, at least in a business sense. In 1968, Hammer received the Queen's Award to Industry in recognition of its contributions to Britain's balance of trade, an unprecedented honor for a film company. Jimmy Carreras, ultimate schmoozer, received his own personal validation in the following year, becoming Sir James Carreras, knight of the realm.

Business was good. Horror was loose in the land once again.

AMERICAN GOTHIC: AIPOE AND OTHER DIVERSIONS

In 1960, America's liveliest and most prolific independent film company made its own entry into the new Gothic movement pioneered by its British counterpart. Surprisingly little has been written on the correspondences and influences between Hammer and American International Pictures, or AIP, which seems more than a little surprising considering the obvious parallels between the two companies. It strains credulity to the breaking point to think AIP wouldn't notice and capitalize on Hammer's box-office success. Exploitation, after all, was AIP's business.

American International, like Hammer, would tackle virtually any genre. Over its twenty-six-year history, AIP released well over four hundred movies, including costume epics, science fiction, thrillers, monster movies, soft-core titillation; they practically invented the juvenile delinquent picture and its various offspring, such as motorcycle gangster movies. Naturally, the company also dabbled in Gothic horror, in a series of films including some of the best entries in the post-1957 Gothic wave.

AIP employed strategies almost identical to those used by Jimmy Carreras at Hammer. AIP's Jim Nicholson was quoted in Mark Thomas McGee's book on the company, *Fast and Furious*, as saying "We do our planning backwards. We get what sounds like a title that will arouse interest, then a monster or gimmick, then figure out what our advertising is going to consist of. Then we bring in a writer to provide a script to fit the title and concept." This process often included Carreras's favored ploy of creating the movie's poster to whip up business *before* the film project itself was begun. Under the direction of Albert Kallis, AIP's art director for seventeen years, the company created a series of entertaining but surreally misleading posters that are still legendary among collectors. (One exhibitor told AIP it was a pity they couldn't just put sprocket holes in Kallis's posters and run *them* instead of the films.)

American International was born in 1954, in what was universally considered a rotten time to be in the movie business. Besides the damage wrought by television, most of the existing movie theaters were located in the inner cities, at a time when the great migration to the 'burb frontiers was in full swing. By one estimate, the average American family's annual spending on movies dropped by more than 40 percent between 1946 and 1952. Another body blow came in the form of a landmark 1949 Supreme Court antitrust decision, the so-called Paramount Consent Decree. The decision disrupted a movie industry that until then had been what the MBAs call "vertically integrated." The major movie studios also owned large chains of movie theaters, to which they distributed packages of their own products pretty much as they saw fit. The decree broke up this tidy arrangement, introducing a large degree of uncertainty into what had been a tight and clubby business, and effectively pitting studios, distributors, and exhibitors against one another. The end result was that, by 1954, as many as half of all United States theaters weren't turning a profit, and the major studios were sharply curtailing their output.

Samuel Z. Arkoff and James H. Nicholson thought it was a *great* time to get into in the movie business.

Sam Arkoff was a lawyer from Iowa who had fallen in love with movies when he read his first copy of *Variety* at fifteen. After World War II, he headed for Los Angeles to enter the industry in any way he could. Arkoff began representing some of the basement-level independent film producers who had largely been frozen out of the old vertically integrated system, the sort that were called "one-lungers" in their day. He also co-produced an early, short-lived television comedy. A growing family and a near-fatal cerebral hemorrhage in 1952 had motivated Arkoff to break into the movie business himself, in the hope of making some serious money in a hurry.

Jim Nicholson was general sales manager for Realart, a small company that made most of its money by re-releasing old Universal films to independent theaters. A lifelong fan of fantasy and science fiction, he'd worked in theaters in almost every role as a teenager, and briefly owned a four-house theater chain in Los Angeles during the late 1940s before going bust. Nicholson became impressed with Arkoff's chutzpah when the lawyer forced a five-hundred-dollar settlement out of Realart on a weak

AIP's James Nicholson, Vincent Price, and Barbara Steele, during the filming of *The Pit and the Pendulum*.

title infringement case. Amused, Nicholson told Arkoff he'd never seen his boss give anybody *anything*. The two men became friends and then business partners. They initially sought the name American International, but found it blocked by an existing American Pictures, so they incorporated as American Releasing Corporation (ARC) in 1954; the AIP name soon became available and was adopted in early 1956. The new company's total assets came to a whopping $3,000.

Amid the general devastation of the movie industry, Arkoff and Nicholson saw opportunities for a nimble company to succeed with inexpensive, popular features. Since the consent decree, the major studios were making fewer titles, and increasingly these were costly, splashy productions designed to lure viewers away from television. The cheaper kinds of films, the Westerns and action pictures, were becoming scarce. Independent theater owners, particularly the suburban drive-in operators, were desperate for affordable movies that would sell tickets. That's what Arkoff and Nicholson proposed to provide—as soon as they could come up with a product to sell.

The new company's original name, American Releasing, points up an important fact, which is where the comparison between AIP and Hammer breaks down. AIP was almost entirely a distribution enterprise, not a production company. AIP rarely became directly involved in making films. Except for a brief and financially disastrous episode in the late fifties, the company never even owned a studio lot. Instead, AIP typically would arrange financing and distribution for films made by independent producers, occasionally buying features outright. (AIP even released a few Hammer films in the United States, including *The Vampire Lovers*.) And AIP's first and most reliable producer was Roger Corman.

It's almost impossible to imagine the history of modern American moviemaking without Corman, who, through several different companies, has functioned as our *de facto* national film academy for forty years. The list of movie talents who began their careers on Corman's low-budget features is fairly staggering; Francis Ford Coppola, Ron Howard, Robert Towne, Jonathan Demme, Peter Bogdanovich, John Sayles, and Jack Nicholson are only a small part of the list. Sayles once said, "He's the kind of person who was willing to take a gamble on someone who'd never written a screenplay before." To which you might add: Or directed. Or acted. Or composed film music. Or whatever. For four decades, Corman's compact with the young, tough, and ambitious has always been the same: Work for me like a dog, for very little money, and I will give you a chance in the movies.

Yet he was and is an unlikely B-movie mogul. Compared to, say, cigar-chomping Sam Arkoff, who looks the part and plays it to the hilt, Corman is a shy, rather preppie fellow—unless a project is in danger of going over budget. Then, reputedly, his mouth begins to foam just a bit. He comes from comfy origins, the son of a successful engineer. In 1940, when Corman was fourteen, his father moved the family from Detroit to Beverly Hills, which was not then quite the multimillionaire's game preserve it is today, but an impressive address nonetheless. Unsurprisingly, while attending high school with the sons and daughters of Hollywood's elite, Corman developed a passion for film. Like Jim Nicholson, he grew up enjoying all sorts of fantasy; He was an avid reader of the sainted John W. Campbell's *Astounding Science Fiction* in its 1940s glory days, and he loved Edgar Allan Poe.

Corman initially set out to follow in his father's footsteps and studied engineering at Stanford, but worked in the field just four days before he quit in disgust. After a hitch in the navy, he moved back to Los Angeles, where his brother Gene had become an agent. In 1954, Gene helped Corman set up a deal to produce his first film, *Monster from the Ocean Floor*, for $12,000, some of which was borrowed from Corman's parents. This film of little discernable

merit (trust me on this) was sold to Robert Lippert—the same man who brought Hammer to the United States—for a quick profit of $110,000. Corman immediately plowed his 60-percent share of the sale price into making another film. By maintaining a breakneck pace and keeping the money flowing in, he managed to get out eight pictures in a little over one year.

Corman's need for quick capital brought him to the newly formed American Releasing Corporation, which was looking for its first release. For his second movie, a racing drama called *The Fast and the Furious* (also 1954), Corman had distribution offers from several bigger companies, including Columbia, but these would have tied up his money for months. Arkoff and Nicholson struck a multi-picture deal with Corman that required them to return his production costs on each movie as he turned it in, giving him the immediate cash he needed to start the next one. Arkoff and Nicholson, in return, managed to persuade various regional sub-distributors to advance them *their* costs. They also convinced their film lab, Pathé, to defer payments for the prints and advance them money for future projects. The soon-to-be AIP was off to a wheezing start.

By keeping their costs low and their publicity outrageous—the ads for *Hot Rod Girl* (1956) promised "Teenage terrorists on a speed crazy rampage!"—AIP endured and prospered throughout the fifties, particularly after its adoption of double features. In those days, second features received flat fees from exhibitors, while the top-of-the-bill feature received a percentage of the box office, a far more lucrative deal. AIP's movies had little chance of making it to the top of the bill on their own, so in 1956 the company began releasing double features of thematically related items (the first was *The Day the World Ended* and *Phantom from 10,000 Leagues*) that offered an entire evening's entertainment, or a facsimile thereof, and earned a share of receipts.

By the late fifties, though, AIP was forced to begin looking for a new strategy. In part, the company was simply a victim of its own success. The money from AIP's juvenile delinquent pictures and other quickies had started to look pretty good to other low-budget companies like Republic and Allied Artists, who were crowding into the market with copycat movies. Even the majors were picking up cheap teen and monster movies from independents, and using their muscle with the distributors to beat AIP at its own game. Arkoff and Nicholson decided they had no choice but to make the plunge into respectability with a decently budgeted feature in color and Cinemascope. The project chosen was *House of Usher*, a loose adaptation of "The Fall of the House of Usher" by Edgar Allan Poe. To make the film, they turned to Roger Corman.

AIPOE: THE POE SERIES' KEY CREATORS, ROGER CORMAN AND VINCENT PRICE, PRETEND TO READ JAPANESE.

Arkoff and Corman differ on whose idea *Usher* was; each has seemed to claim credit, directly or indirectly. Again, it's hard to believe that Hammer's ongoing success with Gothic tales didn't have something to do with the choice. (Another obvious advantage: Poe's stories were in the public domain—they were *free*.) There's an oft-repeated story that Arkoff initially objected to making *House of Usher* because it didn't feature a monster of some sort. Corman claims that he convinced Sam that the house would be the monster, and gave Vincent Price a few lines such as "The house lives…the house breathes…" to drive the point home. Arkoff claims this story is, um, apocryphal (he uses a stronger word), and that he wasn't so stupid as to insist on a rubber bogie in a Poe adaptation.

Whoever's idea it was, AIP more than got its money's worth from the film. The $270,000 film earned about $2 million, in a glorious summer 1960 run that lasted longer than that of any previous AIP movie. Just as astonishingly, American International found itself with mainstream critical success for the first time ever. The *New York Herald Tribune* hailed its "restoration of finesse and craftsmanship to the genre of dread," and *Variety* called *House of Usher* "a film that should attract mature tastes," probably the first time any AIP movie had been accused of this tendency. The praise was merited. The Film is a thoughtful and effective horror tale that takes some liberties with Poe's story but remains faithful to the spirit of his work. It was an unexpected leap forward both for AIP and for Roger Corman, and one that led to a lucrative and long-running series.

Corman had spent the latter fifties churning out films at a ferocious pace, and something odd happened along the way. He had begun directing in 1955 with his third production, *Five Guns West*, not because he had any experience (he had none) but because he'd seen movies directed before and it didn't seem all that hard, and besides, directors cost *money*. Directing turned out to be a little trickier than he thought; it rained on the first day of the shoot and he found himself throwing up from sheer nervous tension. But the picture came in on time and on budget, and over the course of making movie after movie, nearly all shot in ten days or less apiece, he taught himself the basics of the directing craft.

That wasn't the odd part, though. A lot of people working in low-budget movies in the fifties had sketchy credentials. The odd thing was that he slowly became a *good* director.

Good is a relative term, of course. Throughout his career, Corman the incredibly tight-fisted producer often stepped in to sabotage Corman the director; moviemaking has always been first and foremost a money proposition for the man, and all too often he would settle for good enough rather than spend an extra nickle. Even the Poe films, by far his most polished directorial work, are marred by an irritating recycling of plot lines and even of actual footage. He's also a "camera director," good with lighting and camera angles and notoriously indifferent to his actors. But even his two dozen or so early potboilers, crude as they are, are united by a certain cynical, anarchic wit and energy. Corman movies are never boring, that's for sure.

Clear-eyed assessments of Corman's direction are made a little more difficult by the volumes of folderol that have been written about the man's work. No other director of the twentieth century has been the subject of quite so much half-baked psychoanalytic absurdity as Roger Corman, much of it perpetrated by French film critics. The *Cahiers du Cinéma* crowd first started taking notice of Corman's pictures in 1958, with his neatly grim little gangster movie *Machine Gun Kelly*. In a fine demonstration of the Gallic flair for intellectual lunacy, they soon decided that the director was a Genius. Corman never entirely fell for his own press, but critical acceptance does seem to have given him the confidence to stretch his talents to the limit for the Poe series and, with *The Masque of the Red Death*, to make one of the few genuine American art films (but more about that later).

Much of Corman's success as a director was due to his ability to cultivate groups of talented, loyal technicians, writers, and performers who would put up with the demands of his maniacal filmmaking habits. For the Poe pictures, his team included his regular director of photography, Floyd Crosby, who had won an Academy Award for cinematography in 1931 and who had also shot *High Noon* and *Of Mice and Men*. Crosby brought an elegant, fluid grace to the Poe pictures; he joined Corman for *Monster from the Ocean Floor*, and shot fifteen more films for him. It might seem strange to you that a cinematographer of this caliber would hook up with Corman, and damn if it doesn't seem strange to me too (some have speculated that Crosby may have been 'gray-listed' out of A pictures during the Red Scare). Equally important was art director Daniel Haller, who created lavish, flamboyant settings for the series. His painterly eye and talent for making Not Much look like Something were on a par with Bernard Robinson's at Hammer. Scripts for the Poe series were prepared by diverse hands, but received a strong start from Richard Matheson, a successful screenwriter who's also one of the century's better writers of literary fantasy (*The Shrinking Man* and *I Am Legend*, among others). Matheson's screenplays kept Poe's emotionally charged, hothouse atmosphere intact, and were always neatly constructed. He wrote four in all, including *Usher* and the second feature, *The Pit and the Pendulum* (1961).

As for the series' main star, Vincent Price: Was ever an actor so seemingly custom-made for a series of roles? The Poe pictures, for better or worse, sealed Price as a horror star forever, and they contain some of his all-time best work. At times in the series, Price can lapse into chest-thumping melodrama, but he usually goes over the top in a way that seems perfectly in keeping with Poe's own neurotic conceptions. And for those most familiar with Price's spoofy Uncle Vincent persona—no one parodied Vincent Price better than Vincent Price—some of these performances, particularly his roles in *Pit and the Pendulum* and *The Masque of the Red Death*, are a real revelation. In these films, Price proved definitively that he could deliver villainy and menace without a hint of camp.

Corman made seven Poe films between 1960 and 1964 before burning out on the series. They included the comedy *The Raven*, as well as an adaptation of H. P. Lovecraft's novella "The Case of Charles Dexter Ward" that AIP decided would sell better under Poe's title *The Haunted Palace*. Corman's Poe movies are certainly his best work as a director, and with only a few exceptions are the finest Gothic work to come from America during the horror boom of the sixties, which is why I've devoted so much space to them. But AIP gave us a number of other Gothic projects as well, including five more Poe films of *wildly* varying quality.

Casting about for related topics, the company returned to the author who had inspired *The Haunted Palace*, and attempted to build another Gothic franchise based on the stories of H. P. Lovecraft, although the intellectual, "cosmic" nature of his horrors would be difficult to translate to the screen even if the movies in question had made an honest attempt to do so, which they didn't. The results didn't set the box office afire, either; even so, during the late sixties the studio bankrolled three more films based, very faintly indeed, on Lovecraft's works. Happier results came from AIP's European efforts.

In 1959, as AIP plotted the strategy that led to the Poe films, the company began prospecting in Italy for movies that could be acquired cheaply for American release. As America then was still in the throes of its *Ben Hur*-era fascination with ancient epics, most of the films AIP imported featured a lot of extras in silly Spartan attire. Soon after, Arkoff and Nicholson became impressed with the quality and economy of film work then being done in Britain, and helped finance several Anglo-

American co-productions. These efforts brought United States audiences at least two top-quality Gothic films. *Burn, Witch, Burn* (1962), now generally regarded as at least a minor classic, was based on a modern-day witchcraft story by American fantasy great Fritz Leiber. The other, Mario Bava's *Black Sunday* (originally titled *La Maschera del Demonio*), released in the United States in 1961, has nothing minor about it. *Black Sunday* is quite simply one of the most beautiful, evocative, and frightening films ever made, and a major landmark in the history of Gothic.

SIDESHOWS

While Hammer and AIP dominated the Gothic world of the late fifties and early sixties, their success naturally inspired competitors and imitators.

Of course, some of the best horror movies of the period were neither. Every era has a handful of classic films that seem to come from nowhere. Movies like *Curse of the Demon* (1957), *The Innocents* (1961), and *The Haunting* (1963) are accomplishments that seem outside time and trends, and usually they influence little that follows them—partly because genius is not always commercial, and partly because you can copy themes and styles, but you can't copy genuine originality. They sit there in the middle of film history, impressive and isolated, like those giant rocks in the sea off the coast of Oregon.

But the majority of the era's remaining horror films were more formulaic affairs. Hammer's chief rival as a British producer of genre films was Amicus, a company founded by American expatriate Milton

SCARING THE PANTS OFF AMERICA: WILLIAM CASTLE WITH TRADEMARK STOGIE.

Subotsky and his business partner, Max Rosenberg. After making one of the first rock and roll musicals, the pair turned to Gothic horror with 1959's *Horror Hotel* (called *City of the Dead* in the United Kingdom), a marvelously atmospheric if often nonsensical tale of undead witches in New England. Amicus would return to purely Gothic themes occasionally, most prominently with 1965's *The Skull*, a film that seems like a Hammer movie in all but name, and features Peter Cushing and Christopher Lee in excellent performances. In 1964, with *Dr. Terror's House of Horrors*, the company hit on the formula that would sustain it into the early seventies—a long-running series of horror-inflected anthologies, including *Torture Garden*, *Asylum*, and *The House That Dripped Blood*. As is the nature of anthologies, these are mixed affairs, combining horrific pieces with suspense and terror themes, science fiction, and "horror comedy." The Amicus anthologies are often well-written—several were scripted by Robert Bloch—but contain relatively little in the way of "pure" Gothic. Still, they contributed well to the campy, Shock Theater side of the sixties monster boom. By comparison, two other British film companies of the era, Tyburn and Tigon, seem like little more than stillborn Hammer clones.

In the United States, one filmmaker managed to put his own unique mark on a few sort-of Gothic efforts. The best Hammers and AIPoes have a timeless quality that reflects relatively little of the eras in which they were made; this is emphatically *not* true of the movies of William Castle, which are locked like flies in amber in the wonderful nonsense of late fifties exploitation. William Castle was an engaging character with the instincts of a con man, whose autobiography, *Step Right Up!...I'm Gonna Scare the Pants Off*

America, is one of the great show-business memoirs. Parts of it, who knows, might even be true. By his own telling, Castle conceived his grand design of scaring us all when, at thirteen, he saw Bela Lugosi in a stage production of *Dracula*. A backstage encounter with Lugosi led, two years later, to an assistant stage manager's job on a roadshow version of the play. Castle, evidently possessed of solid brass *cojones*, proceeded over the ensuing years to talk his way into a series of jobs for which he had no particular qualifications, eventually becoming a director of 'B' programmers for Columbia. Itching to produce, he became an independent and launched the series of gimmick-promoted pictures that would make him immortal, sort of.

The gimmicks began with a thousand-dollar life insurance policy issued to each audience member attending his soporific thriller *Macabre*—a safe enough bet for Castle, since having your butt fall asleep is rarely fatal. The gimmicks became Castle's trademark, and included vibrating seat cushions (*The Tingler*), glow-in-the-dark skeletons flying out of the screen (*House on Haunted Hill*), and 'Fright Breaks' built into the film (*Homicidal*). Castle was a producer and director of distinctly limited talents who wasted too much of his energy on piss-poor Hitchcock imitations, and it's probably a stretch to classify his two ghost romps, *House on Haunted Hill* and *13 Ghosts*, as 'Gothic.' But hell, they're fun movies that did in fact spook me as a kid, so they're in here.

their debut at almost precisely the same moment at which Bobby 'Boris' Pickett's "Monster Mash" hit Number One in *Billboard*.

I remember when every Saturday afternoon brought a creaky horror movie on television (my mother complained, and rightly, that they would keep me up at night). I remember monster gum cards and decals, and bins of plastic Marx Toy monster figures for a quarter apiece at TG&Y. (Try to get them for that now.) I remember being so scared by a picture of Dorian Gray's hideous death mask in *Famous Monsters of Filmland* that I could only open the magazine in broad daylight. I remember scouring convenience store newsstands for copies of *Castle of Frankenstein*, the best horror fan magazine of all. I remember "The Munsters," which I never cared for all that much, and "The Addams Family," which I loved then and still do. All over America, a generation of boys fell hard for Carolyn Jones as Morticia, and I suppose I shall go to my grave still lusting for her.

God knows what it all means. David J. Skal's magisterial but overly Freudian *The Monster Show*, a recent history of twentieth century horror, goes to some pains to explain that all our monster mania of the sixties may have been a repressed masturbatory fantasy. Well, that's as may be; sex became a pretty enormous concern for me soon enough. But I still remember the Horror Years as a clean, safe and oddly hopeful time. And maybe that isn't entirely nostalgia.

"A NEW WORLD OF GODS AND MONSTERS"

By the mid-1960s, horror had exploded into a national obsession.

These days, it's hard to believe that there ever was an era so innocently morbid. but I was there, for part of it at least. I remember a time when no boy's bedroom was complete without a clutch of Aurora's monster model kits. The Aurora monsters were among the most phenomenally successful model kits in history—"Get them before they get you!" boasted the ads, and just about everybody I knew did. They made

A NOTE ON THE FILMS

Depending on your definitions, at least several hundred Gothic horror films were made between 1957 and 1976. Naturally, any brief selection from this behemoth output is bound to appear fairly arbitrary, and I know that many will believe I must have the brains of a claw hammer to have neglected this or that favorite of theirs. Nonetheless, there *was* a rationale, and I hope a sound one, behind my choices.

Nightwalkers is intended to provide an introduction to the films of the 1957–1976 cycle. It is not a "Best of" selection, but a survey of the most representative efforts, good and bad, of the era's major producers of Gothic horror movies— a "core curriculum," if you will.

In keeping with my definition of Gothic horror, I have intentionally avoided all films of terror and suspense, such as *Psycho* and its numerous clones, as well as the many movies containing horrific elements that are *primarily* concerned with the more common emotion of terror (and there goes a wide variety of films of *The Omen*'s ilk). For similar reasons, I sidestep the problematic case of "horror comedy," such as Roger Corman's *The Raven* and Roman Polanski's *The Fearless Vampire Killers*. Such movies can be quite entertaining (although it's a difficult trick), but the end result isn't horror.

I have restricted this survey almost entirely to British and American efforts, although this is bound to disappoint some readers; but Gothic horror is largely an Anglo-American invention, and the form has thus far reached its fullest expression in these two countries. Even so, I regret the lack of space for a fuller examination of other films, such as the often interesting Italian horror cinema, and its idiot brother, Spanish horror cinema.

Finally, my ratings are completely subjective, of course, and in some cases run counter to what little critical consensus exists. As always, you are free to disagree violently.

2

HE CAN BUILD YOU

Frankenstein Returns

THE POINT IS TO CONDUCT A REMARKABLE MAN TO DAMNA-TION. IT IS SURPRISING, AFTER ALL, HOW LONG IT TAKES—HOW DIFFICULT IT IS—TO BE CERTAIN OF DAMNATION.

—JOHN BERRYMAN

ammer's Frankenstein series has virtually nothing at all to do with Mary Shelley's book or with any previous adaptation of the story. And this is perhaps its greatest strength.

Hammer's decision to part so radically from the story as written by Shelley and developed through various plays and movies was prompted in large part by the threat of legal action by Universal, maker of the 1930s series and a company famed for its zealous protection of its copyrights. (A wise old video bootlegger once told me a basic rule of his business: You don't screw with the Mouse [Disney] or the Globe [Universal].) This threat inspired Hammer's team to counter with what seems, in retrospect, one of their canniest moves: to focus their movies on the monster-*maker* rather than the monster.

This change in focus tends to slight one of Shelley's themes, which was elaborated by Universal's James Whale and much loved by critics—the innocence and suffering of Frankenstein's child-monster. But the best Hammer Frankensteins explore the implications of the monster's existence in a fuller and more interesting way than did Universal. The Unversal Frankenstein (particularly in the earlier, better entries) is basically a new being, a

THE BARON (PETER CUSHING) CONTEMPLATES *CURSE OF FRANKENSTEIN*'S VAT-SPAWNED KILLER.

blank slate who endures the world's cruelties in Christ-like fashion. But the transplanted brains of Hammer's *The Revenge of Frankenstein*, *Frankenstein Must Be Destroyed* and *Frankenstein and the Monster from Hell* retain their memories and individuality. They're *aware* of their nightmarish plight and of the humanity they've lost, which is a far more horrifying concept, I think.

Nonetheless, the star of the Hammer series is the creator, not his handiwork. Anthony Hinds once said that Peter Cushing was his "first and only choice" for Baron Frankenstein, and this choice was certainly the most felicitous casting decision Hammer ever made. By his actions, the Frankenstein of Shelley and Universal may be "in rebellion against God," tinkering with the secrets of life and death; but he's also a wimp, perpetually wringing his hands and reeling in horror over what he's done. Cushing's character is untroubled by such self-doubt. He's solidly in the tradition of the Byronic antihero, a charming but ruthless dandy. Cushing's Frankenstein is a complex and enormously capable man, with the impulses, drives, and dedication of a true artist, and—this is the key—he truly believes in his work, which is selflessly dedicated to the advancement of mankind.

He's a sinner who could easily have been a saint, and his story explores the question of how someone with the best intentions in the world can commit acts of great evil. In that respect, it's a myth with a great deal of meaning for this sad and wounded century.

✦ ✦ ✦

THE CURSE OF FRANKENSTEIN

Hammer, 1957
P: Anthony Hinds
D: Terence Fisher
S: Jimmy Sangster
Starring Peter Cushing (*Baron Victor Frankenstein*), Hazel Court (*Elizabeth*), Robert Urquhart (*Paul Krempe*), Christopher Lee (*the Creature*) and Valerie Gaunt (*Justine*).

Nightwalkers Rating: ½

The Curse of Frankenstein is a film of remarkable significance—so much so that it's easy to lose sight of the movie itself. The film

exhibits considerable technical assurance and a top-notch performance by its star; it is, nonetheless, one of the lesser Hammer horror movies. Even so, it's noteworthy for introducing the Hammer Gothic horror formula, laying the groundwork for what would become the most successful series in the history of the British film industry.

Initially it was intended as a throwaway piece, a three-week shoot in black and white. Early on, however, the participants seemed to realize the project would be something special. The studio decided to film in color and expand the shooting schedule to five full weeks. In an interview with *Little Shoppe of Horrors*, producer Anthony Hinds recalled, "from the first day's rushes, there was immediate enthusiasm from the technicians and crew."

In nineteenth-century Switzerland, Baron Victor Frankenstein tells his story to a priest as he awaits execution. Flashing back to Victor's youth, we learn that the boy was orphaned early and assumed his father's title and riches. Victor, arrogant and passionately devoted to science, engages a tutor, Paul Krempe, to complete his education. After a few years, the two become partners in studying the nature of life itself. They succeed in reviving a drowned puppy, an achievement that Paul wants to report to the medical community. Victor, however, refuses to share their secrets, revealing his ultimate goal— the creation of a new human life from stitched-together parts. Paul is revolted by the idea, but being rather weak-willed and indecisive, he's soon helping Victor steal a corpse.

As the project proceeds, life at the Frankenstein household is complicated by the arrival of Elizabeth, the girl to whom Victor has been betrothed since childhood. Elizabeth, beautiful and a bit dull-witted, is unhappy to discover that Victor is more interested in his experiments than in her. Meanwhile, Justine, a maid who's been sleeping with Victor, boils with jealousy. To complicate things further, Paul begins to care for Elizabeth. Victor is oblivious to all this turmoil, however; he's obsessed with locating a brain for his artificial man. He finds it in the head of Professor Bernstein, a kindly Einstein type. Victor stages his "accidental" death and steals his brain, but the organ is damaged when Paul discovers Victor's grave-robbing and struggles with him.

Paul stays at the house to protect Elizabeth,

but refuses to help Victor any further. Victor pushes on, completing work on his patchwork man. A freak bolt of lightning prematurely awakens the creature, which promptly leaps at its creator's throat. (Could it be that Bernstein's ruined brain still recognizes its killer?) Paul subdues the monster and saves Victor, who's too proud of his achievement to realize what a close call he's had. Paul insists that the monster be destroyed, but while the two men argue, the thing escapes. In a nearby wood, the creature meets and kills (offscreen, thankfully) a blind man and his small grandson. The scientists track the monster, and Krempe shoots it. Unbeknownst to Paul, however, Victor promptly revives the creature, using it to dispose of Justine, who's threatening to tell Elizabeth about their arrangement.

But Victor's luck is running out. The monster escapes once again, just as Elizabeth (finally) decides to see just what's going on in that laboratory. In a rooftop confrontation, Victor shoots at his creature as it stalks Elizabeth from behind, but wounds her instead. As she passes out, Victor eliminates his creation by setting it aflame with an oil lamp. The burning monster crashes through a skylight and falls into a convenient acid vat, destroying any evidence of its existence. Returning at last to Frankenstein's prison cell, we find that Victor has been blamed for the killings. A grim-faced Paul, the only other living person to have seen the creature, denies any knowledge of it, leaving Victor to face the guillotine.

Many distinctive elements of the Hammer style emerged full-fledged in The *Curse of Frankentein*. One such element is its gorgeous and subtle color. At the time, most color movies were lensed in the old Technicolor process,

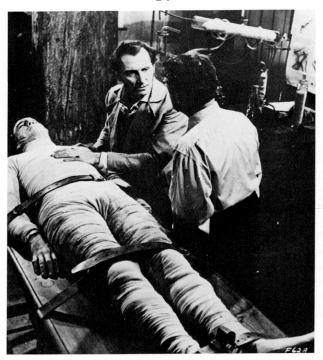

THE PRINCIPALS OF *CURSE OF FRANKENSTEIN* PREPARE TO MEDDLE IN THINGS HUMANS AREN'T MEANT TO KNOW.

which required bright and relatively flat lighting, with few shadows (think of the gaudy, brighter-than-bright look of the era's musicals.) For the Frankenstein film, director of photography Jack Asher took advantage of new Eastman film stock that could be used in relatively low light, allowing him to achieve beautiful, shadowy effects featuring rich, saturated colors in semidarkness.

Production designer Bernard Robinson's settings are a far cry from the cavernous, surreally expressionist sets featured in Universal's Frankenstein tales. Instead, in *The Curse of Frankenstein* the laboratory is somewhat mundane, utterly real-looking, and appropriate to the period. Robinson's production design is an ingenious mixture of real and *faux* opulence, comfortably mingling antiques with artful fakery; a *very* close look at the baron's stained glass windows, for instance, will reveal that they're actually crepe paper. The film also benefits from its bravura score by James Bernard, whose furiously energetic music became nearly synonymous with Hammer. Bernard's scores are always accomplished, if often repetitive (and a little too blood-and-thunderish for my taste).

Hammer ultimately made a distribution deal with Universal that gave them the right to adapt the studio's horror classics, but at this time their relationship was less cordial. While Hammer was free to use any material from Mary Shelley's novel (long in the public domain), they faced immediate legal action if they incorporated *any* elements of the Universal film series. Among other things, this gave Hammer significant difficulty in developing its monster. Universal claimed exclusive rights not only to every facet of the visual conception of the Karloff monster, but even to its lumbering gait!

Given these restrictions, numerous designs were rejected. Hammer make-up artist Phil Leakey finally devised a usable monster less than a day before shooting began. Leakey

CHRISTOPHER LEE'S "PICKLED"-LOOKING MONSTER CONFRONTS A DAMSEL IN OBVIOUS DISTRESS.

told *Little Shoppe of Horrors*, "I was utterly ashamed of it. Used a little bit of string for stitching and rubber bits on the cheeks. But it was too late then, when they'd shown it to all the publicity people…we were stuck with it." Lee's gaunt, cadaverous creature makeup has been criticized, but it's actually much closer to Shelley's original description than Karloff's was. As English film critic Leslie Halliwell remarked, Lee's monster has an interestingly "pickled" look.

Christopher Lee would achieve lasting fame in Hammer's second Gothic movie, *The Horror of Dracula*, but has considerably less to do as Frankenstein's monster. (Michael Carreras once stated flatly that Lee was chosen simply because he was tall.) A talented mime, Lee manages to inject some pathos into the role, but his efforts are constantly sabotaged by a sensationalist script that doesn't allow him to be much more than an impersonal menace. (The creature's murder of the blind man and the little child, in particular, seems like an ugly and cynical warping of famous scenes in the first two Karloff Frankenstein films.)

Baron Frankenstein, the *real* star of this movie, is also ill-served by Jimmy Sangster's screenplay. The biggest problem with the film emerges fully only in comparison to later films in the series, and that's the failure to develop the character of Baron Frankenstein beyond a position of one-dimensional villainy. Although Cushing invests the baron with a smooth charm—note the air of distracted nonchalance

with which he wipes blood on his elegant clothes—he's simply a sociopath, a relentless fanatic. In subsequent films, Cushing's Frankenstein becomes interestingly ambiguous, vacillating unpredictably between evil and a flawed heroism. He's quite capable of selfless, altruistic behavior, and his single-minded dedication to his cause becomes nearly admirable. It's a fascinating tension, and one that ultimately would make Victor Frankenstein Hammer's most memorable character.

THE REVENGE OF FRANKENSTEIN
Hammer, 1958
P: Anthony Hinds
D: Terence Fisher
S: Jimmy Sangster; additional dialogue by H. Huford Janes
Starring Peter Cushing (*Baron Frankenstein/"Dr. Victor Stein"*), Francis Matthews (*Dr. Hans Kleve*), Eunice Gayson (*Margaret*), Michael Gwynn (*"new" Karl*), Oscar Quitak (*"old" Karl*), Richard Wordsworth (*Up Patient*) and George Woodbridge (*Janitor*).

Nightwalkers rating: 💀💀💀½

The Revenge of Frankenstein was a major financial success on both sides of the Atlantic. Since its initial release, however, the film has often seemed overshadowed by its groundbreaking predecessor. Compared to the first, this film has generated relatively little scholarship, and what opinions *are* held vary pretty wildly. I may as well weigh in by saying that I consider *The Revenge of Frankenstein* greatly superior to *The Curse of Frankenstein*, and one of the very best

Hammer horrors.

This film begins where the first left off, with Baron Frankenstein facing execution. A significant glance between the crippled jailer and the executioner tells us that the baron isn't finished yet. Sure enough, the priest who heard Victor's confession ends up substituting for him in a pine box, and our favorite mad scientist departs to revive his career. A few years later, the Baron is ensconced in Carlsbruck, enjoying a thriving medical practice as "Dr. Stein." Victor's a success with society patients, and also runs a free clinic for the poor. Naturally, the baron is also pursuing his experiments. While his clinic *does* help most of his indigent patients, he's not adverse to amputating the occasional limb for the sake of his research—a pickpocket's arm, for example.

This time, however, Victor has a *willing* brain donor, namely Karl, the cripple who helped him escape execution. Their deal is straightforward: "If he saved me from the guillotine, I would give him a new body," as he tells Hans Kleve, an idealistic young doctor who becomes Victor's partner. (Hans has discovered Victor's true identity, and blackmailed him a bit with the knowledge. There's an inconsistency here; in this film everyone seems to know of Frankenstein and his infamous experiments, but in the first film we saw him condemned precisely because no one believed his story.) Victor shows Hans Karl's new body, suspended upright in a vat of liquid. Frankenstein also has another synthetic body in waiting, which (PLOT POINT!) bears a striking resemblance to Victor himself.

The brain transplant goes smoothly, and Karl receives a handsome new body. Unfortunately, he learns that Victor plans to exhibit him

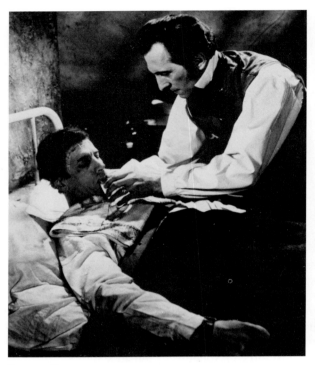

PETER CUSHING SUCCORS HIS LATEST CREATION (MICHAEL GWYNN) IN THE WITTY AND THOUGHT- FUL *REVENGE OF FRANKENSTEIN*.

to the medical community of Europe, like a prize guinea pig. Karl only wants a normal life, free from the prison of his twisted form. He's horrified by Victor's plans, and escapes. He sneaks into the laboratory to destroy his old body, but is discovered and beaten by a gleefully sadistic janitor. The beating injures Karl's brain, unhinging him and subjecting him to cannibalistic (!) impulses. He kills the janitor and later attacks a young girl. Ironically (and in a way that seems to imply some grim supernatural judgment), his new body begins contorting into the same crippled form as his original one.

Filled with remorse, Karl bursts in on a party attended by Carlsbruck's upper crust and pleads with Victor for help, calling him "Frankenstein" in front of everyone. Karl dies, but Victor's secret is out. Soon he's beaten to death by his own charity-ward patients, who now know where their amputated limbs have gone. Thinking quickly, loyal Hans removes Victor's brain and transplants it to the spare body Victor had constructed. As the film ends, we see Hans and the new, improved Frankenstein open shop as fashionable doctors in London's posh Harley Street.

Jimmy Sangster's script for *The Revenge of Frankenstein* is better in every way than his previous effort, with nice touches of black humor and some wry social commentary on the self-satisfied burghers of Carlsbruck. Sangster also manages to weave some neat ironies into his tale, not least that Victor literally *becomes* his own monster. (Note also that his own transplant is the sole truly successful experiment in the entire Frankenstein series.) Karl's plight is tragic and moving, and particularly well-realized in

Michael Gwynn's fine performance.

Cushing retains the waspish charm and sublime arrogance of Victor's first outing, but here he's allowed to deepen the character, bringing interesting new angles to light. Victor is sincerely concerned for Karl, and, in his care for his destitute patients, shows himself to be a better doctor than any of the pompous, "respectable" doctors of Carlsbruck (although his habit of occasionally borrowing their limbs does whiff of malpractice).

Most satisfying of all is the thoughtful way in which the film explores the real-world implications of Frankenstein's activities. Most previous Frankenstein movies treated the brain as if it were merely another organ, like a pancreas, without exploring the idea that these spare parts might have their own memories and agendas. *The Revenge of Frankenstein* meets this imminently logical concept head on, using it to develop a fresh, original approach to a myth cycle that badly needed it.

In all, the film is such an entertaining and engaging work that it's difficult to understand why it hasn't acquired more of a reputation. It's short on visceral scares—the beating Karl receives from the janitor is the single most disturbing scene—but this seems a fairly small loss. "Shockers" age badly simply because our ability to be shocked keeps changing. Through its willingness to grapple with ideas as well as emotion, *The Revenge of Frankenstein* proves itself to be something more, something better.

THE EVIL OF FRANKENSTEIN

Hammer, 1964
P: Anthony Hinds
D: Freddie Francis
S: Anthony Hinds, writing as "John Elder"
Starring Peter Cushing (*Baron Victor Frankenstein*), Peter Woodthorpe (*Zoltan*), Sandor Eles (*Hans*), Katy Wild (*Beggar Girl*), Duncan Lamont (*Chief of Police*), and David Hutcheson (*Burgomeister*).

Nightwalkers rating: 💀½

The Evil of Frankenstein is easily the weakest of the Peter Cushing Frankensteins (some people put *Frankenstein and the Monster from Hell* in the bottom slot, but they are, quite frankly, crazed). This film is not without interest, and it's certainly no bomb; instead it's an understandable misstep on Hammer's part.

Some six years had elapsed since Peter Cushing last played Victor Frankenstein. In the intervening period, Hammer had made a production and distribution deal with Universal International that allowed the studio to freely use elements from the old Universal Frankenstein films—the very thing Hammer had struggled to *avoid* in its first two movies, due to its healthy respect for Universal's legal department. This new freedom, alas, encouraged Hammer to temporarily abandon Terence Fisher's Frankenstein myth in favor of an ill-considered pastiche constructed almost entirely out of incidents and motifs from Universal's series. As we've seen, the first two Hammer Frankensteins are in tight continuity with one another, and the rest of the series can (with some effort) be rationalized into a coherent narrative cycle. *The Evil of Frankenstein*, however, stands entirely outside this cycle, in a sort of stagnant parallel universe.

The film opens without any reference to the events of *The Revenge of Frankenstein*. Instead of London, Victor is back in Central Europe, taking delivery on another corpse in a shabby basement laboratory. A local priest discovers his gory business, and forces the scientist and his current assistant, Hans, to leave town hastily. Victor decides to return to his home town, Karlstaad, although he's highly unwelcome there. Frankenstein's ancestral chateau proves to be long since deserted and looted. As they rummage through the wreckage of his former home, Victor tells Hans (via flashback) about the events that led to his initial exile from Karlstaad. Ten years before, he'd created his first monster; soon after, the town's terrified peasants banded together and drove the baron out. The creature itself, wounded and terrified, had wandered into the nearby mountains, presumably to die. (All this, of course, bears no resemblance whatever to the events of *The Curse of Frankenstein*.)

Karlstaad itself is in the midst of a carnival, and Victor and Hans are able to move about freely—until the baron spies the town's venal burgomeister wearing a large ring that once had belonged to him. His noisy outrage exposes him and forces him to flee once more. A deaf-mute beggar girl helps the scientists find shelter in a mountain cave, where they discover Frankenstein's original monster, perfectly preserved in a block of ice. Victor is inspired to revive his creation, so he and Hans free the monster and return with it to the ruined chateau. They seem to have forgotten that the police are after them; so, apparently, does the script. The monster is brought back to life in the castle's hastily refurbished laboratory, but its mind is strangely dormant. Victor hits on the idea of using hypnosis to reach the monster's mind, and procures the services of Zoltan, a sideshow hypnotist recently ejected from the carnival on the burgomeister's orders.

THE EVIL OF FRANKENSTEIN'S MONSTER TAKES A FIRST STEP.

Zoltan awakens the creature, but the monster will respond only to Zoltan's commands, so Victor is reluctantly forced to accept the hypnotist as a partner. Zoltan, a more practical man than Victor, sends the monster to take bloody revenge on the burgomeister. This rouses Karlstaad's less-than-vigilant police, who arrest Victor just as Zoltan, who has grown rather overconfident, is killed by the monster. The creature eludes the police, and soon Victor does, too. Monster and creator are reunited at the chateau, but come to an unhappy end. While stumbling about the lab, the monster discovers and develops a taste for brandy, then drinks a bottle of chloroform by mistake. His death throes start a fire. Hans and the beggar girl escape, but Victor is trapped in the blazing chateau, which explodes, presumably atomizing the scientist (but you never can tell....)

As I've already indicated, Anthony Hinds's script for *Evil* relies heavily on Universal's original Frankenstein series—and borrows more from the later, weaker entries in that series than from the brilliant first two. The incident of the monster being trapped in ice, for instance, is a direct lift from *Frankenstein vs. the Wolfman*, and significant chunks of *House of Frankenstein* also float in the mix. Furthermore, the script irritatingly paints Victor as a weaker and somewhat more

petulant character than we've seen before. The instance in which he reveals his identity by throwing a snit over his ring grates simply because it's something a person as coldly intelligent as Victor would never do. It's a scriptwriter's contrivance, not a believable action.

The film was director Freddie Francis's first Gothic horror film; he won the assignment after lensing two of Hammer's Hitchcockian thrillers, *Paranoiac* and *Nightmare*, both of which did well at the box office. Francis represents a difficult case for the cognoscenti of horror cinema. A brilliant photographer and a director of undeniable talent, he was involved in some of the better horror films of the sixties—movies such as *The Innocents* and *The Skull*. However, throughout his career Francis has exhibited a dismissive lack of interest in horror, and particularly in traditional Gothic themes—an attitude that affected his work, and sometimes makes it hard for horror buffs to warm up to him. About *The Evil of Frankenstein*, Francis told auteurist critic Wheeler Dixon that "I accepted the money...and I did the best that I could." Unfortunately, in this case, it doesn't seem to be modesty but an accurate assessment of the situation.

Since Terence Fisher put so strong a stamp on the Hammer Frankensteins, it's interesting to contrast his approach with that of Francis. Fisher once told *Little Shoppe of Horrors* that he'd never seen the Universal Frankensteins before beginning the Hammer series, and made a point of avoiding them, as he didn't want another man's vision to interfere with his own. Francis, in contrast, remembered being "fairly worried" about making *The Evil of Frankenstein*, precisely because of his admiration for the Karloff original. (Moreover, Francis hadn't seen Fisher's entries.) While the decision to make the film a Universal pastiche almost certainly emanated from Anthony Hinds and others in Hammer's front office, Francis seems to have agreed enthusiastically with the idea.

The movie's camerawork is reasonably dynamic, and the main laboratory set is impressive—Francis "persuade[d] Hammer to spend quite a large share of our rather low budget on the laboratory set"— but it's still a far cry from the exuberantly expressionist lab of the Karloff Frankensteins. The monster is a bigger disappointment, a clumsy caricature of Karloff's creature that looks like one of DC Comics' "Bizarros" modeled out of adobe.

It's telling that Francis thought these elements were what was important about the Karloff Frankenstein. He told Dixon: "Two ingredients in the film which I thought were completely right…a good-looking, interesting and exciting type of laboratory, and a gentle giant who one really felt sort of sorry for." Which is all very well. But it entirely misses what makes the Hammer series, soon to resume under Terence Fisher, so interesting.

ROY ASHTON'S DISAPPOINTING MAKEUP FOR *THE EVIL OF FRANKENSTEIN*'S MENACE.

fully written and seamlessly directed, with wonderful performances—it's about as good as "mere" horror movies get.

With this film, Terence Fisher resumed directorial duties for the Baron's series for the first time in nearly a decade. After the ill-fated experiment of *The Evil of Frankenstein*, Hammer seems to have decided to move as far away from the old Universal formula as possible. Once again, we're back in Hammerland, that quasi-Germanic neverland of burgomeisters and cockney accents. But this time, rather than simply providing a backdrop, this strange society's cruelties and injustices become a major focus of the movie. Farther in the background than usual is Baron Victor Frankenstein, in a bizarre plot devoid of lumbering monsters.

Instead, *Frankenstein Created Woman* veers into the occult, specifically the bizarre realm of "soul transplants." The film opens with a typically jarring Hammer moment of cruelty: A village drunk, convicted of murder, reels happily enough to his execution on the guillotine, until he realizes that the scene is being watched by his son, Hans. Years later, the adult Hans finds work with Frankenstein, who is, rather unexpectedly, living quietly in the village and conducting experiments under his own name. His pair of ruined hands is the only noticeable link with *The Evil of Frankenstein*'s firey ending. Victor's research partner is a kindly, slightly befuddled village doctor, Hertz, who is awestruck by the scientist's genius and gladly serves as his "hands." Hertz is right to be impressed, as Victor has perfected, among other items, a crude atomic pile!

Hans is the secret lover of Christina Kleve, a pretty but crippled daughter of a local innkeeper. Christina and her father both are mocked and tormented by a local trio of wealthy young swells, led by a despicable creep named Anton. After a particularly ugly confrontation, the three dandies beat the elder Kleve to death,

FRANKENSTEIN CREATED WOMAN
Hammer, 1967
P: Anthony Nelson-Keys
D: Terence Fisher
S: Anthony Hinds, writing as "John Elder"
Starring Peter Cushing (*Baron Victor Frankenstein*), Susan Denberg (*Christina Kleve*), Thorley Walters (*Dr. Hertz*), Robert Morris (*Hans*), Peter Blythe (*Anton*), Barry Warren (*Karl*), Derek Fowlds (*Johann*), and Alan MacNaughton (*Kleve*).

Nightwalkers rating:  ½

Frankenstein Created Woman is high Hammer art. One of the very last Hammer movies made at Bray studios, the company's home throughout its glory years, it is thought-

more or less for sport. Hans is blamed; being the son of a murderer, he's railroaded in court by a vicious police official, and follows his father to the scaffold. Christina returns from a medical treatment just in time to see Hans's execution—just as he had seen his own father's. Heartbroken, she drowns herself.

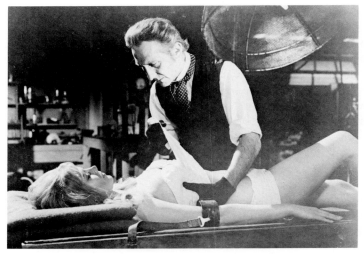

PETER CUSHING PUTS THE FINAL TOUCHES ON SUSAN DENBERG IN THE INTRIGUING *FRANKENSTEIN CREATED WOMAN*.

her second, permanent suicide in the turbulent waters of a rapids.

Frankenstein himself achieves a sort of highwater mark in likeability in *Frankenstein Created Woman*, although he still has that aristocratic chill about him. He harms no one, opposes the actions of the boneheaded police and court, and experiments on Hans and Christina at least partly out of a sense of altruism. Furthermore, there's a certain subdued warmth between Victor and Hertz that makes their relationship enjoyable (Anthony Hinds has said he modeled their relationship after that of Sherlock Holmes and Dr. Watson). In all, Victor in this film is very much the good aristocrat that frequently pops up in Terence Fisher's films, usually in opposition to some snobbish parvenu. Predictably, the town's two-bit authority figures are portrayed in a poor light; more sympathetic characters are abused by the local power structure. (It's particularly ironic to see the baron opposed to precisely the sort of domineering authoritarianism that he himself represented in *The Curse of Frankenstein*.)

This tragic turn of events, however, is highly convenient to Frankenstein's current experiment. Bored with sewing bodies together, Victor is toying with the human spirit itself. He's invented an atomic-powered force field that can capture and *transfer* a person's soul. Hans, freshly deceased, makes a perfect subject. Frankenstein captures Hans's soul from his body and transfers it into Christina's revived body, which Hertz has repaired and corrected under the baron's instruction. The resulting woman, now a flawless blonde, has no conscious memory of Christina's life, but a visit to the guillotine awakens fragmentary memories belonging to Hans, proving to Victor's satisfaction that his soul resides in her body.

But this soul seeks revenge. Hans's spirit takes control of Christina, urging her to avenge them both on Anton and his friends. Christina becomes a beautiful, deadly seductress, evening the score one by one. In between kills, she communes with Hans's head, which she keeps in a hatbox! (By the way, Frankenstein extracts Hans's soul from his headless body, which is subsequently buried. How and where did Christina come by the head?) The suspicious villagers begin to accuse Frankenstein of the mysterious murders. He, having deduced the real answer, tracks Christina down, too late to save the last of Anton's friends. Hans's soul speaks to her once more, expressing satisfaction at the completion of their task. Christina now realizes who she is and what she's done. Victor is unable to prevent

This is probably Anthony Hinds's best horror script. The "soul" angle is a nice surprise—Frankenstein had always seemed like the *ultimate* materialist, and the whole question of whether his synthetic creations possess spirit simply hadn't been raised before. The screenplay is filled with interesting textures and correspondences. It's a movie of pairings and blendings: two lovers, Hans and Christina, who literally become one; two scientists, one of whom serves as the other's hands. Two executions on the guillotine, the father's and the son's. Two drownings, both Christina's. Frankenstein's role in the film is crucial but oddly passive. He serves as a catalyst for the bloody events that follow, as if his mere presence were enough to disrupt the town's nasty hypocrisies.

Unsurprisingly, because of the gender-bending overtones of the improbable plot, the psychoanalytic school of film criticism has given the movie a healthy share of attention and turned up reams of, ah, interesting data. One critic writes, for instance, that Frankenstein's injured hands represent his symbolic castration, while another critic has observed that the movie's makers, while portraying "the difficult existence of female subjectivity in a patriarchal world," are nonetheless "unable to transform their insights into [a] more radical investigation of gender identity"—which, I'm sure, troubled Hammer's accountants no end. Paul Twitchell's *Dreadful Pleasures: An Anatomy of Modern Horror* contains an interesting illustration of the typical strengths and limitations of this approach. Twitchell notes that:

> Christina…first entices, then decapitates, her last victim. As Frankenstein happens onto the scene, she is speaking with Hans's voice to Hans's head, which she is cradling between her hands.…Amazingly, the head replies in her own voice, thereby mixing forever spiritual, corporeal, and sexual identities.

This is a neat and thought-provoking summary, and marred only by the fact that it's totally wrong. The last victim is *not* decapitated, merely stabbed (a surprising number of film writers repeat this mistake), and, more important, Hans's head does *not* reply in Christina's voice, or anyone else's. Is it just me, or do elaborate critical surmises constructed on basic errors drive *you* nuts, too?

Technically, the film can't really be faulted. It's the Hammer team doing its typically professional work, one and all. About the only sign of budgetary problems is its strangely underpopulated quality; lengthy scenes are set in taverns devoid of any customers except the main players.

Cushing's performance is filled with the little nuances that make the baron the most fully developed character in Hammer's corpus. Note, for instance, his calm and unruffled arrogance at Hans's trial; he casually browses through the court's Bible as he gives testimony, too bored and self-assured to give much attention to the pompous prosecutor. Hertz—Thorley Walters, a frequent character actor in Hammer movies—

displays the best sort of quiet, humane English charm (and he would indeed have made a fine Dr. Watson).

The other roles are all solidly given as well. "Yes, Minister" fans should look for Derek Fowlds as Johann, the most sympathetic member of Anton's gang. Susan Denberg is quite memorable as Christina, although her role is dubbed, probably due to her accent (Denberg was Austrian). Denberg was a dancer and former Playmate of the Month with one prior film to her credit. In *Frankenstein Created Woman*, she displays an obvious talent that makes her premature death shortly after the film seem doubly sad.

FRANKENSTEIN MUST BE DESTROYED

Hammer, 1969
P: Anthony Nelson-Keys
D: Terence Fisher
S: Bert Batt and Anthony Nelson-Keys
Starring Peter Cushing (*Baron Frankenstein*), Veronica Carlson (*Anna Spengler*), Freddie Jones (*Professor Richter*), Simon Ward (*Karl*), Thorley Walters (*Inspector Frisch*), Maxine Audley (*Ella Brandt*), and George Pravda (*Dr. Brandt*).

Nightwalkers rating: 💀💀½

From soul transplants, back to brain transplants.

Director Terence Fisher ranked *Frankenstein Must Be Destroyed* as one of his two best films, and his enthusiasm is widely shared. Many fans and film writers consider the film to be the finest of the Hammer Frankenstein movies, and one of the studio's best ever. Indeed, this chorus of praise is so very nearly universal that I'm a little reluctant to admit that the film leaves me rather cold, although I'm not blind to its obvious merits. What troubles me most about the film is the way it casts aside Victor Frankenstein's wonderfully ambiguous quality of heroic villainy, as it had emerged in the series, and returns the character to the one-note evil of the original film.

Frankenstein Must Be Destroyed opens with disconcertingly jaunty zither music and a decapitation murder perpetrated by Baron Frankenstein, who is gathering material for his never-ending experiments. On the run from the law, he moves into a boarding house run by young, beautiful Anna Spengler. Anna is half of a typically limp pair of Hammer-style young lovers, the other being Karl, a doctor at a local asylum. To support Anna's ailing mother, Karl has been selling drugs, a fact that allows Frankenstein to blackmail the hapless couple. (This angle is absurd, as nearly all the "recreational" drugs were not only legal but commonly available in the patent medicines of the nineteenth century.) Karl's job dovetails with Frankenstein's latest plan. In the asylum is Dr. Brandt, a brilliant scientist now insane. Frankenstein wants to study Brandt's transplant techniques, and resolves to kidnap him and cure him via brain surgery. Karl is quickly intimidated by Frankenstein's threats, as is Anna, whom Victor says he needs merely "to make coffee."

In the film's most controversial sequence, deleted from the original United States release, Frankenstein casually rapes Anna—or at least rips her blouse. (We assume worse happens after fadeout.) This scene, oddly awkward and superfluous, was imposed on the production by Hammer's James Carreras. According to Veronica Carlson's account, Carreras popped by the set after shooting was nearly complete and announced, "We haven't enough sex in this picture." A rape scene was planned and shot over the protests of both director and star. Cushing looks distinctly uncomfortable, and Carlson feels it made a hash of her character's motivations, as most of the later scenes in the picture were shot before the rape scene was added. It simply comes and goes, without leaving a trace on the characters or plot. (There's also a touch of unintended humor, since Carlson, a strapping Valkyrie, looks like she could snap Cushing in two without breaking a sweat.)

Brandt is kidnapped as planned but dies of a heart attack in the process. Undaunted,

A VICTIM OF THE BARON'S EXPERIMENTS (FREDDIE JONES) EVENS THE SCORE IN FRANKENSTEIN MUST BE DESTROYED.

Frankenstein kills another doctor at the asylum, Dr. Richter, and uses his body as a receptacle for Brandt's repaired brain. The exploration of Dr. Brandt's subsequent plight is the most interesting part of the picture. Like *Revenge of Frankenstein*, the film takes time to explore the *human* implications of brain transplantation—the profound disorientation and loneliness implicit in the idea—and mines it for pathos. Brandt-in-Richter, shaven head circled with stitches like a crown of thorns, is a truly tragic figure.

Anna and Karl plot to escape from Frankenstein. Before they get away, however, Anna encounters the Brandt-creature and, mistaking his shuffling approach for an attack, wounds him with a scalpel. Frankenstein arrives, finds his latest creation gone in the night, and without hesitation brutally kills Anna with the same knife. Brandt returns to his home and tries to make his wife understand that it's him, trapped in this alien body: "Oh God, it's me! I'm here!" Understandably, she refuses to believe him. The heartbroken scientist releases his wife and prepares to meet Frankenstein, who has followed him. Brandt douses his house with lamp oil and pulls Frankenstein into the inferno, the baron rather cravenly screaming every step of the way—which, at this point, seems no more out of character than his other odd actions in the film.

Fisher's direction was rarely better than in this admittedly flawed film. In one masterfully assembled and very tense sequence, a burst water main uncovers Brandt's body in its burial place beneath Anna's garden, forcing her to haul out the corpse and hide it before a helpful neighbor arrives. It's reminiscent of Hitchcock at his best. Freddie Jones—best known to American audiences as Mr. Bytes, the sadistic showman of *The*

Elephant Man—beautifully portrays Brandt's horror and growing despair. His scenes as Brandt are almost good enough to redeem the entire film. Much of the critical acclaim *Frankenstein Must Be Destroyed* has garnered rests squarely on his shoulders.

But Frankenstein still dominates this movie in terms of screen time, and he simply isn't given this kind of depth. Here, the baron becomes a blackmailer, a rapist, a woman-killer, and finally a coward, in a chilly negation of the complexity and near-heroism he displayed in earlier and better films. We can't sympathize with Baron Frankenstein, or root for him, even reluctantly; this time out, he isn't even all that interesting. One can, of course, argue that this was precisely the point. Hammer critic David Pirie once proposed that Frankenstein's bizarre swing into total evil "finally implicate[s] the audience in their own sympathy for him and arouse[s] their guilt." This could be true; it could also be that the scripters, both new to screenwriting, simply didn't give a damn about the previous characterization. In either case, *Frankenstein Must Be Destroyed* lacks the kind of character-based texture that distinguishes the best entries in this series.

HORROR OF FRANKENSTEIN

Hammer, 1970

P, D: Jimmy Sangster
S: Jeremy Burnham & Jimmy Sangster
Starring Ralph Bates (*Victor Frankenstein*), Kate O'Mara (*Alys*), Graham James (*Wilhelm*), Veronica Carlson (*Elizabeth*), Bernard Archard (*Elizabeth's father*), Dennis Price (*Grave robber*), Joan Rice (*Grave robber's wife*), and David Prowse (*the Monster*).

Nightwalkers rating: 💀 💀

Horror of Frankenstein, a misguided remake of *The Curse of Frankenstein*, is so disliked by most Hammer enthusiasts that I passed up chances to see it for years. Now, having done so, I can say that it's better than I expected—but only just. The film takes the element of black humor always present in classic Hammer and runs with it, descending all too often into ill-considered farce.

The sniggering tone is established in the opening shot, in which schoolboy Victor Frankenstein doodles dotted lines across an engraving of a female nude, as if marking the cuts of beef on a cow. *This* Victor is smug and cheerfully amoral, arranging an "accidental" death for his father when the baron refuses to bankroll his university studies in Vienna. After capping his university career by impregnating the dean's daughter, he returns to assume his father's title and holdings—not least of which is Alys, the old baron's mistress. With a college chum, Wilhelm, Frankenstein begins his research. At one point, Victor runs current through a stolen hand, which springs into the classic English two-fingered up-yours sign. Unperturbed, Victor says he thinks he'll send it to his old dean, as a going-away present.

Life settles into a pleasant routine of corpse-carving by day, and Alys's embraces at night. Frankenstein meets a childhood friend, Elizabeth, now flowered into spectacular womanhood. She still carries a torch for Victor, who seems quite incapable of loving anyone. After dinner with Elizabeth and her father, Victor steals the family's pet turtle(!) and later kills and revives it, in his first successful experiment in reanimation. Encouraged by this breakthrough, the new baron engages a genial husband-and-wife body-snatching team and purchases a whole *bunch* of dead 'uns. Wilhelm begins to get cold feet and assumes the tiresome moralizing role essayed by Paul Urquhart in the original *Curse of Frankenstein*—"you're tampering with forces we don't fully understand," and so on—but Victor offs him before he can get very far with his sermon.

His synthetic man nearly complete, Victor decides to borrow a brain from Elizabeth's father, and slyly poisons his cognac. Victor's body snatcher, however, drops the brain, repeating the damaged-organ gambit from the original film. He pays for his clumsiness when Victor dissolves him in a handy acid vat. The finished monster is an unimpressive, homicidal thug whom Victor uses to silence various inconvenient people, including Alys, who unwisely attempts blackmail. Elizabeth, now a destitute orphan, comes to stay with Victor. She is predictably threatened by the monster, and predictably escapes. At last, Frankenstein attracts the attention of the local gendarmes. He hides his monster in an empty acid vat but, during a nervous interview with the police, the vat is inadvertently flooded, leaving a rueful but wiser

Victor monster-less but free as a bird.

Horror of Frankenstein creator Jimmy Sangster was one of the most important members of the original Hammer family, having scripted most of the studio's initial wave of horror movies. Early on, though, he tired of Gothic themes and devoted his energies to writ-

RALPH BATES'S YOUNGER AND SILLIER EDITION OF THE MONSTER-MAKER, IN *HORROR OF FRANKENSTEIN*.

ing suspense films of the *Psycho* ilk, such as *Scream of Fear* and *Mania*. *Horror of Frankenstein* was Sangster's directorial debut. According to an interview in *Little Shoppe of Horrors*, the assignment essentially was bribery, to lure him back to the company's traditional horror line: "Hammer asked me to do a script on *Horror of Frankenstein* and I didn't want to; they said I could produce it as well [and] I still didn't want to; finally they said I could direct it...so I did it." He went on to direct two more films, including another horror project, *Lust for a Vampire*, discussed elsewhere in this volume. As a director, Sangster made a pretty good writer.

Some of the lighthearted fare in *Horror of Frankenstein* works, although quite a lot doesn't. The best bits involve the amiable body snatchers, splendid turns by character actors Dennis Price and Joan Rice. Furthermore, Ralph Bates, whose horror work often fails to impress me, is intermittently effective at the thankless task of filling Peter Cushing's boots. Bristol native Bates was "discovered" by Hammer after playing Caligula in a British television series, *The Caesars*, and was groomed by the studio as a horror star through a string of films including *Horror of Frankenstein*. Bates lacks the gravity Peter Cushing brought to the role. Instead, he plays his specialty, the insufferable upper-class twit. (He was, in a way, the Bill Murray of Hammer horror.) But Bates, who passed away in 1991, had a certain wry gift for humor, and often

manages to lift the film into the realm of irony rather than slapstick.

Another standout is Kate O'Mara. With the possible exception of American Yvette Vickers, she was the most depraved-looking actress ever to appear in genre films, and her Alys is an alluring menace, dripping greed and calcu-lation. You can see the wheels turning behind her eyes. O'Mara also appeared in *The Vampire Lovers* (which see), but turned down a starring, multi-picture contract with Hammer because she feared typecasting. She opted instead for a varied career in theater and television (including a recurring role on "Dynasty").

Unfortunately, *Horror of Frankenstein*'s monster is the least impressive of Hammer's entire series. Three-time British weightlifting champion Dave Prowse plays the monster as best he can, but the part as scripted is complete-ly without interest or pathos. He's simply *there*, looking like some dome-headed extra from an Italian strongman epic, a plot point rather than a character. While Prowse seems doomed to play, ah, strong, silent types, his career definitely led to better things, most notably the role of Darth Vader in the *Star Wars* series (although the char-acter was voiced by James Earl Jones).

Horror of Frankenstein was double-billed with the far worse *Scars of Dracula*, and did poorly. It seems to have convinced Hammer that the horror-and-humor combination was a com-mercial loser. Looking back with a quarter-cen-tury's worth of hindsight, that still seems a pretty safe bet. Horror and humor *can* be combined effectively, but it's best done in small doses, with a steady hand like that of Universal's James Whale at the helm. For the most part, horror fans prefer their fare straight—no chaser, no smirks.

FRANKENSTEIN AND THE MONSTER FROM HELL

Hammer, 1973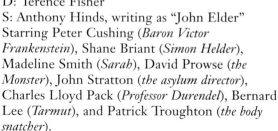
P: Roy Skeggs
D: Terence Fisher
S: Anthony Hinds, writing as "John Elder"
Starring Peter Cushing (*Baron Victor Frankenstein*), Shane Briant (*Simon Helder*), Madeline Smith (*Sarah*), David Prowse (*the Monster*), John Stratton (*the asylum director*), Charles Lloyd Pack (*Professor Durendel*), Bernard Lee (*Tarmut*), and Patrick Troughton (*the body snatcher*).

Nightwalkers rating: 💀💀💀

Frankenstein and the Monster from Hell was, sadly, a film of endings and terminations: the last Hammer Frankenstein, the last movie directed by Terence Fisher, and the last really first-rate horror film made by the legendary studio. This extravagantly titled movie has a mixed reputation with enthusiasts, yet despite all the criticisms leveled at it, some of them quite valid, it seems to me severely underrated. *Frankenstein and the Monster from Hell* is a haunting, affecting movie, and a worthy coda to Hammer Film Productions' remarkable run.

The film returns us to the Peter Cushing cycle that left off with 1969's *Frankenstein Must Be Destroyed*, and ignores the misfire of *Horror of Frankenstein*. Simon Helder, a young doctor, idolizes Frankenstein and is attempting to duplicate his research. In manner and temperament, Simon is the image of the young, arrogant Victor of *Curse of Frankenstein* (with a jigger of Ralph Bates's super-

cilious take on the character), and the authorities take just as dim a view of his work. Simon is convicted of sorcery and imprisoned in Carlsbad Asylum, as Frankenstein had been, some years before. Carlsbad is a Bedlam-style institution with sadistic warders and a giggling, lecherous director who seems more than a little deranged himself.

However, after a brief initiation into the brutal world of this madhouse, Simon discovers that the real power behind the institution is its resident physician, Dr. Victor—better known to us as Victor Frankenstein. The baron, it emerges, had turned the tables on his captors through judicious blackmail. Now, after staging his own death and assuming a new identity, he rules the asylum with an iron hand. Simon, who is very nearly as resourceful and strong-willed as Victor himself, becomes his assistant (giving the baron the first really top-notch help he's had since *The Revenge of Frankenstein*). However, Simon begins to doubt his idol's judgment, and his sanity, as he learns more about the baron's current project.

Once again, as in *The Revenge of Frankenstein*, Victor is using a medical position as a handy source for experimental materials. A brutish killer named Schneider, has supplied the newest monster with a powerful, apelike body. It was patched together under Victor's instructions by Sarah, a mute girl whom the adoring inmates call Angel. (Remember, Victor's hands were injured in *Evil of Frankenstein*, and the inferno in *Frankenstein Must Be Destroyed* probably didn't do them much good either.) With Simon's help, stolen hands and eyes are added to the creature. As always, a new brain comes last. Victor selects a distinguished prisoner, Professor Durendel, a musical and mathe-

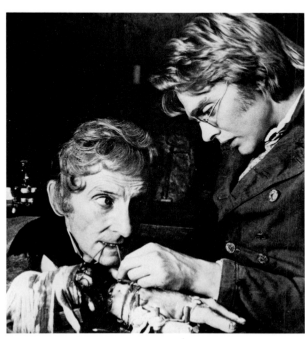

PETER CUSHING, OBVIOUSLY A GOOD SPORT, IN AN ODD POSE FROM *FRANKENSTEIN AND THE MONSTER FROM HELL*.

matical genius given to fits of violence, who desperately wants to be released. After saying "I'm not a murderer"— a pretty astonishing declaration, in light of his past behavior— Victor drives Durendel to suicide by letting him know he's been diagnosed as incurably insane.

Simon discovers he has a conscience after all, and is revolted by Victor's clever ploy. Nonetheless, he assists in the transplant. Durendel wakes up in his new hulk of a body, and is understandably distraught. There's a pathetic scene in which he discovers that his apelike hands can't manipulate his beloved violin. Soon, the body's old homicidal tendencies somehow begin resurfacing. Schneider had gouged his victims with broken glass, and now Durendel-the-monster uses the same weapon in an abortive attack on Simon. This crisis past, Victor casually mentions a *truly* insane plan—to mate the monster with Angel—and even makes the repellent suggestion that this might cure her, for she's the asylum director's daughter, and became mute after her father raped her.

Simon, by now disgusted with his former hero, and more than a little in love with Angel, attempts to kill the monster. He fails, but his attempt drives the monster berserk. The Durendel-creature kills the asylum director, who richly deserves it, but is literally torn to pieces by the other inmates when they think he threatens Angel. Victor is unruffled—and quite mad. Simon listens in cold horror as a vacant-eyed Victor prattles on about their next experiment: "Next time, we will need new material…Herr Adler in 106, perhaps?"

To dispose of some of the film's oft-cited problems: Yes, the script is derivative and rather weak. It seems content to recycle ideas from previous entries in the series; Durendel's torment is

HOPELESSLY INSANE, HORRIBLY ALONE: FRANKENSTEIN'S SAD FATE IN *MONSTER FROM HELL*.

a pale shadow of Dr. Richter's predicament in *Frankenstein Must Be Destroyed*. The monster's death seems arbitrary, while the barely sketched-in romance between Simon and Angel is all too predictable. And yes, the monster makeup is pretty terrible, making the monster look faintly like an overgrown troll doll; there's just no way this rotund, hairy lump could *ever* have been a man. (Nevertheless, David Prowse creates some genuine pathos under this ridiculous suit. It's miles above his performance in *Horror of Frankenstein*.)

Moreover, the film is marred by clumsy bursts of graphic violence and gore, obviously designed to compete with the nastier theatrical fare then becoming more popular. These silly scenes are segregated into brief bites that could be easily deleted for television, and the film loses absolutely nothing without them.

Terence Fisher's direction arguably is a bit more perfunctory, a bit more static than in his previous works. Possibly this was due to his failing health, as Fisher was a dying man at this point, his health broken by two auto accidents and long periods of convalescence. His wife, Morag, has stated that it was obvious at the time that this was Fisher's last film. His academic admirer Wheeler Dixon has put it rather eloquently: "…there is an undeniable tone of farewell…as if all involved knew this would be their last chance to work together." Hammer would not outlive its greatest director's departure.

Frankenstein and the Monster from Hell died at the box office, and helped hurry Hammer into extinction. But I suspect its failure had less to do with the problems I've mentioned than with the simple fact that the film seemed so out of step with its times. After all, 1973 was the year of *The Exorcist*, which overturned nearly everyone's ideas about what a horror film could and should be; the Hammer formula, once so controversial, had come to seem bland and conservative in the year of *Don't Look in the Basement* and *Silent Night, Bloody Night*.

And yet, and yet...I've found that this profoundly pessimistic film lingers in the memory more than all but a handful of Hammer's best. Save for those odd and dispensable gory scenes, the movie blends well with its classic predecessors. It's a handsome, competent production, largely free of the technical shoddiness of other late Hammer efforts like *Scars of Dracula*. Yet something grimmer and sadder has crept into the mix, reflected even in Scott MacGregor's simple but effective set designs. In setting the film almost entirely inside the asylum, Fisher opts for a cold, nearly monochrome palette that couldn't be more different from the decadent splendor of Hammer's glory days. It's a chill and funereal setting, suitable for the sad business at hand: the disintegration of the most interesting character in the history of horror films.

In *Frankenstein and the Monster from Hell*, Victor Frankenstein meets with a final mental and moral collapse. At first, he seems to have regained the complex and contradictory character that made him so interesting in the earlier films, and was so oddly missing in *Frankenstein Must Be Destroyed*. His relationship with Simon at first feels almost paternal; at times he seems to

be looking to the younger man for approval. But a deeper and more disturbing change in Victor soon becomes apparent. It's reflected even in his features, which display all too clearly the toll his obsessions have taken on him. (Peter Cushing's mourning over the recent death of his wife had given his face a gaunt and haunted look that, ironically, suited the film's purposes well.)

The film forces those of us who've stuck through the entire Frankenstein series to reflect on how we've watched Victor evolve. He's still essentially an unsolvable puzzle, but there's at least a feeling that in some way we know this man—a feeling that makes it hard to accept the change we see in him now. At first, only a few notes play false; his helpless laughter at a bad joke jars simply because it's so unlike him. But at last, the formidable dedication, which had always seemed fanatical but rational, begins to look like madness. What purpose do these experiments serve any longer, now that Victor is buried away in an asylum? There's no longer any talk of improving mankind, or revolutionizing science. Frankenstein seems trapped on a treadmill, an endless loop of pointless suffering and cruelty.

By the end of the film, we realize that the baron is no longer capable of change, or even of reason; the Victor we thought we knew is gone. It's a chilling conclusion to what is, despite a few bumpy spots, the finest horror series ever made.

3

THE PRINCE OF DARKNESS

Count Dracula

THERE WAS IN HIM A VITAL SCORN OF ALL;

AS IF THE WORST HAD FALL'N WHICH COULD BEFALL,

HE STOOD A STRANGER IN THIS BREATHING WORLD,

AN ERRING SPIRIT FROM ANOTHER HURL'D...

—LORD BYRON, *LARA*

he most famous character in all of horror entertainment was conceived by Bram Stoker, an Irish theatrical agent, and born in May 1897. Stoker had no idea he'd created one of the twentieth century's most popular and enduring Rorshach blots.

Dracula, so redolent of blood and sex and mystery, is a myth pattern of enduring appeal, that seems to hold within its pages all the fears and confusion of the last hundred years. Depending upon who guides you through the work, you may meet Dracula, the sinister Easterner, bent on tainting England's pure Aryan blood; Dracula, the liberator of unholy feminine passions, the underminer of Victorian home life and the male's pride of place; Dracula as an expression of the irrational, a seed of madness blooming into a straight-laced era's greatest fear, the loss of self-control. All of which may well be true. It's also a fine Gothic adventure, if indifferently written in places. Reluctant as I am to agree with some of our more feverish academics, it seems clear that *Dracula* is a much better book than is generally acknowledged, and probably a better book than its author intended or realized.

Quite a lot of scholarship has been devoted to the shadowy historical figure, Vlad Tepes, whom Dracula once was, implicitly in the book and explicitly in at least two films. Transylvania provided Stoker with an exotic and little-known setting, and in Vlad the Impaler he found a suitably monstrous personage to give the book its requisite Gothic underpinning of antiquity. Beyond this, however, Vlad ultimately seems rather irrelevant to the character of Dracula. He was just a psychopath, brave enough in battle, but interesting only because the scope and barbarity of his crimes were on an Oriental scale that was unusual in the Europe of his day. Had he been an able general and pyramid-of-skulls builder for Genghis Khan, say, he'd barely rate a footnote.

"Wrath and fury": Christopher Lee's brilliant turn as Bram Stoker's evil count in *Horror of Dracula*.

Those who've gone spelunking in Bram Stoker's private life have turned up more suggestive material. The popular conception of Stoker, to the extent that one exists at all, is fairly colorless, but if he was bland, he certainly kept interesting company. He spent twenty-eight years as devoted manager to Sir Henry Irving, the most famous actor of his day, an arrogant snob who treated Stoker with studied cruelty. Their relationship was so odd as to inevitably raise suggestions of homoerotic masochism. Some have suggested that Dracula is in part modeled on the imperious actor, and even that the relationship between Irving and Stoker seems to have echoes of that between the vampire king and his hapless servant, Renfield. Yet Stoker was also a man who won and married a society beauty that Oscar Wilde had wanted for himself (when Wilde thought that was what he wanted). More interesting, he was a close friend of Whistler who knew Beardsley and moved among the so-called decadents of England's yellow nineties, those strange years of exquisitely drawn phalluses and the Love That Dare Not Speak Its Name.

It's no surprise, of course, that the hidden sexuality of the late Victorian period should seem so overheated, so schoolboyish, given the era's profound repression of normal sexual impulses. Squeeze the toothpaste tube at one end and see what happens to the other. Yet sex for Stoker's era, like our own, held a special horror; syphilis, vehicle of madness and death, then incurable and rampant among the sexually active, just as AIDS is today. Certainly, a major subtext of *Dracula*—and the element that Hammer uniquely brought to the fore— was the characteristically English theme of repression and its consequences, the forbidden that cannot be forever contained. Stoker gave us the perfect symbol for this sex-equals-death conundrum, and Hammer used it and abused it without ever quite destroying its power: Count Dracula, charming, seductive, unstoppable, a contaminant, a corruption in the blood.

HORROR OF DRACULA
(United Kingdom title: *Dracula*)
Hammer, 1958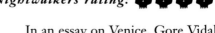
P: Anthony Hinds
D: Terence Fisher
S: Jimmy Sangster
Starring Peter Cushing (*Doctor Van Helsing*), Christopher Lee (*Count Dracula*), Michael Gough (*Arthur Holmwood*), Melissa Stribling (*Mina Holmwood*), Carol Marsh (*Lucy Holmwood*), John Van Eyssen (*Jonathan Harker*), Olga Dickie (*Gerda*), and Charles Lloyd Pack (*Doctor Seward*).

Nightwalkers rating: 💀💀💀💀

In an essay on Venice, Gore Vidal once remarked that it's simply no longer possible to say anything original on the topic; every bush-league epiphany you might have has already been put on paper by someone else. I know just how that feels when I turn to *Horror of Dracula*, arguably the best-loved horror film of the baby-boom era. Tens of thousands of words have already been expended on this one, including some amusingly overheated deep-think analysis. But peel back all the verbiage and "metatext," and you'll find a stylish and exciting movie, quite possibly the most satisfying vampire film ever made.

If *Curse of Frankenstein* introduced the Hammer formula, *Horror of Dracula* crystallized it at a level of near-perfection, providing the studio's horror efforts with a benchmark they would rarely achieve again. It's a polished and beautifully acted movie that has a wonderful sense of its own gravity and seriousness, balanced with furious bursts of action. It's a timeless film, too, which has lost very little of its impact in nearly forty years.

May 1885: *Horror of Dracula* opens with Jonathan Harker's arrival at Castle Dracula. An innocent young solicitor in the novel, this Harker is neither young nor innocent. Instead, he's a middle-aged librarian hired to catalog Dracula's ancient library, and with a secret mission—to *kill* Dracula, and "forever end this man's reign of terror." Harker is received hospitably by the count, who significantly admires a photograph of Harker's fiancé, Lucy Holmwood. Jonathan settles in to await his chance, but, after narrowly escaping an attack by Dracula's concubine, he's made a prisoner, locked in his bedroom. Near dusk, Harker awakens, and escapes through a window. After leaving his journal in a nearby tree, Harker manages to find Dracula's crypt, and to stake the count's bride, who instantly crumbles into old age and death. But he's dawdled too long, and as the sun goes down, we see that the count has left his coffin. Harker is trapped in the crypt with Dracula, who slowly swings the door shut behind him....

Next we meet a slight but steely and curiously formidable man, Dr. Van Helsing, Jonathan's partner in the hunt for Dracula. The terrified peasants near Castle Dracula won't talk to him, but Harker's journal has been found, and a kind barmaid slips it to Van Helsing. The professor pieces together the story and goes to the castle himself, in time to see Dracula's coffin carried away by a speeding hearse. He finds Jonathan, now in a vampiric trance in Dracula's crypt, and frees his friend from the vampire's curse with a sharpened stake. Van Helsing then travels to nearby Klausenberg to report Harker's demise to Lucy. She is too ill to receive him and,

as he refuses to give any details about Jonathan's death, the professor initially is rebuffed by Lucy's brother, Arthur Holmwood. However, Van Helsing soon returns when it becomes apparent that Lucy's "illness" is Dracula's doing. Van Helsing is unable to prevent her death, but, with Arthur's help (and in the most effective cinematic rendition yet of one of the novel's most remarkable scenes) he saves her soul when she, too, begins to walk the night as one of the undead.

Meanwhile, Dracula shifts his attentions to Arthur's wife, Mina. Lured away from her house on a false pretext, Mina is attacked by the count in an undertaker's parlor. She returns home with a look of complete erotic satisfaction, and attempts to hide her rendezvous, exactly as one might disguise an affair. She's given away when a cross Arthur gives her burns her hand, a telltale sign of vampiric infection taken directly from Stoker. Van Helsing and Arthur search for Dracula by day, and watch over the house by night, but the attacks on Mina continue. In one memorable scene, she's found sprawled across her bed and covered in blood, in a direct and effective visual metaphor for rape. The two men then find that Mina has given the vampire refuge *within the house itself*, in its cellars. Discovered, Dracula abducts Mina and flees, returning to the safety of his castle and its undiscovered hiding places. Van Helsing and Arthur pursue him, saving Mina. Finally, the doctor and the centuries-old count face one another directly, in a final, definitive confrontation.

Jimmy Sangster's screenplay is an intelligent reduction of Stoker's novel that changes many of its particulars, eliminating characters and entire subplots (such as Renfield's), while mostly remaining faithful to its basic structure and themes. (However, it's interesting to note how Harker's mission changes the original story's thrust. In the book, Jonathan, Lucy, and Mina are simply innocent victims, but in *Horror of Dracula*, Harker is, after all, *looking* for trouble, making Dracula's subsequent attacks seem more like revenge—or a need to replace the female companion that Harker had so inconveniently dispatched.) Many of Sangster's other changes were necessitated by economics. The generalized Middle European setting condenses the book's sprawling geography so that the story's major settings all are within easy horseback rides of each other. Sangster also removes many of Dracula's more fanciful powers, such as his ability to shape-shift, thus bringing the film closer to plausibility (none of those painfully obvious bat puppets in *this* film, at any rate) while easing the strain on a meager special effects budget.

Despite the changes, *Horror of Dracula* is well-grounded in Stoker's novel. As

LUCY (CAROL MARSH) AWAITS HER UNDEAD CONSORT, IN A POWERFULLY EROTIC SEQUENCE FROM *HORROR OF DRACULA*.

with *Curse of Frankenstein*, Terence Fisher pointedly declined to see the Universal version, or to refer to it in any way, preferring to craft a fresh interpretation of the material. As always, despite the Central European references, Fisher's setting is transparently Victorian England, and the characters all are the recognizable English types Fisher loved so well—the comic peasants (good for a few flashes of a purely British music-hall humor); the well-meaning, repressed bourgeois; and the arrogant, commanding noble, who rips apart the fabric of the Holmwood's homey and all-too-conventional lives. All this provides a backdrop for the purest expression ever of Hammer's constant theme of Good versus Evil, as embodied by the two actors most synonymous with the studio.

Horror of Dracula made an international star of Christopher Lee, and his talent for athletic villainy was never put to better use than here. The film follows Stoker's book closely by first introducing Dracula and establishing his capacity for destruction, then keeping him offstage for much of the remaining story as an unseen menace. For this structure to work, it's essential that the vampire establish an overwhelmingly strong presence at the outset, so that his threat will loom in the viewer's mind during his absence from the foreground plot. *Horror of Dracula* accomplishes this through an opposing pair of scenes. In his first appearance, Lee's Dracula is disconcertingly normal. Audiences hoping to snicker at some arch, stylized bogeyman along Lugosi's lines were surprised by the handsome and crisply polite aristo-

crat who greets Harker. (Although he lacks the mustache Stoker gave his character, Lee is infinitely closer to the book's Dracula than Lugosi's jowly villain.) The only touch of the strange is nearly subliminal; all sound for the scene was carefully dubbed in so that, if you pay close attention, you'll notice that Harker's feet ring on the castle's stone floors, while Dracula and his bride move *without any sound at all*, giving them a subtly unearthly quality.

Dracula's second appearance is something else again. As Harker nearly succumbs to Dracula's female companion, Dracula *explodes* into the room. In tight closeup, we see his mouth smeared with blood, and eyes burning crimson (a painful contact-lens-induced effect). The enraged vampire tosses the woman aside with more than human strength, as if she were a doll, and sends Jonathan flying with a casual blow. When Harker, still believing the woman to be human, attempts to struggle with Dracula, the vampire begins to strangle him. Another unforgettable closeup from Harker's point of view shows us Lee's face contorted into a mask of hatred and bloodlust (a remarkable piece of mime). Then he contemptuously casts Harker aside and sweeps his consort from the room. The two sequences neatly define Dracula's character and the threat he represents, while creating the necessary sense of danger to project his presence throughout the film's quieter midsection.

Yet Peter Cushing's Van Helsing is nearly as dynamic as the count himself. The stern vampire hunter is one of Cushing's greatest conceptions for Hammer, wedding Victor Frankenstein's knowledge, drive, and resourcefulness with an almost saintly purity of purpose—very much the "manly Christianity" to which so many Victorians aspired. Van Helsing is decent and kind, yet ruthless when fighting evil, a trait best displayed in the film's climax.

Cushing was widely recognized among his fellow actors for his ingenuity with props (watch how often and how deftly his characters occupy themselves with some bit of business involving a magnifying glass, a pipe, or what have you), and he devised much of the final sequence on the spot, on the last day of filming. During his final battle with Dracula, Van Helsing makes a running leap from a long table (the only scene in which Cushing is doubled), and seizes the castle's heavy, brocaded curtains, pulling them down with his own weight and trapping the vampire in the sun's lethal rays. Cushing then was supposed to produce a cross from his pocket, but he'd already done so twice in the film. Not wanting to appear to be "a crucifix salesman," the actor provided a better solution. Van Helsing grabs a pair of ornate candlesticks from the table and slams them together, improvising a cross, and forces Dracula back into a spectacular death by disintegration (courtesy of Sid Pearson's startling special effects). This climax is actually a considerable improvement on the drawn-out, second-hand denouement of Stoker's novel. In some ways, I think it's the best scene Hammer ever did.

Horror of Dracula wouldn't be nearly so memorable without the efforts of Jack Asher, the director of photography who turned in what might well be his best work ever for this film. Asher once told *Little Shoppe of Horrors,* "*Curse of Frankenstein* was a tryout, a debut of my ideas for photographing color....When we started *Horror of Dracula,* I felt a settling down, a maturing of style. I began to feel we had something special." Asher concocted a vibrant color scheme dominated by brilliant red, the blood color that becomes the movie's binding symbol for evil and carnality. The look is velvety rich, highlighting Bernard Robinson's typically miraculous sets. (Note the floor in Castle Dracula, with its enormous astrological chart, seemingly of colored marble and mosaic; almost unbelievably, it's drawn on paper.) Together, Asher and Robinson make this under-$200,000 quickie look like a million uninflated bucks. The *New York Daily News* called Asher's elegant photography "good enough to frame," and his work was nominated for an Oscar—a doubly impressive honor considering the general contempt in which horror movies were held at the time.

What little on-screen violence is featured in *Horror of Dracula* has quite lost its power to shock jaded nineties types like you and me, so much so that some may find it hard to understand why contemporary observers found the movie so shocking. The American popular press responded fairly warmly to *Horror of Dracula,* but many British critics professed revulsion; the *Observer* apologized to America(!) for the movie's "sickening bad taste." This nausea was shared by many horror cognoscenti raised on Universal's mannered fairy tales of the thirties and forties. Even in the late 1970s, Ivan Butler's influential *Horror in the Cinema* rather sniffily called the film "an orgy of blood-letting, stake-driving and general mayhem." To which one can only respond: huh? Explicit violence in *Horror of Dracula* essentially is limited to one scene, Lucy's staking, when some blood wells from around the stake in a quick cut. The other stakings are off-camera. Other than some fleeting neck-nibbling and Dracula's admittedly disturbing destruction, that's the entire "orgy of mayhem."

Of course, what *really* bothered some critics was the way *Horror of Dracula* capitalized on the novel's sexual subtext, in a way never dreamed of in the dear old Universal days. Van Helsing compares Dracula's hold over his victims to drug addiction, but the film makes it clear that his magnetism is primarily erotic, a quality that liberates and inflames women's sexual instincts—which may have seemed subversive and dangerous both in the Victorian period and the 1950s. Fisher crafts some clever scenes to make the point, as when Lucy readies herself for the count's nightly visit, opening the French doors to her bedroom, her face flushed with excitement and longing, as leaves swirl in a breeze outside the door. It's a moment of considerable beauty and subtlety, electric with eroticism. (By the same token, you can of course interpret the stakings that break the vampire's spell as symbolic rape, and believe me, plenty of people have.)

All this praise doesn't mean I wouldn't have liked to see a few things in the film done differently. Michael Gough, a good actor who could be astonishingly bad in junkers like *Konga,* is mediocre at best as Arthur Holmwood, clearly at a loss for a proper handle on the character. A broader objection concerns the screenplay. The first third of Stoker's *Dracula* is usually called the most compelling stretch of the book—the part in which Dracula demonstrates the remnants of his humanity. Before he bares his teeth, as it were. (Stoker's novel is quite definite on the subject of Dracula's charm, and even refers to his "sweet courtesy.") Lee handles this aspect of the character extremely well in Hammer's truncated version of this sequence, but Sangster's screenplay is in a hurry to move on to the excitement, and I for one would have liked to see more of the count's human parts. (Later Hammer Dracula films neglect the vampire's humanity almost completely, to their loss.)

Still, I cheerfully cast these misgivings aside each time I see *Horror of Dracula*. Four significant adaptations of *Dracula* have come and gone since Hammer's series ended, and despite major stars and fat budgets, none displays the conviction and authority of this effort. The most fitting summation I could give for *Horror of Dracula* is something I stumbled on from Ezra Pound, of all people, who said in his *ABC of Reading*: "A classic is a classic not because it conforms to certain rules, or fits certain definitions....It is a classic because of a certain eternal and irrepressible freshness."

DAVID PEEL AS THE ELEGANT VAMPIRE BARON MEINSTER IN *BRIDES OF DRACULA*.

Largely ignored by the critics of its day (but weren't most Hammer films?) and disliked for years by fans of Christopher Lee, *Brides of Dracula* has taken a long time to find its audience. Strictly speaking, this isn't a Dracula movie at all, since it chronicles the depredations of a "disciple" of the count, Baron Meinster. (A more conventional Dracula sequel apparently was put aside when Lee asked for more money than Hammer was willing to spend.) However, the film features a highly impressive appearance by the count's nemesis, Professor Van Helsing, and for this reason alone deserves a prominent place in the canon. Today, the film is generally regarded as one of the very best Hammer horrors; some heretics even consider it superior to *Horror of Dracula*, with handsomer production values and a richer, more satisfying story. (Settle down. I *said* it was heresy.)

A beautiful French schoolmistress, Marianne Danielle, is headed for a new post in Badstein, somewhere in nineteenth-century Transylvania. While stopping in a hamlet, Marianne is abandoned by her coach driver, and accepts the hospitality of the formidably sinister Baroness Meinster. Ensconced in Castle Meinster, Marianne discovers that the baroness keeps her young and charming son a prisoner, claiming that he is hopelessly mad. However, in a lovely moonlit scene on the castle's battlements, the young baron convinces Marianne that his mother has imprisoned him to retain the family properties, and persuades her to free him.

Bad idea. The baron attacks his mother, fangs bared. Soon Marianne discovers her bleeding body, and Greta, the baroness's lunatic servant, tells her that she's just freed a vampire! Marianne flees the castle and is found, hysterical, by vampire-hunter supreme Van Helsing,

BRIDES OF DRACULA
Hammer, 1960
P: Anthony Hinds
D: Terence Fisher
S: Jimmy Sangster, Peter Bryan and Edward Percy
Starring Peter Cushing (*Professor Van Helsing*), David Peel (*Baron Meinster*), Yvonne Monlaur (*Marianne Danielle*), Martita Hunt (*Baroness Meinster*), Freda Jackson (*Greta*), and Andree Melly (*Gina*).

Nightwalkers rating: 💀💀💀½

who is investigating some mysterious deaths in the area. Van Helsing takes Marianne to the school and returns to investigate Castle Meinster. There he fends off the baron with a crucifix, and finds the baroness, now a vampire herself and wracked with grief and shame. She explains that she had encouraged her son in dissolute habits, and sheltered and fed him when he contracted the "disease" of vampirism. Presumably, she lured Marianne to the castle to supply her son with blood. The pathetic baroness willingly submits to Van Helsing's liberating stake.

Meanwhile, in Badstein, the baron ingratiates himself with the residents of the school, and particularly with Marianne, who agrees to marry him. He also vampirizes Gina, another instructress, who joins a village girl in his undead harem. Van Helsing is on Meinster's trail, however, and confronts the vampire and his brides in their lair, a deserted windmill. After a struggle, Van Helsing is bitten and left for dead, while Meinster goes to claim his most recent victim. The professor frees himself of the vampiric "infection" with a red-hot iron (ouch!) and holy water; when Meinster returns, Van Helsing sears his face with the holy water. In the ensuing battle, the mill goes up in flames. With a tremendous leap, the professor grabs one of the burning windmill's vanes and uses his weight to turn it so that the count is transfixed and destroyed by an enormous, cross-shaped shadow.

Brides of Dracula had a troubled genesis. The triple screenwriting credit reflects the fact that Peter Cushing refused to play Jimmy Sangster's original script, a thoroughly unusual move for this most affable of actors. Cushing objected to sequences that had Van Helsing using magic to counter Meinster's powers; originally, the vampire was to be torn apart by spectral bats conjured up by the professor. Cushing felt strongly (and rightly, I think) that this was utterly out of character for Van Helsing, who makes do with moral stength and homelier tools such as stakes and crucifixes. Nonetheless, the revised script is a little masterpiece of Gothic impulses that wrings a surprising amount of pathos out of the Meinster clan's sordid story. The specifically venereal connotation given to vampirism—its parallels with disease, the connection with "dissolute habits," the suggestion of incest and the insidious destruction of the family structure—remains faithful to Stoker's Victorian

sensibilities while elaborating on the novel's erotic undercurrents.

The Hammer family was at the top of its game in 1960. Terence Fisher's direction, one of his best efforts, is smooth, seamless, and understated. The cinematography and production design (featuring some of Hammer's most opulent sets) are consistently excellent. (Particularly noteworthy is the unforgettable, beautifully composed scene of the windmill blazing against the predawn sky.)

The performances are never less than impressive, with the unfortunate exception of Bardot lookalike Yvonne Monlaur, another of Hammer's gorgeous, talentless starlets. (Andree Melly, as the vampiress Gina, manages to be far more memorable in a much smaller role.) As Baroness Meinster, Martita Hunt (who played Miss Havisham in David Lean's *Great Expectations*) moves from patrician assurance to emotional collapse with effortless conviction. And let's not forget Freda Jackson's unforgettable, carpet-chewing performance as Greta, the baroness's servant who plays nanny to the vampire's new brides. She has to be the *maddest* madwoman in films. The scene in which she "midwifes" as a vampiress claws her way out of her grave—"Come, my sweet one, come…"—is genuinely eerie (and marred only by the fact that the grave appears to be approximately six inches deep.)

Which brings us to David Peel's effective and underappreciated Baron Meinster. Christopher Lee's was a difficult cape to fill, and Peel's performance has attracted much more criticism than it merits. Actually, he's simply a different *kind* of vampire. Lacking Lee's stern and commanding bearing, Peel is young (-looking; actually, he was forty), graceful, charming, exquisitely mannered, and distinctly androgynous. In fact, he seems like an interesting precursor of the Anne Rice school of vampires. (He would have made a marvelous Lestat.)

Finally, though, this is Peter Cushing's movie. In *Brides of Dracula*, Van Helsing goes beyond Stoker's initial conception to become something more, an outsized figure fully equal in stature and interest to Dracula himself. Cushing's Van Helsing is endlessly resourceful, improbably athletic, and relentless in the face of evil—more like one of Robert E. Howard's pulp heroes than the little Dutch professor of Stoker's novel. This sort of derring-do could easily collapse into unintended farce, but Cushing never allows it to do so. It's a remarkable star turn, and arguably the best performance in a long and varied career.

DRACULA—PRINCE OF DARKNESS

Hammer, 1965 (U.S. release 1966)
P: Anthony Nelson-Keys
D: Terence Fisher
S: credited to Jimmy Sangster, writing as "John Samson"; shooting script by Anthony Hinds
Starring Christopher Lee (*Count Dracula*), Barbara Shelley (*Helen Kent*), Andrew Keir (*Father Sandor*), Francis Matthews (*Charles Kent*), Suzan Farmer (*Diana Kent*), Charles Tingwell (*Alan Kent*), Philip Latham (*Klove*), and Thorley Walters (*Ludwig*).

Nightwalkers rating: 💀½

This last and least of Terence Fisher's Dracula films is notable mostly for Christopher Lee's return to his most famous role, after seven years. In addition to the usual stories of salary disputes, some sources have indicated that Lee avoided the part for years because he feared (rightly) that he would become typecast. Lee himself has said the delay was entirely up to Hammer—but then, Lee's own remarks concerning his long association with the Dracula role are always ambivalent and sometimes contradictory.

Unfortunately, *Dracula—Prince of Darkness* is saddled with what film buffs call an "idiot plot," meaning that the protagonists' actions make sense only if you assume they're idiots. It employs that most parodied of clichés, the unwary travellers who take shelter in a spooky old house. That this unpromising situation works at all is a tribute both to

THE COUNT PREPARES FOR A WATERY DEATH DURING THE FILMING OF *DRACULA—PRINCE OF DARKNESS.*

Terence Fisher's technical ability and Christopher Lee's undeniable presence as the Count.

Dracula—Prince of Darkness opens by reprising the climax of *Horror of Dracula* and quickly moves forward ten years. Dracula is no more, but the Transylvanian peasants still live in terror, both of vampires and of rifle-toting Father Sandor, who fills in for Van Helsing as the film's stern and knowledgeable champion of Good. We meet (and spend rather too much time getting to know) a pair of English brothers, Charles and Alan Kent, and their respective wives Diana and Helen. The Kent clan are, unaccountably, travelling the vampire-haunted Carpathians as tourists. Charles and Diana are vibrant and fun-loving, while Alan and Helen are dull, disapproving and conventional. Given Hammer's predilection for subverting Victorian prudishness, it's not hard to guess who Dracula's first victims will be.

Despite a warning from Father Sandor, the Kents continue their tour, soon finding their way to Castle Dracula, where they are received as guests by the count's servant, Klove. Alan soon regrets this, as Klove kills him and drains his blood for use in a ritual that revives his master. The blood is poured into a coffin with Dracula's ashes—which we saw blowing in the wind at the end of *Horror of Dracula*; one assumes Klove was lurking nearby with broom and dustpan—and soon, the vampire is revived.

Helen falls under Dracula's spell first. In classic Fisherian style, vampirism causes her to shed her modesty and become seductive and sexually wanton. Charles and Diana escape and enlist Father Sandor's aid. In the jumbled remnant of the film, Dracula makes several unsuccessful attempts to attack Diana; Father Sandor and the monks of his monastery slay the vampiric Helen; and Sandor himself ultimately dispatches Dracula in a novel way, by blasting the ice around the vampire's feet as he stands on a frozen moat, running water being fatal to the undead.

By 1965, the Hammer formula was displaying a certain hardening of the arteries, and the commercial and artistic judgment that had guided earlier ventures often seemed sadly lack-

DRACULA—PRINCE OF DARKNESS'S **BARBARA SHELLEY** AS AN ENRAGED VAMPIRESS FACING A SECOND DEATH.

ing. *Dracula—Prince of Darkness* illustrates these tendencies all too well. Anthony Hinds and Jimmy Sangster's screenplay is clichéd and clunkily constructed. A full third of the film has elapsed before it really begins, with Dracula's resurrection. A few elements from Stoker's novel are added to the movie, such as "Ludwig," a thinly disguised Renfield character, but they serve no particular purpose and only point up the scriptwriters' lack of interesting original ideas. Furthermore, *Dracula—Prince of Darkness* is distinctly impoverished-looking for a Hammer production. The movie, filmed on sets recycled from *Rasputin—The Mad Monk* (the films were made back to back), has a tacky, overlit look reminiscent of 1960s television. Composer James Bernard's score is repetitive and ultimately irritating, grossly overusing his thudding Dracula musical motif.

Despite its ineptitude, *Dracula—Prince of Darkness* does contain some grace notes, mostly in its performances; Lee's, of course, but most notably Barbara Shelley's. She ably portrays Helen's repressed and frightened nature, and, later, is truly extraordinary as the animalistic vampiress. The film's most successful moment involves Helen's staking by Sandor and the monks—not as she lies sleeping in a coffin, but while awake, struggling, and very much against her will. This scene is remarkably powerful and, for its day, quite bloody. Andrew Keir is also somewhat better than the script. Sandor is appropriately strong, with an Old Testament fer-

vor, but he's never able to make us stop missing Peter Cushing.

Most damaging to *Dracula—Prince of Darkness*, however, is the diminution of the Dracula part itself. Lee has stated that his role in the film had "a great deal of dialogue originally, but it was so bad that I refused to deliver it." Consequently, Dracula speaks not a word, which robs the character of nearly all human interest and reduces Lee's portrayal to a one-dimensional, hissing menace.

In all, *Dracula—Prince of Darkness* seems doubly unfortunate because it, and not *Horror of Dracula*, set the tone for the remainder of Hammer's series. Better movies were to come, but from this point on, Dracula's on-screen appearances are increasingly brief, ineffective cameos that only highlight Hammer's almost inexplicable inability to make effective use of their most popular and enduring character. Christopher Lee said it best: "I am asked, 'Why didn't they give you more to do?'...The answer is quite simple: they didn't know what to give me to do, or to say."

DRACULA HAS RISEN FROM THE GRAVE
Hammer, 1968
P: Aida Young
D: Freddie Francis
S: Anthony Hinds, writing as "John Elder"
Starring Christopher Lee (*Count Dracula*), Rupert Davies (*the Monsignor*), Veronica Carlson (*Maria*), Zena (*Barbara Ewing*), Barry Andrew (*Paul*), and Ewan Hooper (*the Priest*).

Nightwalkers Rating: 💀💀½

After a lull of more than two years, Hammer revived Dracula in this second sequel.

Squeamish British censors awarded the film the "adults-only" certificate Hammer had come to expect (and apparently treasure). In America, however, where the Batman-generated "camp" craze was still going strong, the film received a "G" rating and was marketed with a nauseatingly cute ad campaign that featured tag lines like "You can't keep a good man down." Regardless of its aesthetic merits, the campaign worked, and *Dracula Has Risen from the Grave* became a major hit.

CHRISTOPHER LEE LOOMS OVER THE LOVELY VERONICA CARLSON IN *DRACULA HAS RISEN FROM THE GRAVE*.

Terence Fisher was scheduled to direct the film, but was sidelined by the first of two traffic accidents that largely ended his career. Freddie Francis assumed directorial chores, and criticisms of *Dracula Has Risen from the Grave* mostly seem to boil down to the simple fact that Freddie Francis isn't Terence Fisher. It *is* true that the themes and obsessions that became so much a part of the Fisher's work for Hammer are largely cast aside in this movie. In particular, the archetypal Monster and Avenger figures here are, in writer Kim Newman's words, "reduced to irritable onlookers," which seems to bother auteurist fans of Fisher no end. Francis also had little regard for the vampire myth as established in previous Dracula films, and this one commits at least two blunders that offend many purists. Even so, as a work of entertainment, the third Dracula film is entirely superior to its disappointing predecessor.

A year after Dracula's apparent demise in *Dracula—Prince of Darkness*, a monsignor visits the nearby village and finds its people still terrified. The local priest is a fear-ridden drunkard. The monsignor (a distinctly minor-league Van Helsing surrogate) decides to perform a rite of exorcism at Castle Dracula, with the priest's reluctant help. The two embark on a grueling all-day climb up a mountain to Dracula's lair. (Thought question: What happened to that road that went right to the castle gates in the last film?) Once at the summit, the monsignor performs the ceremony and places a crucifix across the castle's door, sealing it against evil. The priest, meanwhile, stumbles off and falls, cutting his head. As he lies dazed, a trickle of blood falls through a crack in some nearby ice, where—as fate would have it—the vampire lies frozen, presumably after his watery demise in the last movie. The blood falls on Dracula's lips—also as fate would have it—reviving him instantly. The vampire then places the priest under his hypnotic control. (At this point, the priest sees Dracula's reflection in a pool of water, a gross infraction of standard cinematic vampire rules.) Upon discovering the cross on his door, the reborn vampire swears vengeance upon the monsignor.

Dracula and priest decamp to the monsignor's home town, where we meet Maria, the monsignor's insipidly beautiful niece, and Paul, her insipidly beautiful lover. Soon, Dracula is comfortably ensconced in the cellars below the inn where Paul lives and works. He enslaves Zena, a busty barmaid, and kills her when she fails to deliver Maria to him. Dracula then lays siege to the monsignor's house, where he begins seducing Maria. Both Zena and Maria display an orgasmic enthusiasm for Dracula's toothy embraces that brings the sexual subtext of the previous films right on to center stage, making this an early harbinger of the racier Hammer movies of the 1970s.

The monsignor manages to fend the vampire off, but is attacked by the enslaved priest. Dying, the monsignor entrusts Maria's care to Paul, and arms him with the knowledge he'll need to fight the vampire. Paul manages to locate Dracula's coffin and drive a stake into him, but Dracula *plucks it out*, because Paul is an atheist who didn't *pray* while performing the ceremony(!!). (This new and nonsensical twist on the vampire legend does make for a startling visual sequence, which is probably all that concerned Francis.) Finally, Dracula seizes Maria and takes her to his castle. He forces her to remove the crucifix on the door and toss it away, but Paul comes to the rescue and Dracula ends by falling on the discarded cross, which impales him. The repentant priest musters up the courage to pray, and Dracula dissolves once more.

Dracula has a bit more to do in here than in the previous movie. At least he can talk again (though he's given little of interest to say.) Nevertheless, his role still is essentially static, giving Lee little opportunity to develop the character. This is all the more damaging to the film in view of the general lack of compelling foreground characters. Francis is unapologetic about this structure, once saying, "I was more interested in the love affair…than with Dracula, he was just a fly in the ointment." Unfortunately, Maria and Paul just aren't all that interesting, although Veronica Carlson *is* astonishingly gorgeous. The monsignor is even more of a cipher, displaying little of the spiritual strength that marked Van Helsing or Father Sandor.

Despite these problems, *Dracula Has Risen from the Grave* is considerably more enjoyable than Fisher's last effort with the character, with visibly higher production values and an infinitely superior score. No classic, it's typically competent Hammer horror; fast-moving, beautifully photographed and mostly well-acted. Hammer could, and would, do much worse by the count.

TASTE THE BLOOD OF DRACULA
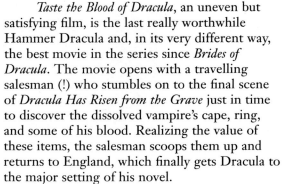
Hammer, 1969 (U.S. release 1970)
P: Aida Young
D: Peter Sasdy
S: Anthony Hinds, writing as "John Elder"
Starring Christopher Lee (*Count Dracula*), Geoffrey Keen (*William Hargood*), Gwen Watford (*Martha Hargood*), Linda Hayden (*Alice Hargood*), Peter Sallis (*Samuel Paxton*), Anthony Corlan (*Paul Paxton*), Isla Blair (*Lucy Paxton*), John Carson (*Jonathan Secker*), Martin Jarvis (*Jeremy Secker*), and Ralph Bates (*Lord Courtley*).

Nightwalkers rating: 💀💀💀

Taste the Blood of Dracula, an uneven but satisfying film, is the last really worthwhile Hammer Dracula and, in its very different way, the best movie in the series since *Brides of Dracula*. The movie opens with a travelling salesman (!) who stumbles on to the final scene of *Dracula Has Risen from the Grave* just in time to discover the dissolved vampire's cape, ring, and some of his blood. Realizing the value of these items, the salesman scoops them up and returns to England, which finally gets Dracula to the major setting of his novel.

Some years later, we meet three thoroughly despicable London "gentlemen"—Samuel Paxton, Jonathan Secker, and their leader, William Hargood. (An interesting note: it's been said that Vincent Price originally was signed to appear in *Taste the Blood of Dracula*, but budget cuts forced Hammer to release him from the film, and his part was divided among these three.) Hargood and the others are wealthy would-be decadents who maintain staunchly respectable home lives while doing "charity work in the East End"—their cover for monthly drinking and whoring sessions. However, having indulged in all the vices their limited imaginations can devise, they've grown bored.

Enter Lord Courtley, a young, impoverished and vicious aristocrat who frequents the same brothel as our "charity workers." This truly sick puppy aspires to revive the most evil man of all time—Dracula, of course—through a magical ritual. To do so, he only needs the deep pockets of Hargood and his friends to purchase the Dracula memorabilia mentioned earlier. Titillated, they agree. Courtley holds his ritual in a large abandoned church, quaffing a nasty-looking potion made from the dried remnants of Dracula's blood. The three horrified apprentices, however, balk at drinking the vile stuff. Instead, they beat Courtley viciously and flee. Moments later, the potion transforms Courtley's body into the once-again revived Dracula, who—although he just got here—promptly swears vengeance on his disciple's attackers. ("They have destroyed my servant. They will be destroyed!")

And Dracula proceeds to do just that, striking at these Victorian hypocrites through their children, a collection of bland, well-fed twits who readily fall under Dracula's erotic spell. Hargood's daughter Alice hands her father a sharp rap with a spade; later, we see her lolling sensuously on Dracula's sarcophagus lid.

Paxton's daughter, Lucy, drives a stake through her father's heart, only to have Dracula drain her blood. Secker is last to go, stabbed by his son. Only Paxton's son Paul avoids Dracula's spell, and eventually rescues Alice from Dracula's lair in the abandoned church. Dracula perishes in a poorly edited and confusing finale. Apparently he's

DRACULA'S LATEST DISCIPLE AWAITS HER MASTER'S VOICE IN *TASTE THE BLOOD OF DRACULA*.

burnt by a stained-glass cross and falls to his (most recent) death. (By the way, this is the fourth Dracula movie we've discussed so far featuring two major female characters, one of whom dies while the other escapes. The pattern clearly echoes the fates of Lucy and Mina in Stoker's novel, but by this time it's getting tedious.)

Christopher Lee's recorded remarks concerning this film are dismissive, although he has noted that the cast is exceptionally good. It's easy enough to understand his dissatisfaction. By this film, Dracula's function as walk-on player in his own movies seemed set in stone. Lee is more than ever a *diabolus ex machina*—more a plot device than an active character. This said, at least there's a decent movie revolving around him. Anthony Hinds's screenplay is fresh and inventive, particularly for this period in Hammer history. Also worth mentioning are the appropriately rich and moody cinematography by Arthur Grant, and James Bernard's haunting, romantic score, his best of the Dracula series.

Perhaps most impressive is Peter Sasdy's

DRACULA LOOKS A BIT NONPLUSSED AT THE SIGHT OF A CRUCIFIX.

canny direction. Sasdy, a Hungarian-born director who achieved critical success in the British television industry, made his feature debut with this film. Sasdy made only a handful of films after *Taste the Blood of Dracula*, none of them as good, although he often displayed a certain talent for striking visual compositions.

Hammer scholar David Pirie has praised the way Sasdy "uses the specter of Dracula to subvert the façade of Victorian society." More precisely, it seems to me, the film comments on Hammer's highly stylized *interpretation* of the period, as crystallized by the studio's greatest director.

Terence Fisher's work and interviews make it clear that he was a thoroughgoing Tory by inclination, and his romantic nostalgia for the nineteenth century rolls through most Hammer movies like a thick fog. By contrast, Sasdy gives us the rotten underbelly of Victorian society, with all its hypocrisy and corruption. The film is devoid of likeable or admirable characters. Hargood in particular is a memorable petty tyrant who bullies his wife and daughter, and Sasdy has said he wanted the pretty, thoughtless children to seem bloodless before Dracula comes into their lives.

I've little patience for the silly excesses of film theory, but the psychological implications of *Taste the Blood of Dracula* seem both lucid and intentional. As never before, Dracula here is an overtly erotic Chaos figure, whose very existence shatters society's hypocritical stability and, in this case, brings three "respectable" families to ruin. It's a thoughtful and chilling story, and by rights the real climax to the Dracula series. From here, we move downhill.

SCARS OF DRACULA
Hammer, 1970
P: Aida Young
D: Roy Ward Baker
S: Anthony Hinds, writing as "John Elder"
Starring Christopher Lee (*Count Dracula*), Jenny Hanley (*Sarah Framsen*), Dennis Waterman (*Simon Carlson*), Christopher Matthews (*Paul Carlson*), and Patrick Troughton (*Klove*).

Nightwalkers rating: 💀

Filmed just a few months after *Taste the Blood of Dracula*, *Scars of Dracula* displays virtually none of the former movie's style and assurance. Christopher Lee has described it as "the weakest and most unconvincing of the Dracula stories." Quite. It's not only hard to accept this as a Hammer film; at times it's difficult to believe that it was made in a first-world nation.

Scars of Dracula breaks with the story continuity established in the earlier Hammer Draculas (and the series never returns to it again). Remember, *Taste the Blood of Dracula* left Dracula, returned to ashes once more, in Edwardian London. *Scars of Dracula* begins with the count in ashes, but takes place in and near Castle Dracula in Transylvania, and judging from the costumes, it's set about a century before *Taste the Blood of Dracula*. (Call it a "prequel," if your ability to rationalize is sufficiently well-developed.)

As the tale opens, a large and mammothly unconvincing bat puppet revives Dracula by puking blood on his remains. Really. Soon, the long-suffering locals are turning up stiff, which prompts a Universal-style torch-bearing mob to descend upon the castle and burn it. The villagers return home only to find that their wives and children are all dead, torn to pieces (via some crude, unpleasant gore effects) by a flock of the count's vampire bats.

Flashing forward some years, we meet our blandly attractive protagonists, the Carlson brothers, Paul and Simon, and the woman they both care for, Sarah Framsen. Simon's something of a sobersides, while Paul is a glib, charming wastrel. Caught in a compromising position with the burgomeister's daughter, Paul is forced to flee town, ending up (naturally) at Castle Dracula, which has been rebuilt (by whom?) since the fire. In short order, he's seduced by a mysterious beauty, Tania (Anoushka Hempel); after sex, she attempts to put the bite on him. He's saved by Dracula, who rather amazingly proceeds to stab Tania repeatedly with a rubber bendy-knife before drinking her blood. Paul attempts to escape the castle, but only succeeds in trapping himself in Dracula's crypt.

Cut to Simon and Sarah, who're searching for Paul. They, too, become guests at the castle. To your complete surprise, no doubt, Dracula sets his sights on Sarah. Complicating matters is the fact that Dracula's hairy, hunchbacked servant, Klove (looking quite different from his *Dracula, Prince of Darkness* days) also loves Sarah. Klove flatly refuses to deliver Sarah into the vampire's arms, so Dracula tortures him with a red-hot sword. (What the hell kind of vampire behavior is

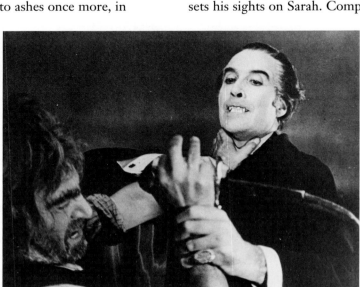

DRACULA SUBDUES AN UNRULY SERVANT (PATRICK TROUGHTON) IN *THE SCARS OF DRACULA* (1970).

this?) Simon discovers Paul's dead body, and tries but fails to stake Dracula. Finally, during a rooftop confrontation with Simon and Sarah, Dracula tosses his rebellious servant off the battlements, then is struck and incinerated by lightning bolt. *Whew.*

This thumbnail sketch highlights some of the film's bizarre plot twists, but it doesn't do justice to the film's depressing, amateurish execution. *Scars of Dracula* was directed in lackluster fashion by Roy Ward Baker, a director capable of far better things (such as *Five Million Years to Earth*, a fine Hammer science fiction film). The budget has been reported at $480,000, not too shabby for the day, but for some reason (possibly connected with a devastating fire that had disrupted Hammer's operations), *Scars of Dracula* sports the production values of a Mexican soap opera, making *Dracula, Prince of Darkness* look sumptuous by comparison. The photography looks flat and muddy (although I'm told that English prints of the film are distinctly superior to American ones). The gore effects would be stomach-churning if they weren't so laughable, as in one scene in which a stiffly flapping bat puppet takes a *really* long time to chew an unlucky priest's face off. Brief flashes of female nudity and a recurrent, smutty jokiness seem utterly pointless.

The saddest thing about *Scars of Dracula* is that one gets the feeling that its basic concept was sound. After his glorified walk-on part in *Taste the Blood of Dracula*, Christopher Lee once again became disgusted with the role. In contemporary interviews, Hammer's Michael Carreras coyly hinted that Ralph Bates might replace the recalcitrant actor. Eventually, of course, Lee agreed to play Dracula again, while the studio in turn promised to make the vampire a central character and return to some of the novel's original concepts.

Lee *is* given more to do, and gets to display some icy charm, such as when acting as host

to his reluctant "guests," that's nicely reminiscent of the opening chapters of *Dracula* the novel. Nearly every discussion of *Scars of Dracula* mentions an intriguing scene taken directly from the book, in which Dracula demonstrates his ability to clamber along the castle's walls like a spider. This is a nice bit, but it lasts only a few seconds, and hardly redeems the rest of the film. In particular, the stabbing and torture scenes are utterly out of character and nonsensical (what does Dracula need a knife for?).

Scars of Dracula received the commercial reception it deserved. Warner took one look at it and flatly refused to release it to the American market (it later received a limited release from a small independent, Continental Films). The movie can be credited with some good intentions—specifically, its sporadic return to Stoker's novel for some of its themes and scenes—but little else. Some film writers find this movie superior to *Taste the Blood of Dracula*, a suggestion I regard as bizarre. (According to Roy Ward Baker, the French loved *Scars of Dracula*. You may use the page margin for your own derisive comment concerning Jerry Lewis.)

DRACULA A.D. 1972
Hammer, 1972
P: Josephine Douglas
D: Alan Gibson
S: Don Houghton
Starring Christopher Lee (*Count Dracula*), Peter Cushing (*Professor Lawrence Van Helsing* and *Professor Lorrimer Van Helsing*), Christopher Neame (*Johnny Alucard*), Stephanie Beacham (*Jessica Van Helsing*), and Michael Coles (*Inspector Murray*). Special musical (?) appearance by Stoneground.

Nightwalkers rating: ½

Sometimes, a single picture *can* tell the whole story. Right now, I'm looking at a publicity still from *Dracula A.D. 1972*. Four starlets glance more or less blankly over Christopher Lee's shoulders as he sits on a coffin, chin on one hand, with an expression that looks very much like rueful embarrassment on his face. I can understand his feelings.

VAMPIRE AND VAMPIRE-HUNTER, IN A CLIMATIC CONFRONTATION IN A RUINED CHURCH.

to his own wounds. Immediately after, a sinister-looking fellow—a disciple of Dracula's, we assume—drops by to scoop up a bit of the vampire's dust. This opening sequence does have some of the old Hammer zing, and is marred only by Michael Vickers's wretched soundtrack, which would sound far more appropriate in an Italian spy movie.

While it's an undeniable improvement on *Scars of Dracula, Dracula A.D. 1972* was a bitter disappointment for most Hammer fans. After fourteen years, Hammer had finally reunited its two greatest stars. At long last, Dracula would once again face his most formidable foe, Professor Van Helsing. Unfortunately, the resulting film was scarcely worthy of the talents of Christopher Lee and Peter Cushing.

Even so, it isn't a complete waste of time. Just as it was once remarked that Wagner's music is better than it sounds, *Dracula A.D. 1972* is actually a somewhat better movie than it, well, watches; it's just wrapped in some intensely embarrassing trappings. No films in history have aged more quickly and less gracefully than those of the late 1960s and early 1970s—the ones that desperately attempted to be "relevant for today's kids," while displaying a baffled ignorance of the era's actual youth culture. *Dracula A.D. 1972* is, like, a particularly dismal example.

Dracula A.D. 1972 opens in 1872, during a "final confrontation" between Van Helsing and Dracula. (As 1872 is considerably earlier than the settings of Hammer's Dracula films before *Scars of Dracula*, one assumes we are again in some parallel Dracula universe.) There's a thrilling coach chase, ending in a crash; Dracula is run through with a wheel spoke and disintegrates. Van Helsing has the satisfaction of seeing his ancient enemy crumble before succumbing

A century later, we're in swinging London, grooving with some crazy kids to Stoneground, an awesomely terrible band whose music produces a sensation akin to biting down on aluminum foil. (If you can get past this sequence, you've got this movie licked.) The kids in question, poorly drawn hippy stereotypes, are dominated by a handsome rogue named Johnny Alucard—there's something familiar about that name—who's the spitting image of the fellow of a century before who collected Dracula's remains. Obviously, evil runs in the family; Johnny proposes that the group hold a Black Mass for kicks, or, as they put it, "Something way, way out—a bacchanal with Beelzebub." (Man!) A pretty, blonde member of the clan, by the way, is named Jessica Van Helsing.

Using the vampire dust he's inherited, Johnny revives Dracula in an abandoned church, pretty much as in *Taste the Blood of Dracula*, and soon lures a couple of the women into the vampire's embrace. Their blood-drained corpses draw the attention of Scotland Yard, and Police Inspector Murray drops around to chat with Jessica, who lives with her grandfather, Lorrimer Van Helsing. Van Helsing (also played by Cushing, of course), the grandson of the original professor, shares the family interest in vampires and immediately realizes what's going on. Jessica, however, is reluctant to confide in her grandfather because

Adults Just Don't Understand.

Johnny persuades Dracula to vampirize him—more or less instantly, by the way; in late Hammer, any requirement that the victim die first has pretty much gone by the wayside—and Dracula sends Johnny after Jessica, so that he may take revenge on the Van Helsing clan via its youngest member. However, Lorrimer is every inch the vampire hunter his grandpa was. He makes short work of Johnny, and eventually defeats Dracula as well, by forcing him into an empty grave filled with sharp stakes.

The decision to update the Dracula series was made at the request of Warner, Hammer's American distributor, and seems inspired, at least in part, by the success of American-International's parodic Count Yorga films. Hammer's managing director, Michael Carreras, apparently hated the idea of modernizing the series, and has claimed credit for the way in which the film keeps Dracula lurking in the timeless setting of a ruined church. Ironically, though, this approach eliminates any chance that the movie might become really interesting. After all, there's no intrinsic reason why a modern Dracula story couldn't work. Stoker's Dracula was very much of his time, familiar with financial dealings, a reader of travel guides and train schedules. Note also the enormous success of Anne Rice's contemporary vampires. *Dracula A.D. 1972* makes no attempt whatsoever to come to terms with the idea of a modern vampire, which is *precisely* the point of the Yorga films.

This all sounds pretty harsh, and yet the movie *does* have its moments. What bright spots occur are largely due to the irreducible talent and dignity of Christopher Lee and Peter Cushing. Lee is, as usual, criminally misused, reduced once again to a minor character. It's no small thing to say that he does as much with the part as any actor could. As for Peter Cushing …it's magic, pure and simple. No matter how much distaste you may feel for this film in general, when Cushing comes on screen, you immediately start buying the whole thing. His strength of character and conviction literally transform *Dracula A.D. 1972* into a different, and better, movie. Perhaps the best postmortem was delivered by the *San Francisco Chronicle*, which noted, "Peter Cushing carries the picture, what there is of it."

THE SATANIC RITES OF DRACULA

(Initial U.S. release title: *Count Dracula and His Vampire Bride*)
Hammer, 1973 (limited U.S. release, 1978)
P: Roy Skeggs
D: Alan Gibson
S: Don Houghton
Starring Christopher Lee (*Count Dracula/D.D. Denham*), Peter Cushing (*Professor Lorrimer Van Helsing*), Michael Coles (*Inspector Murray*), Freddie Jones (*Professor Julian Keeley*), and Joanna Lumley (*Jessica Van Helsing*).

Nightwalkers rating: 💀½

Although *The Satanic Rites of Dracula* is not without a certain moronic charm, watching it is ultimately a depressing experience. Hammer was on its last legs by this point—out of energy, out of ideas—as every frame of this silliness reminds you. And, at the risk of repetition, let me assure you that some good performances by Hammer regulars once again constitute the movie's best feature.

The Satanic Rites of Dracula is a direct sequel to *Dracula A.D. 1972*, featuring many of the same characters and behind-the-camera personnel. Barely a Dracula film at all, it is a weird hodgepodge of science fiction and spy-movie riffs, drenched with an intensely seventies soundtrack featuring *Shaft*-style wocka-wocka guitars—in fact, if it weren't for the glum atmosphere hanging over the whole project, it might pass muster as a mediocre episode of "The Avengers."

A few years after Dracula's (apparent) destruction in the last movie, a British intelligence agency uncovers evidence of a shadowy plot involving a number of powerful men, including an industrialist, cabinet minsters, and a Nobel Prize-winning scientist. The group meets at a country mansion, Pelham House. An operative sent in to investigate this cabal is captured and tortured, but manages to escape and tell his superiors a lurid story of satanic rituals and human sacrifice.

Not knowing what to make of all this, the intelligence service calls in Scotland Yard's Inspector Murray, who acquired occult experience in *Dracula A.D. 1972.* Murray, in turn, enlists the aid of Lorrimer Van Helsing again, as well as that of his daughter Jessica. They learn that the power behind the satanic conspiracy is billionaire recluse and property developer D. D. Denham. (Christopher Lee has accurately described the character as "a mixture between Howard Hughes and Dr. No." In a rather nice touch, Denham has built his headquarters building on the site of the church where Dracula lurked in the previous film.)

Van Helsing interviews the cult's scientist member, Professor Julian Keeley, and finds that he's gone mad, raving about the "the thrill of disgust, the beauty of obscenity." At Denham's behest, Keeley has developed a mutated strain of the bubonic plague capable of destroying all life on earth, which ups the ante considerably, plotwise. Concluding that Denham is actually Dracula (his latest resurrection and subsequent accumulation of wealth is never explained), the professor speculates that the vampire has tired of his centuries-long existence and plans to wipe out humanity as a kind of spectacular suicide—an interesting thought that isn't much developed, although it does seem out of character for a consummate survivor like the count to eliminate his food supply.

That's the setup. There's little point in a blow-by-blow of the remaining plot, except to say that it's lively and confusing. Our protagonists have various narrow escapes from Denham/Dracula's army of pistol-toting motorcycle thugs (who wear sheepskin vests that make them look sort of Crosby-Stills-Nash-ish). Pelham House's basement turns out to be filled with miscellaneous vampire brides, who emerge periodically to threaten our heroes, without much effect. Jessica finds herself on the cult's altar, scheduled to become Dracula's consort, and is (to no one's surprise) rescued at the last moment.

The script improvises pretty freely with vampire legendry, at one point sending Van

CUSHING'S VAN HELSING IN A PORTRAIT OF STEELY DETERMINATION FROM *THE SATANIC RITES OF DRACULA*.

Helsing after Dracula with a pistol loaded with a silver bullet (wasn't that for werewolves?). The vampire women are eliminated with a sprinkler system (running water, remember?). Oddest of all, however, is Dracula's demise. The frail-looking Van Helsing is able to impale Dracula easily when the vampire becomes entangled in a hawthorn bush, because the hawthorn once was used to fashion Jesus' crown of thorns(!). Not a bad idea, but the way the sequence is shot makes it all too apparent that Lee could simply step out of the bush at any time he chose, making the whole thing seem rather silly.

Dracula A.D. 1972's director, Alan Gibson, and screenwriter, Don Houghton, both returned for this film. Houghton's screenplay pays little heed to traditional vampire legends and the Hammer mythos in general, but deserves some credit for imagination. (A number of nonsequiturs and dangling loose ends, such as the lack of an explanation for Dracula's reappearance, suggest heavy and hurried rewriting.) The D. D. Denham angle, probably inspired by Howard Hughes's brief stay in London during the early 1970s, is witty and amusing, in a comic-book sort of way. Gibson, however, seems to have no feeling whatever for the horror genre, and his flat, unimaginative direction robs the film of what little impact it might otherwise have had. Peter Cushing is as good as always, as is Freddie Jones, whose brief turn as the mad Professor Keeley is effective and moving. Christopher Lee's Dracula, however, is once again marginalized and shunted aside.

As *The Satanic Rites of Dracula* was being filmed, *Dracula A.D. 1972* was flopping at box offices around the world. *The Satanic Rites of Dracula* met with an even worse fate. It was rejected by Warner Brothers for American distribution and shelved for years. (In 1978, the film received a brief and embarrassing American release by Max Rosenberg's Dynamite

Entertainment under the title *Count Dracula and His Vampire Bride.* The poster boasted, "The King of the Undead marries the Queen of the Zombies," which gives you the flavor of the accompanying ad campaign.)

Christopher Lee made no attempt to hide his contempt for this project, telling interviewers he was doing the film "under protest," and calling it "fatuous, pointless, absurd." For Lee, the film's "final, total collapse of the character" (as he put it) marked the end of the road; his periodic resolve to quit the series finally held. At this late date, it's sad to reflect that Lee was never able to give us a truly definitive interpretation of the count. Even so—and for all the limitations and absurdities of the series—Christopher Lee probably has come closer to embodying Bram Stoker's character than any other actor, before or since.

LEE'S DRACULA GOES DOWN FOR THE LAST TIME, IN *SATANIC RITES OF DRACULA*'S BRAMBLE PATCH OF HOLY THORNS(!).

LEGEND OF THE SEVEN GOLDEN VAMPIRES

(initial U.S. release title: *The Seven Brothers Meet Dracula*)
Hammer, 1974 (limited U.S. release, 1979)
P: Don Houghton and Vee King Shaw
D: Roy Ward Baker
S: Don Houghton
Starring Peter Cushing (*Professor Van Helsing*), David Chiang (*Hsi Ching*), Julie Ege (*Vanessa Van Buren*), Robin Stewart (*Leyland Van Helsing*), Shih Szu (*Mai Kwei*), and John Forbes-Robertson (*Dracula*).

Nightwalkers rating: 💀💀½

This bizarre goulash is probably the strangest Dracula film ever made (although I admit that *Dracula's Dog* is certainly in the running). Some Hammer fans despise it, but others regard it as a guilty pleasure. It's an entertaining romp, despite the fact that it bears precious little resemblance to the studio's more famous works.

Legend of the Seven Golden Vampires was inspired by the Western world's forty-two-minute fascination with Chinese kung-fu movies, a mania sparked by the meteoric career of Bruce Lee. The Far East had long been a major market for Hammer's horror movies, and the notion of mixing traditional vampire themes with martial arts must have seemed entirely logical to filmmakers on both sides of the globe. This film was the result, an unlikely collaboration between Hammer and Hong Kong's Shaw Brothers, major producers of karate and kung-fu films.

In 1804, a Chinese priest, Kah, trudges across Asia and Eastern Europe to Castle Dracula. (Major walk, that.) Kah is the high priest of a cult of seven vampires who've long terrorized the village of Ping Kuei; but they sleep now, and the villagers have lost their fear. Kah asks Dracula to revive the vampires. Dracula, seeing an opportunity to leave his mausoleum for greener pastures, assumes Kah's identity (apparently by absorbing him) and leaves for China(!).

A century later, Professor Van Helsing—the original—is in Chungking lecturing on vampirism. (It's a delight to see him back in his proper era, by the way.) Van Helsing relates the legend of the "golden vampires" of Ping Kuei, so called because of masks of beaten gold that cover their hideous faces—and soon learns that his sole attentive listener, Hsi Ching, is a Ping Kuei native who has heard of Van Helsing's prowess in fighting Dracula. He seeks to Van Helsing's aid in ridding the village of its curse. Hsi Ching is accompanied by six brothers and a sister, each proficient in a different style of combat. Van Helsing agrees to help and, with his son Leyland, sets off with Hsi Ching's party. Before departing, they're joined by a beautiful heiress, Vanessa Van Buren, who's fleeing the attentions of a local gangster.

Meanwhile, we get to know the golden vampires better. They're an interesting bunch, withered and corpselike. From their base in a sinister pagoda, they like to sweep through Ping Kuei on horseback, kidnapping girls for use in blood orgies around a bubbling cauldron of gore. Kah/Dracula raises reinforcements at will by summoning the vampire's zombielike victims from the earth with a large gong. These zombies locomote via peculiar jumping steps, which makes them all seem to be doing the Bunny Hop (an image that does not precisely terrify).

The remainder of the film consists largely of lengthy fights between the vampire horde and its hunters, and campfire scenes during which various players pair off. Van Helsing's callow son falls in love with Hsi Ching's sister, Mai Kwei, and she falls for him in turn, for no reason at all that I can see. Hsi Ching and Vanessa also go soft on one another. Hsi Ching's little army does away with several of the vampires and then fortifies Ping Kuei against a final assault. In the course of this battle, several brothers and all but one of the vampires are killed. Vanessa is briefly nipped by a vampire and *in seconds* grows inch-long fangs, which is silly. Hsi Ching impales her on a bamboo stave and then, grief-stricken, spindles himself as well. Finally, there's a requisite last-minute rescue of the remaining attractive female, and Van Helsing confronts his old enemy once more. Dracula assumes his normal form, looking rather out of place in formal evening dress. Van Helsing grabs a wooden spear and, well, you know. (Another thought question: How could Dracula and Van Helsing have fought previously if Dracula had spent the last century in China? Or does he commute?)

Legend of the Seven Golden Vampires was, by all accounts, a grueling experience for its makers. A ten-week shooting schedule ballooned to twenty-one weeks. Only a handful of actors and

JOHN FORBES-ROBERTSON, HAMMER'S REPLACEMENT DRACULA, EYES A PROSPECTIVE VICTIM IN *LEGEND OF THE SEVEN GOLDEN VAMPIRES.*

crew spoke English. Moreover, Roy Ward Baker found Chinese filmmaking methods bewildering, exasperatedly saying, "Their idea is that everybody mills around for twenty minutes [with] three different cameras …and they throw it all into the cutting room." Baker fought to bring order into the pandemonium and ironically succeeded in capturing some of the better martial arts footage that had been shot up until then.

What is odd, the film became a true Dracula film literally at the last minute. With production already under way, the Shaws suddenly insisted on an appearance by the count in traditional garb, as the character was popular in Hong Kong, and so new opening and closing scenes were hurriedly added. The role went to a rouged and inadequate-looking John Forbes-Robertson, who poses little threat to Christopher Lee's memory.

As for the rest of the cast, it seems almost unnecessary to say that Peter Cushing is wonderful. David Chiang, a rising kung-fu star of the day, is also quite good. Robin Stewart's Leyland Van Helsing has a thankless, second-banana role and does nothing with it, while Julie Ege as Vanessa is a Nordic beauty with spectacular cheekbones and no discernable acting talent.

Even so, *Legend of the Seven Golden Vampires* is undemanding fun. The hopping Oriental vampires are an unusual and interesting menace, and the fight scenes are brisk and exciting, if you like that sort of thing. The film did fairly well in England, and had international response been better, Hammer was considering matching Van Helsing against other exotic menaces. (An Indian vampire movie was in the planning stages.) Unfortunately, the kung-fu craze was already fading by the time *Legend* was completed. The film failed to reach America for years, until Dynamite Entertainment stepped in once again, releasing a recut and shortened version of the film as *The Seven Brothers Meet Dracula.*

⇒ 4 ⇐

BLOODSUCKERS

Vampire Kith and Kin

PEOPLE DON'T COME TO SEE OUR MOVIES FOR THE HORROR.

THEY COME TO SEE THE GIRLS.

—SIR JAMES CARRERAS

Carreras's assessment might be a wee bit cynical, but there's no mistaking the strong erotic current running through many of the era's best vampire movies. In this, of course, they emulate Christopher Lee's Dracula, father of them all. In this chapter, we meet a clutch of other Nightwalkers who have more than blood on their minds.

The most influential of these movies were the entries in Hammer's so-called Karnstein trilogy, all based with varying degrees of fidelity on Joseph Sheridan LeFanu's "Carmilla," a beautifully written novella of vampiric seduction first published in 1871, more than twenty years before *Dracula*. "Carmilla" was a fairly astonishing piece for its era; it concerned Carmilla Karnstein, a "lesbian" vampire—that is, a female who preys on other females, through advances that are unmistakably sensual. Hammer chose these films as its vehicle for its most open and explicit linking of sexuality and vampirism ever, and for the first time plunged into the brave

GENERAL SPIELSDORF (PETER CUSHING) COMFORTS "MARCILLA," WHO IS NOT AS INNOCENT AS SHE SEEMS IN *THE VAMPIRE LOVERS*.

new world of frontal female nudity—for American release, that is. (Before his death, Michael Carreras confirmed long-lived rumors that previous Hammer films going all the way back to *The Mummy* had featured nude scenes filmed for Oriental markets only.) These sex-vampire projects lacked the polish of the Hammer classics of a decade before, but they did inject some badly needed verve into the studio's aging product line.

Of the three Karnsteins, only the first, 1970's *The Vampire Lovers*, was a significant success for Hammer, making at least a minor horror icon of its lovely star, Ingrid Pitt. But the series seems to have provided inspiration for an international cycle of early seventies sex-vampire and lesbian vampire movies, including *The Velvet Vampire* (1971), *Le Rouge aux Lèvres* [*Daughters of Darkness*] (1971), *Vampyros Lesbos* (1970; I trust this needs no translation), and *La Comtesse aux Sein Nus* [*The Bare-Breasted Countess*—I *love* that title] (1975), to name just a few of an eminently forgettable crew. Predictably, Hammer proved more adept at copying Hammer. Projects like *Vampire Circus* and *Captain Kronos—Vampire Hunter* display a good deal of the energy and erotic flash that marks the best moments of the Karnstein movies.

KISS OF THE VAMPIRE
Hammer, 1963
P: Anthony Hinds
D: Don Sharp
S: Anthony Hinds, writing as "John Elder"
Starring Clifford Evans (*Professor Zimmer*), Noel Willman (*Dr. Ravna*), Edward de Souza (*Gerald Harcourt*), Jennifer Daniel (*Marianne Harcourt*), Barry Warren (*Carl Ravna*), Jacquie Wallis (*Sabena Ravna*), Isobel Black (*Tania*), Peter Madden (*Bruno*), and Vera Cook (*Anna*).

***Nightwalkers* rating:** 💀 💀 💀

Kiss of the Vampire, a key vampire thriller from Hammer's glory days, is noteworthy for a stylishness and restraint that almost, but not quite, lift the movie into classic status.

Kiss of the Vampire dates from those Wilderness Years during which Hammer and Christopher Lee were disputing his salary requirements for donning Dracula's cape. In a groundbreaking study of the movie for *Little Shoppe of Horrors*, film scholar Bruce G. Hallenbeck cited evidence that *Kiss of the Vampire* was originally intended to be another Dracula-less Dracula movie, a direct follow-up to *Brides of Dracula*. While the resultant film has no direct connection with the Dracula mythos, it nevertheless shares a number of plot elements and thematic concerns with *Brides of Dracula*, most prominently the increasingly specific equating of vampirism with sexual degeneracy. *Kiss of the Vampire* also incorporates the original ending to *Brides of Dracula* that Peter Cushing had vetoed.

Kiss of the Vampire opens with a fairly shocking pre-title sequence. A grim-faced man interrupts the funeral of a young girl—his daughter, as we shall learn—by thrusting a shovel through her coffin lid. Blood runs out, to the horror of the assembled witnesses. As the credits roll, the camera peers into the grave to show us the unmistakable sign of vampirism, fangs curled over the (now twice-dead) girl's lips. This strong stuff is followed by that ancient chestnut, the Young Couple Whose Car Breaks Down Near a Mysterious Old House. The lovebirds in question are Gerald and Marianne Harcourt, British newlyweds who are traveling through Bavaria by motorcar (not unlike the happy-go-lucky tourists of *Dracula, Prince of Darkness*). Their car is out of gas; the year is about 1910, and gas is a scarce commodity in this neck of the woods. The Harcourt's plight is observed with interest, via telescope, by Dr. Ravna, aristocratic owner of a nearby mountaintop château.

The couple check into a local inn run by a close-mouthed couple, and soon receive a dinner invitation from Dr. Ravna and his adult children, Carl and Sabena. The Ravna château and clan alike are elegant, luxurious, and faintly decadent. During the dinner party, Carl plays the piano beautifully, and Marianne begins to succumb to his strangely hypnotic charm (which is, of course, the familiar sexual magnetism of the vampire). Meanwhile, a lithe girl steals from the château and visits the grave of the opening scene. This girl, Tania, attempts to coax the vampiress from her grave, and is confronted by the dead girl's father, Professor Zimmer. She escapes after plunging her fangs into his wrist. (Back at the inn, we learn that Tania is the innkeeper's lost daughter; her heartbroken mother still sets a place for her at the table each day.)

The next morning, Carl and Sabena visit the inn and invite the Harcourts to a masked ball. They beat a suspiciously hasty retreat when Professor Zimmer arrives and announces, with some enjoyment, "The weather is improving. It's getting brighter, I think." (The vampiric Ravna family plays by a looser set of rules than Hammer's Dracula, being able to eat and drink normal human fare and move about during the daytime, albeit in a limited fashion.) The unsuspecting Harcourts attend the ball, which is the film's most famous set piece, famously parodied in Roman Polanski's horror comedy, *The Fearless Vampire Killers*. It's a surreal and beautifully directed sequence, in which it slowly dawns on the viewer that, save for the Harcourts, *all* of the bizarrely garbed revelers are vampires, members of a satanic cult led by Ravna. Marianne is spirited away, while Gerald is drugged.

The next day, a groggy Gerald is curtly informed that none of the Ravnas has ever seen or heard of Marianne; he's then simply tossed out of the château. His nightmare deepens when he returns to the inn and find Marianne's things gone, and the frightened innkeepers claiming ignorance of her existence. (Hallenbeck dubs this odd, suspenseful sequence "Hitchcockian," due in part to its overt similarity to developments in the master's *The Lady Vanishes*. It's interesting to note that it *also* closely echoes events in Terence Fisher's best-known pre-Hammer film, a suspenser called *So Long at the Fair*.) However, before this subplot has much time to develop, Professor Zimmer tells Gerald that Marianne is being held by Ravna. Zimmer also relates his personal history, underlining the vampirism-as-venereal disease motif: his beloved daughter had "drifted in with the so-called smart set," and ended up living with Ravna. "She came home eventually…riddled with disease….and she was a vampire."

TANIA TAUNTS PROFESSOR ZIMMER (CLIFFORD EVANS) IN *KISS OF THE VAMPIRE*.

Zimmer tries to force Gerald to rest and prepare for Marianne's rescue, but the desperate husband instead barges into Château Ravna alone, very nearly getting himself vampirized. He escapes an attack by hastily improvising a cross on his chest with his own blood (an inventive touch).

Zimmer comes to the rescue and seals the vampires in the château with garlic, as Gerald spirits Marianne back down the mountain. Marianne is still under Ravna's power, à la Mina Harker, but Zimmer plays his trump card. Apparently, the embittered professor has been dabbling in magic for some time, seeking a way to turn the power of evil against the Ravna clan. Now he chants a fateful incantation—the action Peter Cushing felt Van Helsing would never take—and summons up an army of Hell-spawned bats that attack and destroy the vampire cult, still trapped in Ravna's château. (No hint is given as to why Zimmer hadn't taken this step before.)

Kiss of the Vampire was an interesting attempt to mold a new creative team to rival the Terence Fisher/Christopher Lee/Peter Cushing consortium that had worked for them so well, and so consistently. It must have seemed a good moment for such a move; besides the periodic money squabbles, Lee was at this time living in Switzerland and spending much of his time working on the continent, in part to avoid Britain's ruinous taxes. Moreover, Fisher's 1962 version of *Phantom of the Opera* had recently flopped badly at the box office, and rumors had it that Fisher was not in the best odor with the company for a few years afterward.

At any rate, directorial duties were assigned to Don Sharp, an Australian who'd directed a handful of minor features as well as second-unit work on several other films. *Kiss of the Vampire* was Sharp's first relatively high-profile assignment, and his first horror work—in fact, he's said that he'd never even *seen* a horror movie before accepting the assignment. Nevertheless, Sharp brought to the project a nice feel for the mannered and erotic decadence of his vampire characters, and a fine flair for action; his rousing 1965 pulp adventure, *The Face of Fu Manchu*, is one of the era's most entertaining genre films.

Sharp and producer/scriptwriter Anthony Hinds assembled a cast of talented and classically trained actors, headed by Noel Willman, a well-respected stage performer and director. Willman's performance is impeccably smooth, as one might expect, but too bloodless (sorry) to suit me—he has a markedly passionless, Leslie Howardish quality, in a role that would have benefited from a bit more oomph. (Willman once told interviewer David Del Valle that, as he was worried about "how easy it could be to send this all up," he chose to play Ravna "withdrawn and immobile." It makes you miss Christopher Lee.) By contrast, Isobel Black, in her minor role as Tania, is filled with the proper vampire spirit; all fire and fangs, she's as memorable as Andree Melee's similar character in *Brides of Dracula*.

Kiss of the Vampire's script is one of Anthony Hinds's better efforts, although it's marred by some overly clichéd plot devices. Moreover, the "Hitchcockian" interlude is intriguing, but its brevity and inconsequence to the rest of the film make it seem like something of a non sequitur. The use of the rejected ending from *Brides of Dracula* is certainly interesting from a film-crit standpoint, and makes you wonder (as has Hallenbeck) whether Hinds had some uncredited involvement in the earlier film's script. (Some say that Hinds originally intended to write *Brides of Dracula*—it would have been his first screenplay—but that Cushing agreed to act in it only if a "real" writer did the script.)

Sharp and Hinds conceived *Kiss of the Vampire* as opening and closing with bursts of action and violence, with the bulk of the movie devoted to a more restrained and atmospheric buildup. In this they largely succeeded, but it must be admitted that the ending is a let-down. Seasoned Hammer fans have learned to look past the technical and budgetary limitations of the studio's special-effects shop (God knows I've made my peace with the lame effects in *my* favorite Hammer, *The Devil's Bride*)—but a horde of demonic bats was a particularly stiff challenge for Hammer's technicians. Brief animated shots of the bats circling the château are reasonably effective, but the ensuing attack is all too obviously conducted by rubber bats on nylon thread. (They were purchased at a Woolworth's, by the way.) Well, this is what your ability to suspend belief is for; it'll serve you in good stead here.

One final consumer warning: a bowdlerized version of *Kiss of the Vampire*, with additional scenes added, was prepared for a 1967 American television release under the title *Kiss of Evil*. Prints of this version pop up occasionally; don't waste your time on them.

HOUSE OF DARK SHADOWS

MGM, 1970
P, D: Dan Curtis
S: Sam Hall and Gordon Russell
Starring Jonathan Frid (*Barnabas Collins*), Grayson Hall (*Dr. Julia Hoffman*), Kathryn Leigh Scott (*Maggie Evans*), Nancy Barrett (*Carolyn Stoddard*), John Karlen (*Willie Loomis*), Thayer David (*Professor T. Eliot Stokes*), Roger Davis (*Jeff Clark*), Louis Edmonds (*Roger Collins*) Donald Briscoe (*Todd Jennings*), David Henesy (*David Collins*), Lisa Richard (*Daphne Budd*), and Joan Bennett (*Elizabeth Stoddard*).

Nightwalkers rating:

With every passing year, the mid-1960s are looking more and more like the last truly great era in American pop culture—the tube had "The Man from U.N.C.L.E." and "Jonny Quest," Marvel comics were fresh and original, and Sean Connery was James Bond, as God intended—and for many fans, one highlight of that golden period was the 1966–1971 run of the oddest television soap opera ever, "Dark Shadows."

This Gothic-flavored soap was floundering in the ratings when, a few months after its premiere, its makers decided to enliven the proceedings by adding a genuine vampire to the cast. As played by Canadian actor Jonathan Frid, the vampire in question, Barnabas Collins, became a minor-league culture hero and made the show a success, spawning a flood of paperbacks, trading cards, board games, fanzines, conventions, and collectors' items of every sort—a phenomenon that hasn't abated to this day, even in the wake of the show's disastrous and short-lived prime-time network revival in 1991. Followers of "Dark Shadows" continue to rival fans of "Star Trek" in enthusiasm, if not in numbers.

In all honesty, though, while I'm sure there are some modern-day converts to the "Dark Shadows" cult, my gut feeling is that if you didn't love it at at a tender age, you probably never will. The problem is not so much the show's laughable production values and incredibly convoluted plot lines. It's mainly that "Dark Shadows" is first and last a daily soap opera, with all the irritants that implies. You've got to wade through hours of exposition for the least significant plot development, until you feel you'll go mad waiting for something to actually *happen.*

But that's okay, because the show's creator, Dan Curtis, thoughtfully provided us noncultists with a palatable introduction to his universe, *House of Dark Shadows,* a feature-film spinoff from the show. The film features much of the show's enormous cast in a simplified tale of the undead, *sans* time travel, parallel universes and the other "Dr. Who"-like trappings of the television serial.

The film, like the soap opera, is set in and around the ancestral seat of the Collins family, Collinwood, an enormous New England Gothic Revival mansion (actually Lyndhurst in Tarrytown, New York). Near the mansion is a far older, crumbling house that was Barnabas Collins's home in the late eighteenth century. The action begins when a feeble-minded, Renfieldish character named Willie Loomis steals into this ruin and opens the vampire's

A GRUESOME MONTAGE FROM DAN CURTIS'S *HOUSE OF DARK SHADOWS.*

sealed crypt, seeking treasure. Barnabas, free again after having been imprisoned by his own family nearly two centuries before, loses no time in slaking his thirst on the local populace. This done, he charms his way into the confidence of the current Collins clan by passing himself off as a long-lost English cousin, the namesake of the "original" Barnabas.

Barnabas discovers that the Collins family governess, Maggie Evans, is the image of Josette, his old love of some two hundred years before, who killed herself when she discovered that her fiancé had become a creature of darkness. (Curtis later reused this plot device in his film version of *Dracula.*) He's instantly mad for this new Josette, and she responds, to the dismay of her own fiancé.

A chance for happiness seems to present itself to Barnabas in the form of the Collins family physician, Dr. Julia Hoffman. Dr. Hoffman discovers Barnabas's true identity and, intrigued with his case, develops a treatment that suppresses the "destructive cells" that cause vampirism. This cure begins to take effect, allowing Barnabas to appear in daylight; delighted, he plans to wed Maggie. Unfortunately for Barnabas, Dr. Hoffman, an attractive woman "of a certain age" (as the French say), has fallen in love with him as well—say, this *is* beginning to sound like a soap, isn't it?—and, embittered with jealousy, she sabotages his treatment, causing Barnabas to revert to his old habits. In an impressively downbeat denouement, virtually the entire platoon-sized cast of characters is vampirized and/or killed.

House of Dark Shadows is a confused but occasionally entertaining mess. The straightforward-enough plot I've outlined is festooned with about three times as many characters as it needs, apparently to let Curtis give nearly every member of his sprawling soap-opera family a few minutes' exposure. There's also some ripe unintentional humor, most notably a sequence in which Collinwood's local police force is organized into a vampire-hunting posse and issued crucifixes and silver bullets. Moreover, as I've noted elsewhere, Dan Curtis's direction is often weak, particularly in the area of pacing. The film creeps along from scene to scene with a glacial, dipped-in-concrete feel. On the other hand, Curtis has a knack for coming up with handsome, atmospheric visuals; a vampire's appearance amid the ruins of an enormous covered swimming pool is eerily beautiful. Furthermore, the whole "cure for vampirism" angle is reasonably fresh and interesting.

Barnabas is unquestionably the best thing about *House of Dark Shadows*, though; he's a brooding, reluctant, and romantic vampire, with a faintly ambisexual appeal, who seems to pave the way toward the sort of complex and self-divided monsters who would become hugely successful in the works of Anne Rice.

THE VAMPIRE LOVERS
Hammer/American International, 1970
P: Harry Fine and Michael Style
D: Roy Ward Baker
S: Tudor Gates
Starring Ingrid Pitt (*Carmilla*, "*Mircalla*," and "*Marcilla*"), Pippa Steele (*Laura*), Madeleine Smith (*Emma*), Peter Cushing (*General Spielsdorf*), George Cole (*Roger Morton*), Dawn Addams (*the Countess*), Kate O'Mara (*Mdme. Perrodon*), Douglas Wilmer (*Baron Hartog*), Jon Finch (*Carl Eberhardt*), Kirsten Betts (*the prologue's Vampire*), John Forbes Robertson (*the Man in Black*), Harvey Hall (*Renton*), and Ferdy Mayne (*the Doctor*).

Nightwalkers rating:
☠☠½

With fangs and breasts bared, *The Vampire Lovers* briefly revitalized Hammer's aging Gothic formula, while providing the studio with one of its last solid commercial and critical hits on both sides of the Atlantic. Seen in retrospect, *The Vampire Lovers* is one of the brighter spots of late Hammer. It's an uneven but handsome and entertaining production, with a sexy energy that (mostly) smooths over rough spots in the script and performances. Moreover, this first entry in Hammer's Karnstein trilogy—all based loosely on Joseph Sheridan LeFanu's classic tale "Carmilla"— helped precipitate something of a mini-boom in flashy, openly erotic vampire movies, including its two sequels as well as *Vampire Circus* and *Captain Kronos: Vampire Hunter.*

The Vampire Lovers opens with a moody, beautifully photographed precredit sequence (which is, in all, probably the best part of the picture). In the eighteenth-century Austro-Hungarian province of Styria, Baron Joachim Von Hartog journeys to the mist-shrouded graveyard of the Karnsteins, a clan of vampires, to avenge the death of his sister at their hands. Confronted by a gorgeous blonde vampire, he nearly succumbs but is saved by his crucifix. With a sweep of his blade, he decapitates her, as the camera freezes and the credits roll.

Some years later, the narrative resumes at a ball given by General Spielsdorf, an acquaintance of the baron's. A mysterious countess attends, accompanied by her beautiful daughter Marcilla. (Conspiratorial glances and whispers between these two tell us they're not what they seem.) The countess rushes off with a story about a dying friend, leaving Marcilla in the general's care. Marcilla, a sultry, husky-voiced beauty, initiates a passionate "friendship" with the general's young niece, Laura, who develops a mysterious wasting ailment. Marcilla seems to care for Laura tenderly during her illness; only after Laura dies does the general discover the tiny puncture marks on her neck. By this time, Marcilla has skipped town.

Soon afterward, like vampiric con men, the countess-and-daughter team arrives at the home of Roger Morton, a well-to-do English friend of the general's living in Styria. The same pattern is repeated, as the vampiress, now calling herself Carmilla (the anagram names are a feature of LeFanu's original story), begins to seduce—and feed on—Morton's buxom daughter, Emma. To cement her place in the household, Carmilla also vamps the family's sultry governess, Mademoiselle Perrodon, turning her into a sexual slave. Emma begins to look pale and has nightmares haunted by an enormous cat.

An alert butler, Renton, manages to stave off the vampiric attacks with garlic flowers, and summons a doctor, but both men fall victim to Carmilla. Emma's father, returning from a journey, meets Baron Hartog and General Spielsdorf, who are searching for Laura's killer. Hartog explains that he had slain all the Karnstein vampires except for one whose tomb was hidden, Mircalla, who they now believe to be the Marcilla who killed Laura—and the Carmilla now staying at Morton's house. Morton sends Carl Eberhardt, Emma's beau, on to protect Emma. Carl confronts the vampiress, who simply vanishes, returning to the safety of her tomb. Meanwhile, the general, Hartog and Morton hasten to the Karnsteins' burial ground, locate Carmilla's tomb and find her resting there. The offended gentry put her to rest with stake and sword in time to save Emma.

The Vampire Lovers was the product of a rare collaboration between the era's two greatest creators of horror films, Hammer and American International. By 1970, "Hammer" no longer

A CHORUS LINE: THE BEAUTIFUL LADIES OF *THE VAMPIRE LOVERS*.

existed, in the sense of a small, tight-knit team of technicians and creative talent; instead, the organization essentially devoted its time to brokering deals between various film producers and distributors. One such deal came about when Fantale Films, a company run by producers Harry Fine and Michael Style, approached Hammer's James Carreras with a proposal for a new and relatively explicit version of "Carmilla" (which had been filmed twice before in a more circumspect way by French and Spanish companies). Carreras, always enthusiastic about any project involving scantily clad women, loved the idea and quickly lined up $400,000 in financial backing from American International—so quickly, in fact, that Fantale was given less than two months to develop a script, cast actors, and handle other preproduction chores.

This rush job undoubtedly hurt the project, particularly in terms of Tudor Gates's hastily written screenplay. The "Laura" and "Emma" sections are so similar as to give the movie a slow and overly repetitive feel, and while apologists for *The Vampire Lovers* often compare this structure to Hitchcock's similar ploy in *Psycho*, Pippa Steele's Laura doesn't generate enough interest to make us feel much surprise (or anything else) when she dies. The script also takes stab at giving Mircalla some complexity, but with little follow-through. Occasional suggestions that her romantic inclinations toward her female victims may be genuine mostly are lost amid the more conventional vampiric doings. There are also a few large and rather irritating loose ends. We never learn anything about the mysterious countess in league with Mircalla, or about a black-clad male vampire on horseback who lurks at the edge of the proceedings throughout the film, without affecting the plot a whit. (These two are often identified as Karnsteins, but Hartog clearly states that he'd already slain all of them except Mircalla. Still, I suppose he could be wrong.)

Gates elaborates freely on the vampire myth (as most of Hammer's movies did, after all). Like Varna in *Kiss of the Vampire*, Mircalla prefers the shade, but isn't overly troubled by sunlight. More problematic is the fact that *The Vampire Lovers* is the only Hammer vampire film to entirely abandon the concept of vampirism as a transmittable disease; Carmilla's victims just *die*. Besides begging the question of just how the Karnsteins got to *be* vampires, this idea has the effect of reducing our potential sympathy for Mircalla. Most cinematic bloodsuckers at least offer their victims a chance to share the pains and pleasures of their undead condition, which of course is the source of much of the potency of the vampire myth. In some cases (as with Dan Curtis's *Bram Stoker's Dracula*), the vampire seeks to create an undead mate and partner. By contrast, Carmilla is simply a killer, which renders her less interesting, and makes her protestations of love for her victims ring a little hollow.

Even so, Gates's screenplay contains a number of nicely horrific little touches, such as the dreamlike opening, and another great scene in which Carl confronts Mircalla just as she's vampirized the governess; Mircalla looks up in surprise, then hastily wipes the blood from her mouth with a guilty pout, like a child caught at the cookie jar. Moreover, the production values in *The Vampire Lovers'* are top quality. Scott MacGregor's settings (some of them artful redressings from *Taste the Blood of Dracula*) are quite as good as anything Bernard Robinson did in Hammer's earlier days. And Roy Ward Baker's direction lends a dignified air to proceedings that could easily have veered off into camp, although he allows the pace to slacken in the film's middle.

For the most part, though, *The Vampire Lovers* rests squarely on the shapely shoulders of Ingrid Pitt, whose continuing reputation as a horror *femme fatale* is probably rivalled only by that of Barbara Steele. It's an apt comparison in another way; Pitt is a beautiful and charismatic woman with a natural gift for projecting strength and authority on screen, and, in her horror work, is more notable as a *presence* than as an actress, just as Steele was. Pitt's heavy, Teutonic quality works against her in her love scenes with Emma, which seem stiff and awkward, and she's not helped by Madeleine Smith's Emma. Smith, whose face and form are of such awesome perfection as to be almost cartoonlike, was a young and inexperienced actress at the time, and her characterization is innocent to the point of idiocy. By contrast, Pitt's matter-of-fact seduction of Kate O'Mara (who was the brightest spot in the misfired *Horror of Frankenstein*), is both convincing and powerfully erotic.

The lesbian angle was fairly daring and explicit for the period, but, other than Pitt's breathy love-talk, it's restricted to some brief on-screen breast-stroking. It *is* a bit surprising for an AIP coproduction of the period, since until this time the studio had been more inclined to sell the sizzle than the steak, if you get my drift. AIP seems to have been of two minds about the whole thing; producer Harry Fine once told *Little Shoppe of Horrors* that he believed the explicit lesbianism was "the miracle extra ingredient that attracted AIP." But Roy Ward Baker has recalled that, soon after shooting had begun, AIP "sent a letter saying 'all references to lesbianism must be deleted.' [!] Considering the whole picture was about lesbianism, we just all laughed and tore the letter up and that was that! Our attitude was 'Don't be bloody silly, dear, the boat has already sailed.'" Indeed.

As for the film's once-controversial nudity: while it seems both mild and reasonably tasteful by 1990s standards, it did serve to catapult Hammer briefly back into controversy, since the film was the very first horror film ever to receive an "R" rating in the United States, shattering the long-standing assumption on the part of American distributors and viewers that horror films were, ipso facto, kiddie fare. You could scarcely ask for a better illustration of that bizarre and peculiarly American Puritanism that laps up scenes of death and mass destruction, but quails before unclothed body parts owned by half the population.

LUST FOR A VAMPIRE
Hammer, 1970
P: Harry Fine and Michael Style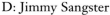
D: Jimmy Sangster
S: Tudor Gates

Starring Ralph Bates (*Giles*), Barbara Jefford (*the Countess*), Suzanna Leigh (*Janet*), Michael Johnson (*Richard Le Strange*), Yutte Stensgaard

(*Mircalla/Carmilla*), Helen Christie (*Miss Simpson*), Count Karnstein (*Mike Raven*), and Pippa Steele (*Susan*).

Nightwalkers rating:
💀💀

Even its makers seemed to heartily dislike *Lust for a Vampire*, the second movie in the Karnstein cycle. Ralph Bates, the top-billed actor, considered it "one of the worst films ever made," while director Jimmy Sangster once noted, "I hated the film, hated it!" Many Hammer fans and film writers have expressed similar emotions, if less pithily. But *Lust for a Vampire* isn't all *that* awful, as anyone who has seen a really bad horror film can tell you, although it is a comedown from its stylish predecessor.

The film opens with a blatant steal from *Dracula—Prince of Darkness*. In 1830, the vampire Count Karnstein abducts a peasant girl and uses her blood to revive Carmilla, who literally grows new flesh on her withered skeleton. (Her head has reattached itself since the last picture.) The reborn Carmilla, now an icily attractive blonde, enrolls in a girl's school located about seven feet from the haunted ruins of Castle Karnstein. Carmilla, under the anagram name Mircalla, finds ripe pickings at the school, whose students are unfailingly beautiful, highly sexed, and given to prancing about in filmy chemises. Mircalla's roomie, Susan, soon makes lesbian advances—which turns out to be a fatal mistake. Their interlude, culminating in a moonlight swim, is less explicit than similar scenes in *The Vampire Lovers* but still impressively erotic.

Passing through the area is a handsome English writer, Richard Le Strange, who is smitten with Mircalla, so much so that he wangles a teaching position at the school. There he meets another teacher, Giles, who is unhealthily fascinated with the occult, and Mircalla as well. Giles discovers the vampiress's secret and begs her to make him a creature of evil too; she drains his

ROBOTIC BEAUTY: *LUST FOR A VAMPIRE'S* GORGEOUS YUTTE STENSGAARD.

blood instead. (This sequence features the movie's most eerily beautiful scene, in which Mircalla glides, rather than walks, through the mists shrouding the castle grounds.) Later, Richard learns Mircalla's secret from Giles's papers, but he's too besotted with love to care. Here the plot takes an interesting twist; the beautiful vampire comes to *return* his love.

Naturally, things don't work out. In love though she may be, Mircalla continues with her, ah, alternative lifestyle, vampirizing another girl. The school's headmistress, Miss Simpson, covers up the odd happenings, and Count Karnstein himself silences a snoopy police inspector; but ultimately a torch-wielding mob bears down on the castle. Richard tries to save his undead lover, but she's speared by a falling roof beam as the castle burns. Karnstein and his vampire countess stand by impassively, watching the flames mount. He says there's "no death in fire" for such as them, but still looks faintly worried as the film peters out.

Preproduction on *Lust for a Vampire* began while *The Vampire Lovers* was still filming. Producers Fine and Style had cut a quick production deal with EMI—a mistake, as it turned out, because American International's savvy had a lot to do with the success of *The Vampire Lovers* in America. (*Lust for a Vampire* was released in the United States by a minor-league independent, Continental Films, and did lousy business.) Unfortunately, two events dealt the movie severe blows before the cameras rolled.

The role of Giles, the obsessed teacher, was originally written for Peter Cushing. Cushing, however, was forced to drop out of the production because his beloved wife was seriously ill; Ralph Bates stepped into the part almost literally at the last minute. At roughly the same time, Terence Fisher, who was scheduled to direct the film, was struck by a car in front of his home and badly injured (three days before shooting was to start, according to Jimmy Sangster). He was replaced by Hammer alumnus Sangster, who was back in London after a longish sojourn in California, wrapping up post-production on his directorial debut, *Horror of Frankenstein*. *Lust for a Vampire* producer Harry Fine once characterized Sangster's direction as "efficient if unimaginative," a good enough description of the man's style. He simply moves the story along, reasonably briskly, but in a flat and literal way.

In all, the twin losses of Cushing and Fisher probably destroyed the film's chances of being something more than a programmer. Given Fisher's flair for romance, it's easy to speculate on what he could have done with the movie's most interesting feature, the love affair between Richard and Mircalla. As it stands, this angle is simply sketched in, with no particular emotional depth. Fisher might have made the situation seem genuinely tragic, as he did with similarly thin characters in *The Gorgon* (which see). And, while Ralph Bates acquits himself well as the doomed and obsessed Giles, doubtless Cushing's presence could have added that inde-finable weight and respectability he brought to so many semi-stinkers.

The other performances in *Lust for a Vampire* are workmanlike. Playing Karnstein in this outing is Mike Raven, a former BBC disk jockey who parleyed his role in the film into a brief career as horror villain. With his hawklike features locked in an "evil" expression, Raven comes off as a low-grade Chris Lee clone (a comparison oddly pointed up in one cutaway shot, in which a closeup of Karnstein's eyes is clearly spliced-in footage of Lee's bloodshot Dracula peepers). Yutte Stensgaard as Mircalla doesn't offer Ingrid Pitt much competition. For some fans, she's a bit of a laughing stock, which seems unfair. Lord knows she's not much of an actress (though this is relative—compared to the women in Ed Wood's movies, she's Kate Hepburn), but nonetheless, there's something arresting and unsettling about this robotic beauty, her flawless face so utterly unmarred by any trace of thought or emotion.

Harry Robertson's lush, romantic score ranks with the best Hammer music. Ironically, though, the one thing most fans seem to remember about *Lust for a Vampire* is a nauseating pop song added to the film during postproduction by its producers. As Richard and Mircalla tryst in the moonlight, a woman's voice begins warbling "Strange Love" (sample lyrics: "Strange love, tender and burning/love, you've ever been yearning"). Ralph Bates and Jimmy Sangster went to see the film together, unaware that this terrific addition had been made; according to Bates, "When that awful song came on I had to pull Jim off the floor to make him watch it. The whole audience was laughing and throwing cups and boxes up in the air."

This sort of thing does not lend itself to the suspension of disbelief.

TWINS OF EVIL
Hammer, 1971
P: Harry Fine and Michael Style
D: John Hough
S: Tudor Gates
Starring Peter Cushing (*Gustav Weil*), Madeleine Collinson (*Frieda Gellhorn*), Mary Collinson (*Maria Gellhorn*), Damien Thomas (*Count Karnstein*), Isobel Black (*Ingrid Hoffer*), David Warbeck (*Anton Hoffer*), Kathleen Byron (*Katy Weil*), Dennis Price (*Dietrich*), and Katya Keith (*Countess Mircalla*).

Nightwalkers rating: 💀 💀 💀

Twins of Evil is probably the most entertain-ing of Hammer's Karnstein trilogy; it's darker and more sumptuous, less titillating (the lesbian angle largely goes by the board) and considerably more grim and violent than its predecessors.

Twins of Evil concerns another evil scion of the Karnstein clan, but it's set in the seventeenth century, well before the events of the first two films. The chunk of Middle Europe that pro-vides our setting is oppressed by several different forms of evil. A string of mysterious vampire slayings has the village of Karnstein terrified. In response, a ruthlessly fanatical group called the Brotherhood (clearly modeled on Cromwell's Puritans) is attempting to root out the evil in their midst by burning village girls for witch-craft, more or less at random. The Brother-hood's leader, Gustav Weil, hates aristocrats nearly as much as Satan, and few are more hate-ful than Count Karnstein, a vicious noble whose connections with the Holy Roman emperor allow him to thumb his nose at Weil's homicidal crusade. The two men's relationship is beautifully summed up when Karnstein casually abandons his latest bedmate, a peasant girl, to the Brotherhood's fires, then blithely asks a furious Weil to pray for his soul.

Weil's twin nieces, recently orphaned, arrive in Karnstein to live with him. Frieda and Maria are identically beautiful, but opposite in character. Maria is a quiet, dutiful girl (the movie's title is misleading), while Frieda is passionate, fun-loving and, as they used to say, out for kicks—not the sort of girl to please her dour uncle. The two girls are enrolled at the village's school, which is run by a brother and sister, Anton and Ingrid Hoffer. Anton, handsome and idealistic, is the closest thing to a hero in sight. He turns sweet on Frieda, but she is immediately fascinated by the charming and lecherous Count Karnstein.

Meanwhile, the count grows bored, so his lackeys stage an ersatz Satanic mass for his entertainment. On a whim, he dismisses them and turns the ceremony into the real thing by killing the girl brought in to play the sacrifice. This murder summons the spirit of his vampire ancestor, Mircalla, who vampirizes the count—unfortunately, via one of those rather silly, late-Hammer instantaneous transformations; the count sprouts inch-long fangs in seconds. This done, Mircalla promptly disappears from the plot, without explanation. (Another conundrum: Who was vampirizing those villagers at the film's beginning? The movie offers no clue.) At any rate, the count quickly recruits Frieda into vampirism. As with the previous Karnstein movies, these vampires can move about by day, allowing them to disguise their true natures.

Anton is a rationalist who doesn't believe in vampires, and despises Weil's inquisition. He learns better when his beloved sister is slain by Frieda. The Brotherhood condemns Frieda, but a case of mistaken identity almost consigns Maria

MADELEINE COLLINSON DISPLAYS HER IMPRESSIVE, UM, FANGS, IN HAMMER'S GRIM *TWINS OF EVIL*.

to the flames, until she's saved by Anton (a sequence that's more than a little reminiscent of similar events in *Black Sunday*). In a bloody denouement, the vampires are routed and slain, though not before Karnstein takes Weil off the game board as well. Anton, we assume, will pair off with the virtuous twin.

Director John Hough was chosen for *Twins of Evil* due to a flair for action he first demonstrated in television projects like "The Avengers," and he keeps what could have been a rather depressing movie lively and entertaining. (Hough also did admirable work on the sorely underrated *Legend of Hell House*.) The film also benefits from some of Hammer's finest visuals ever, due to a remarkable and expensive-looking production design by Roy Stannard. In particular, the lavish, cavernous interiors of Castle Karnstein (filmed at Britain's Pinewood studios) offer a stark contrast to the beautiful but often cramped sets featured in earlier Hammer films shot at Bray.

Twins of Evil is also aided by remarkable performances from the movie's principals, Peter Cushing and Damien Thomas. This was Cushing's first film after the death of his wife, Helen, and, sad though it is to say, his genuine and profound grief seems to add depth and conviction to his performance (as it did in *Frankenstein and the Monster from Hell*, shot soon afterward). His portrayal of Weil could easily have been as a despicable and one-dimensional tyrant, but the obvious pain in Cushing's drawn features inevitably creates some sympathy for this rigid, driven, unhappy man, who clearly does care about his wayward (to say the least) niece. Stage actor Damien Thomas is nearly as interesting as Karnstein. Thomas, probably best known to Americans as Father Alvito in the televised epic *Shogun*, plays Karnstein as a charming monster in the best Terence Fisher tradition.

The other leads, Madeleine and Mary Collinson, um, do not detract unduly from the picture, despite their lack of acting experience. Obviously, casting identical beauties represented a considerable challenge for Hammer. The Collinson twins won the assignment on the basis of an October 1970 *Playboy* pictorial (which, by the way, was a truly unforgettable piece of contraband, if you happened to be a thirteen-year-old boy at the time). Despite their white-bread names, the Collinsons are Maltese, and their English was broken at best, so both were dubbed by another actress. They look suitably voluptuous and rarely embarrass the film.

Vampirism is essentially a secondary element in Tudor Gates's screenplay for *Twins of Evil*, which seems far more concerned with describing its bleak and amoral worldview. The script is certainly not without its weaknesses, such as the rather obvious plot holes I've already mentioned, and occasional silliness like those inch-long fangs. Moreover, the film's one innovation on the vampire legend—the idea that only evil persons become vampires when bitten and the virtuous merely die—is a stupid concept that, fortunately, did not catch on: Much of the peculiar horror of the vampirism lies *precisely* in the idea of friends and loved ones being changed, of finding an evil stranger in a familiar body.

Despite these problems, *Twins of Evil* ranks with Peter Sasdy's *Taste the Blood of Dracula* as one of the most unsettling and compelling of the Hammer horrors. While Anton, our supposed hero, doesn't seem nearly as ineffectual as his counterparts in Sasdy's movies, his efforts still do little to relieve the sense of injustice and monumental evil that hangs over *Twins of Evil* like a fog. Some writers have made much of the film's "struggle between Puritanism and libido," but both sides are portrayed in unrelentingly negative terms. Justice, mercy, and simple decency seem oddly irrelevant in the movie's morbid universe.

VAMPIRE CIRCUS
Hammer, 1971
P: Wilbur Stark
D: Robert Young
S: Judson Kinberg
Starring Adrienne Corri (*the Gypsy woman*), Laurence Payne (*Mueller*), Thorley Walters (*the burgomeister*), John Moulder-Brown (*Anton*), Anthony Corlan (*Emil*), Lynne Frederick (*Dora Mueller*), Domini Blythe (*Anna Mueller*), and Robert Tayman (*Count Mitterhouse*).

Nightwalkers rating: 💀💀💀

The lively and visually impressive *Vampire Circus* was made smack in the middle of Hammer's late sex-and-violence phase. In its original form, it was pretty strong stuff for its day, with dollops of female nudity and some better-than-average gore effects. Twentieth Century–Fox butchered the film for its United States release, removing more than ten minutes of footage and re-editing the remainder. I've been fortunate enough to view the original British print, and my remarks apply to that version.

Even in its original form, however, the script for *Vampire Circus* is probably too ambitious, and often confusing. While the story is simple enough in its basic outline, it brims with enough subplots to equip a medium-sized Dickens novel—which probably explains why most summaries of the movie I've seen are riddled with errors. I won't attempt a complete description; suffice it to say the following:

In nineteenth-century Serbia, the village of Stetl suffers under the attentions of Count Mitterhouse, a vampire who feeds on the villagers' children and seduces their wives; "One lust feeds the other," he mutters, as he romps with a comely matron. Having tired of this behavior, the residents of Stetl stake the vampire and burn his castle. Impaled, he still has enough energy to curse the villagers' children. Anna Mueller, the vampire's mistress, is captured and flogged by the incensed villagers, who seem angrier about her sexual peccadillos than their children's deaths. She escapes and pulls the vampire's body into a crypt beneath the castle ruins.

Fifteen years later, Stetl has fallen on hard times again, this time due to a plague carried by bats. The surrounding inhabitants have quarantined the village, preventing entry or exit at gunpoint. Nonetheless, a caravan arrives in town, bearing the Circus of Nights, a weird touring troupe led by a strange gypsy woman and an equally unsettling dwarf. The circus also features a vampiric were-leopard, Emil, the count's cousin; a tigerwoman, who prances about in her striped birthday suit (in the English print, that is), and a pair of male and female twins, vampire aerialists who can transform into bats. (David Prowse, later to inhabit Darth Vader's suit, also has a small role as the circus strongman.)

The circus pitches its tents on the ruins of

Mitterhouse's castle, and in short order this odd assortment of characters begins preying on the grown children of Count Mitterhouse's persecutors, enslaving or slaying them. One of the circus tents contains an enchanted mirror, which apparently serves as an interdimensional portal leading to Mitterhouse's crypt below the circus. The vampires take their victims there, using their blood to revive the count. Finally, the village doctor returns from a dangerous foray beyond the town limits, with a contingent of soldiers to the rescue. The deadly circus is burned out, and Mitterhouse, now brought back to life, is decapitated with a crossbow string. The dying gypsy is revealed to be Anna, the village wife who loved the vampire.

Vampire Circus contains a bushel basket of imagery that seems lifted from a film student's graduate thesis. The sinister dwarf seems plucked straight from Fellini, while the hall of mirrors feels like a steal from Cocteau. The primary conceit here, of course, is the Circus of Nights itself, which seduces and betrays the locals by playing on their own fears and desires. Knowledgeable fantasy fans will recognize that this idea, too, seems copied more or less whole from previous (and superior) works, namely Charles G. Finney's sardonic classic of the 1930s, *The Circus of Dr. Lao*, and Ray Bradbury's *Something Wicked This Way Comes*. Still, I guess that borrowed profundities are better than none at all, and the film *is* stylish.

Early critical reaction to *Vampire Circus* among connoisseurs was enthusiastic; a gushing review in *Cinefantastique* even compared the film to Bergman's *The Seventh Seal*. To me, though, the movie's resonances ultimately seem half-digested and rather arbitrary. Most genuinely subtle films grow more satisfying in recollection. *Vampire Circus*, if slept on awhile, seems to diminish.

Even so, if *Vampire Circus* is "only" a vampire film, rather than a major existentialist tract, it's an effective and efficiently directed example of the form, with a number of memorable scenes. I immediately think of an impressive 360-degree shot involving the magic mirror. The vampire twins appear before their victims in the mirror, then step out, revealing no reflection in its surface, and lead their prey into its shimmering depths. Les Bowie's special effects are crude at best, featuring ancient tricks such as "Bewitched"-style stop-camera, start-camera

"materializations," but they're oddly effective within the film's dreamlike context. A scene featuring the vampire aerialists' performance is particularly lovely, even though their transformations are simply suggested via intercut process shots of flying bats. The movie's surreal quality is reinforced by uniformly effective efforts from the actors playing the circus's hellish denizens. In particular, Anthony Corlan's Emil, the wereleopard, is wonderfully animalistic and sensuous.

Although it promises considerably more than it delivers, *Vampire Circus* is offbeat and consistently entertaining. It's one of the best of the late Hammer horrors.

CAPTAIN KRONOS: VAMPIRE HUNTER
(United Kingdom title: *Kronos*)
Hammer, 1973
P: Albert Fennel and Brian Clemens
D, S: Brian Clemens
Starring Horst Janson (*Captain Kronos*), John Carson (*Dr. Marcus*), John Cater (*Professor Grost*), Caroline Munro (*Carla*), Shane Briant (*Paul Durward*), Lois Daine (*Sara Durward*), Ian Hendry (*Kerro*), Wanda Ventham (*Lady Durward*), William Hobbs (*Hagen Durward*), and Brian Tully (*George Sorrell*).

Nightwalkers rating: 💀💀

Sometimes you find yourself liking a film more for what it *could* have been—for the freshness or outrageousness of its premise, say—than for what it actually is. For me, *Captain Kronos: Vampire Hunter* is one of those, an ungainly but sporadically entertaining mess that mixes the Hammer vampire mythos with themes from pulp adventure and even Westerns.

The film is set in the central European community of Durward (an unlikely name for the area, methinks) and, judging from the costumes and a stray reference to telegraphy, it's 1840 or thereabouts. Young girls are being attacked by a mysterious cloaked figure who drains them, not of blood, but of the life force itself; teenagers are transformed to dying, wrinkled hags in seconds. Dr. Marcus, the local physician, smells supernatural trouble, and summons an old comrade, Captain Kronos—who happens to be Europe's foremost (only?) professional vampire killer.

Kronos, "late of the Imperial Guard," arrives in a wagon loaded down with sharpened stakes and the other tools of his trade. He's accompanied by his faithful hunchbacked companion, Professor Grost, of whom Kronos says, "What he doesn't know about vampirism wouldn't fill a flea's codpiece" (a line typical of

BEWARE THE EYES THAT PARALYZE: HORST JANSON AS THE STEELY *CAPTAIN KRONOS: VAMPIRE HUNTER.*

the screenplay's rather elephantine wit). Along the way, they pick up a peasant girl, Carla, who does her best to become the taciturn Kronos's love interest. Grost quickly diagnoses the killer as a special sort of vampire that traps its victims with hypnotic powers, and feeds directly on their life energy. The little professor tells Marcus that there are *hundreds* of different species of vampire, each with its own powers and weaknesses—an interesting revelation that helps to explain the manic rule-changing going on throughout Hammer's vampire cycle.

The killing continues as Kronos and Grost begin to track their quarry. Doctor Marcus is attacked and vampirized (why he doesn't simply die from instant old age, like the others, is unexplained), and discovers his plight only when he notices that he's growing *younger*. Marcus begs Kronos to lift the curse by killing him, which proves to be rather difficult. In a ghoulish sequence that has a certain macabre humor about it, Kronos and Grost attempt to find, via trial and error, just what it takes to kill this particular type of vampire. The standard stake doesn't work, nor does hanging. At last the two discover by accident that this sort can be slain only by impalement with a cross. Grost, who's an extremely handy fellow to have around, takes an old metal cross and smiths it into a beautiful blade for Kronos, complete with a mirrored guard to shield him from the vampire's hypnotic gaze.

Their investigations lead them ever closer to the suspicious clan of nobles who gave the town its name—Paul and Sara Durward, and their invalid mother, Lady Durward. The lady is still deep in mourning for Hagen, her long-dead husband, reputedly the best swordsman in Europe. Kronos enlists Carla's help as a sort of Trojan horse, insinuating her into the Durward household to discover the vampire's identity. Despite a number of red herrings planted to implicate the children, the vampires turn out to be Lady Durward and her undead husband, who crosses blades with Kronos. Guess who wins.

Brian Clemens, the film's co-producer, director, and screenwriter, had considerable success in Britain's television industry, and despite some minor flashes of gore, *Captain Kronos: Vampire Hunter* feels oddly like a television pilot in its lightheartedness and general lack of dramatic heft. (It *was* a pilot, in a sense; plans for a movie series dissolved after the film flopped in the United States.) The look is television as well; virtually all of the film's scenes are shot in a flat, gray northern light, which is nicely Vermeerish at times, but its drab colors are a far cry from the velvety shadows and rich hues of classic Hammer cinematography. With the exception of a dimly lit love scene, there's also a near-total lack of night settings—which is more than a little strange, considering this is, after all, a *vampire* story. (At one point, Kronos and his party bed down "for the night" in a sunny forest glen, at what appears to be about three o'clock in the afternoon.) Clemens manages a few chilling scenes, most notably a vampiric attack in a church. The shadow of a crucifix on the wall behind the victim slowly mutates into that of a figure with arms reaching out toward her.

It's refreshing, too, to see a horror film make the *hero* the central character, rather than the menace, and Captain Kronos is an engaging superguy, complete with his own logo (a "K" with an upward-thrusting arrow, embossed on his saddle). Kronos has a number of other colorful comic-book heroic traits; he uses Chinese herbs, meditates, and totes a samurai sword, not that we ever learn why. Horst Janson is fairly wooden as Kronos, but his intensely Teutonic looks fit the role well, and he does manage a certain enigmatic charm, sort of like a bush-league Klaus Maria Brandauer. Professor Grost, well-played by John Cater, is given much amusing schtick concerning the technical side of vampire hunting, and one of the movie's genuine pleasures is watching him employ ribbons, bells, and dead frogs to track down his vampiric prey.

Ultimately, though, *Captain Kronos: Vampire Hunter* simply lacks the kind of larger-than-life visual excitement needed to put over its preposterous story. In particular, the action sequences lack fire. For instance, there's a scene in which Kronos takes out three tavern bullies

with a single, too-fast-for-the-eye-to-follow slash of his samurai sword. It's obviously modeled on the eye-popping swordplay of Akira Kurosawa's samurai movies, but seems unconvincing and silly here. The final confrontation betwen Kronos and Hagen Durward is similarly flaccid, and badly shot, with too many static long shots of action that begs for more animated camerawork and editing.

Unfortunately, this basic lack of cinematic energy holds the film back. It's pretty easy to imagine *Kronos* made with the kind of breakneck verve and comic edge seen in Richard Lester's *Three Musketeers* films, for instance; *that* would have been something. Even so, *Captain Kronos: Vampire Hunter* is offbeat enough to be entertaining, most of the time, making it one of the more interesting specimens from Hammer's kitchen-sink period.

⇛ 5 ⇚

HERE THERE BE MONSTERS

THE WISDOM OF MEN IS SMALL, AND THE WAYS OF NATURE ARE STRANGE, AND WHO SHALL PUT A BOUND TO THE DARK THINGS THAT MAY BE FOUND BY THOSE WHO SEEK FOR THEM?

—SIR ARTHUR CONAN DOYLE, "LOT NO. 249"

𝔄nd now, a miscellany of Nightwalkers for your consideration, monsters all. Hammer's deal with Universal, which freed them to adopt and adapt elements from the 1930s horror series, encouraged the company to diversify its monstrous brood well beyond Frankenstein and Dracula. Indeed, Hammer quickly surpassed Universal in its ingenuity at conjuring up new bogies to shamble across the screen.

Two of Hammer's best monster movies were shaped by Terence Fisher's capable hands

into haunting, minor-key tragedies. *The Curse of the Werewolf* uses Universal's wolfman concept to generate pathos for its reluctant monster. (Like Universal, Hammer chose to employ an anthropomorphic half man, half beast, doubtless for visual interest and shock value. The werewolf of folklore, of course, simply becomes a wolf, and Western audiences are just a little too fond of pups to be frightened by even the largest frisky canine.) Fisher's *The Gorgon*, in contrast, borrows from Greek myth to create a wholly unique screen monster that is, alas, the weakest element of a reasonably strong movie.

Another pair of films, John Gilling's

OLIVER REED IN A DEFIANT MOOD AS THE RELUCTANT WOLFMAN OF HAMMER'S *CURSE OF THE WEREWOLF*.

Cornwall classics, involve a similar mix of old and new. *The Plague of the Zombies*, a bizarre tale of Haitian voodoo in the Cornish mining country, uses the traditional living-dead zombies of Val Lewton's old movies to conjure up some pretty effective shocks, without ever quite disproving the simple principle that unstoppable automatons make fairly boring antagonists (or at least they did before George Romero taught them to eat human flesh). The second of Gilling's pair, *The Reptile*, involved perhaps Hammer's most outré monster of all, a beautiful and sensual female were-snake.

These monsters were all one-shots, however. The only Nightwalkers to establish any sort of franchise at Hammer to rival those of Frankenstein and Dracula were the mummies, who figured in four of the studio's films in all. Hammer's Egyptian tales were another product of the company's Universal remake arrangement, and as such perpetuate an interesting and infrequently acknowledged case of second-hand plagiarism.

The mummy horror tale, as rendered in movies, was invented by Sir Arthur Conan Doyle in two 1890s short stories. One, "The Ring of Thoth," concerns an undead priest of ancient Egypt who seeks to revive the mummy of his long-dead love. Karl Freund's 1932 classic *The Mummy* is simply too similar to this story in events and themes for the resemblance to be accidental. Even Doyle's description of the priest, his face "cross-hatched with a million delicate wrinkles," seems to have provided the model for Karloff's Imhotep makeup. Yet the film makes no acknowledgment of this blatant borrowing. Eight years later, Universal embarked on a new series of four movies in which a desiccated mummy repeatedly and tediously pursues its victims, one bandaged arm outstretched. These seem modeled entirely on another Doyle tale, "Lot No. 249," which concerns a man who revives a mummy and sets it upon his enemies,

one by one. The story even mentions the sacred scroll and mystic leaves that became standard cinematic mummy-revival gear. Once again, no screen credit was given.

Hammer's mummy films are based largely on the later Universals, rather than the brilliant first outing. The Hammer series began on a strong note—the Hammer *Mummy* is the best mummy film yet other than Freund's—but soon succumbed to the same tedium that enveloped Universal's later efforts. It's the same problem as with zombies, I'm afraid. There's only so much you can do with a shuffling corpse. They lack star appeal.

THE MUMMY
Hammer, 1959
P: Michael Carreras
D: Terence Fisher
S: Jimmy Sangster
Starring Peter Cushing (*John Banning*), Christopher Lee (*Kharis*), Yvonne Furneaux (*Isobel Banning* and *Ananka*), Eddie Byrne (*Inspector Mulrooney*), Felix Aylmer (*Stephen Banning*), Raymond Huntley (*Joseph Whemple*), and George Pastell (*Mehemet*).

Nightwalkers rating: ½

The international success of Hammer's renditions of Frankenstein and Dracula made it inevitable that the studio would tackle another of Universal's horror classics. In exchange for American distribution rights, Universal agreed to allow Hammer to adapt elements from its Mummy series of the 1930s and '40s. The resulting film lacks the sheer beauty of Karl Freund's exquisite 1932 version of *The Mummy*, but it has its own charms, and easily ranks as one of Hammer's best.

In 1895, English archaeologists uncover the tomb of Ananka, an Egyptian princess. The expedition is led

CUSHING'S JOHN BANNON CONFRONTS THE UNSTOPPABLE KHARIS IN *THE MUMMY*.

by Stephen Banning and Joseph Whemple, as well as John Banning, Stephen's adult son. John is laid up with a broken leg that hasn't set properly, but, fired with enthusiasm for the tomb's opening, he's refused to leave the dig for treatment. At the same time, a quiet, mannered Egyptian, Mehemet, begs them not to desecrate Ananka's tomb; unheeded, he warns of dire consequences. Stephen is first to enter the crypt, where a mysterious event renders him mad. This was, we learn later, an encounter with the living mummy Kharis.

CHRISTOPHER LEE'S UNCOMMONLY ATHLETIC MUMMY IN SEARCH OF HIS NEXT VICTIM.

appears—who, as John has mentioned, is the very image of Kharis's ancient love Ananka. The dead man looks at her, eyes filled with pain and yearning, and abandons his errand. Mehemet, puzzled by Kharis's failure, accompanies his undead charge back to Banning's house. Seeing the trouble, he makes the mistake of ordering Kharis to slay Isobel. The mummy turns on his master instead, breaking his back, and carries Isobel back to the swamps. At

Three years later, Stephen recovers from his madness sufficiently to summon his son to his side. He warns John that the mummy is after them. Naturally, John ascribes this to his father's illness. Meanwhile, Mehemet has taken a large house near Stephen's asylum. A wagon delivering a mummy-sized crate of "artifacts" accidently overturns, sending it tumbling into a nearby bog. That evening, Mehemet summons Kharis from the misty swamp and sends him to slay the half-mad Stephen in his padded cell.

Later, John examines Stephen's papers in search of a clue to his killer; as he does so, he tells Whemple the legend of Kharis and Ananka. In an extended flashback, we learn that Kharis, a high priest, so loved the princess Ananka that he could not accept her death. After presiding over her elaborate and bloody burial ceremonies, Kharis creeps back, opens her tomb, and attempts to revive her with the Scroll of Life—a hideous sacrilege. Discovered, he's turned into a living mummy and entombed with his beloved, to guard her throughout eternity.

Whemple is next on the mummy's hit list. John arrives and attempts to save him, only to find that bullets have no effect on the mummy. John now realizes that the legend is true, and that the mummy will visit him soon. Mehemet sends Kharis to slay John, and Kharis is on the point of doing so when John's wife Isobel

the bog's edge, Kharis releases her, and then is blasted apart by a hastily assembled posse. The mummy is last seen sinking into the dark waters, still clutching the scroll that gave him life.

The Mummy was one of Hammer's most lavish-looking productions ever, largely due to the efforts of production designer Bernard Robinson and cinematographer Jack Asher. The lush sets for the lengthy Egyptian flashback are typical Robinson miracles of papier-mâché that utterly disguise the shoestring nature of the production. Asher films them in vivid, jewel-like colors that nicely capture an otherworldy feel, and contrast starkly with the somber tones of the modern scenes.

An intelligent script and uniformly excellent performances support this framework. In particular, Peter Cushing's John Banning is a refreshing departure from the usual stalwart hero. He's interestingly shaded, with a strong and memorable undertone of sadness. One senses that his obsession with discovery has cost him much more than the use of his lame leg. George Pastell as Mehemet has a more conventional villain's role, but subverts it simply by refusing to *act* like a villain. Instead, he's a thoughtful, cultured, and pious man who sincerely believes he's following the dictates of his god.

Christopher Lee makes the most of another silent role, effectively conveying Kharis's terrible longing for Ananka through his eyes and mime. Roy Ashton's makeup lacks the eerie, parchment-dry look Jack Pierce gave Karloff in the original, and Lee makes an oddly muscular and lanky mummy. On the other hand, the mummy of the later Universal films was a sluggish menace at best. Lee's creation is athletic, fast-moving, and impressively threatening. In particular, the scene in which he smashes through a sanitarium window to kill Stephen Banning in his cell is convincing and scary. There's something genuinely chilling in the way Banning finds himself trapped by this unstoppable creature. (Lee's strenuous performance cost him a strained back and a dislocated shoulder during the shoot.)

Many Hammer enthusiasts are oddly lukewarm on *The Mummy*, possibly because its themes depart so dramatically from those of the studio's other classics. In particular, *The Mummy*'s story gave Terence Fisher little opportunity to create the binary tension between representatives of Good and Evil that figures so strongly in most Hammer tales. However, one of the most interesting aspects of *The Mummy* is precisely the fact that it lacks true heroes and villains. It's possible to feel pity for all the characters. The archaeologists, our supposed heroes, are fundamentally decent but display a callousness toward native belief that makes it clear they've earned some of their troubles. Kharis is a pathetic creature who has suffered millennia of unguessable torment. Once he regains some spark of humanity, he kills only to protect the woman he believes to be his old love. Even Mehemet, the closest thing present to a villain, acts from a deep and sincere piety. To me, at least, this kind of moral ambiguity is at least as interesting as the black-and-white dichotomies more typically seen in Hammer movies.

THE CURSE OF THE WEREWOLF

Hammer, 1960
P: Anthony Hinds
D: Terence Fisher
S: Anthony Hinds, writing as "John Elder"
Starring Oliver Reed (*Leon*), Clifford Evans (*Don Alfredo Carido*), Hira Talfrey (*Teresa*), Catherine Feller (*Christina*), Yvonne Romaine (*the Jailer's Daughter*), Anthony Dawson (*the Marquis*), Richard Wordsworth (*the Beggar*), Warren Mitchell (*Pepe Valiente*), John Gabriel (*Priest*), Ewen Solon (*Don Fernando*), Peter Sallis (*Don*

Enrique), Michael Ripper (*the "Old Soaker"*), George Woodbridge (*Dominique*), and Justin Walters (*Young Leon*).

***Nightwalkers* rating:** 💀💀💀½

In tight closeup, baleful werewolf eyes stare out at us—and shed tears. This arresting image opens Terence Fisher's sad and elegiac *The Curse of the Werewolf*, the story of a reluctant monster who simply could not get a break.

In late eighteenth-century Spain, a beggar enters the unhappy village of Santa Vera. Church bells announce the wedding of the town's loathsome, sadistic marquis. Hoping for a handout, the hapless beggar crashes the marquis's party, only to be mocked, humiliated, and finally thrown into a dungeon to rot. Years pass, and the beggar is forgotten by all except the jailer's mute daughter, who befriends the wretch. The girl grows into splendid womanhood, and one day attracts the aged marquis's lecherous eye. When the girl resists, he has her thrown in the cell with the beggar, who is by now little better than an animal. The brute rapes her, then dies. Upon release, the girl stabs the marquis and flees, hiding in a forest. Eventually, she's taken in by kindly Don Alfredo and his housekeeper, Teresa. When she dies in childbirth, the don raises her son as his own, naming him Leon.

Leon is born on Christmas Day—an unlucky impiety, according to superstitious Teresa. At the child's christening, the skies darken with peals of thunder and lightning, and the water in the baptismal font boils. Despite these uncomfortable hints, Leon grows into a sensitive, dutiful lad, unremarkable until the village watchman, Pepe, shoots a squirrel in his presence, and arouses a latent bloodlust within the child. Soon, *something* is killing goat kids and kittens. One night, Pepe shoots at a wolfish shape, and Leon wakes the next day with a musket ball in his leg. A wise village priest tells Don Alfredo that an elemental spirit—the spirit of a wolf—entered Leon at birth, and that the boy's human soul and animal spirit are at war with one another. Love, warmth, and understanding will strengthen his soul and keep the beast at bay. Don Alfredo agrees to show the boy all the love he can—and puts bars on his bedroom window, just in case.

Leon grows into a handsome young man without further incident. He leaves home to make his own way in the world, and gets a job bottling wine for a Don Fernando—and falls in love with his daughter, Christina. She returns his love, but she's betrothed to a wealthy, arrogant fop, and both lovers know her father would never allow them to marry. Leon allows himself to be taken to a brothel by a tipsy workmate,

DOOMED LOVE: *THE CURSE OF THE WEREWOLF'S* LEON WITH HIS CHRISTINA (CATHERINE FELLER).

and a prostitute's advances awaken his slumbering wolf nature. As a vicious wolfman, he kills three persons in a single night, including the harlot and his friend. The next day, Leon is horrified and remorseful, and tries to stay away from Christina, but she refuses to abandon him. Exhausted, he collapses and sleeps all night under Christina's care, without changing into his wolf-form. True love has restored his human nature once more. Leon is elated, believing he sees a way out of his curse; but his time has nearly run out. The police have discovered the murders and arrest him.

In jail, Leon begs for execution, to free his soul, while Don Alfredo and the village priest try to have him placed in the care of a monastery. The mayor, however, insists that Leon remain imprisoned until trial. That night, he becomes a werewolf once more, and bursts out of jail in a homicidal fury. He eludes the police, springing from rooftop to rooftop, and at last takes refuge in the bell tower of the village church. As the bells ring wildly, Don Alfredo gives his son the peace he seeks, with a silver bullet.

Every frame of *The Curse of the Werewolf* bears the stamp of classic Hammer horror. All the strengths of the studio's ensemble approach are present, including typically top-flight production design by Bernard Robinson and a first-rate werewolf makeup by Roy Ashton. *The Curse of the Werewolf* contains some of the finest acting seen in any Hammer film, most notably by a young Oliver Reed in his first starring role. Although the part is a bit sketchy, Reed uses it to take his character through a full and impressive range of emotions with real conviction. Seeing the film today reminds you once again of Reed's considerable talents, which have not always been evident during his often-disappointing roller coaster of a career. Also worth mentioning are Richard Wordsworth's brief turn as the hapless beggar, which generates a good deal of pathos, and Anthony Dawson's striking portrait of the vile marquis.

The Curse of the Werewolf was adapted, very loosely indeed, from Guy Endore's ponderous 1933 novel, *The Werewolf of Paris*. Only a few incidents from the novel remain intact, including the rape that conceived the unfortunate werewolf, his birth on Christmas Day, and the prostitute's murder. The action was transferred to Spain to take advantage of some Spanish-flavored sets prepared for a failed Michael Carreras production, *The Rape of Sabena*. (The cancellation of this project, by Carreras's own father, helped exacerbate a significant and lasting rift in Hammer's first family.)

The generally excellent script was Anthony Hinds's first, under his pen-name of John Elder—a pseudonym he adopted simply because he was already a line producer for Hammer, and didn't think it professional-looking for one name to keep popping up all over the credits. Hinds once told *Little Shoppe of Horrors* that he wrote the screenplay largely because, at the time, Hammer couldn't afford to pay anyone else to do it(!). Nonetheless, he went on to become one of Hammer's best and most prolific screenwriters for films like *Kiss of the Vampire* and *Frankenstein Created Woman*, and once said that *The Curse of the Werewolf* was the script of which he felt proudest.

Interestingly, *The Curse of the Werewolf* is one of the few Hammer films to be substantially altered due to censorship. Despite the nature of

A PARTICULARLY FINE BELGIAN THEATRICAL POSTER FOR HAMMER'S *CURSE OF FRANKENSTEIN* (1957).

THE REANIMATED CHRISTINA COMPLETES HER QUEST FOR VENGEANCE IN *FRANKENSTEIN CREATED WOMAN*.

A FRENCH POSTER FOR
HORROR OF DRACULA (1958).

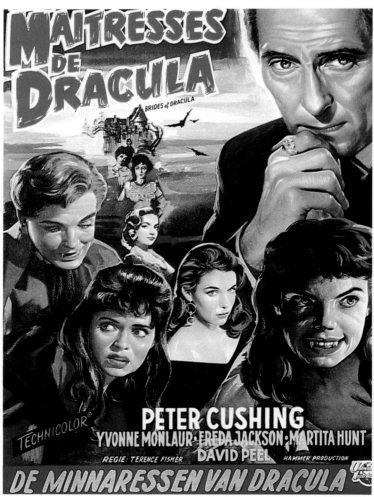

THE ORIGINAL BELGIAN POSTER
FOR *BRIDES OF DRACULA* (1960).

IN A CLASSIC SET-PIECE FROM STOKER, DRACULA OFFERS HIS OWN BLOOD TO DIANA IN
***DRACULA—PRINCE OF DARKNESS*.**

LEE'S DRACULA LOOKS RATHER PENSIVE AS HE SIPS FROM CAROLINE MUNRO
IN *DRACULA A.D. 1972*.

SEDUCTIVE
VAMPIRESS TANIA
(ISOBEL BLACK)
MAKES AMOROUS
ADVANCES IN *KISS OF
THE VAMPIRE*.

ANTHONY CORLAN BARES A FORMIDABLE MOUTHFUL OF FANGS
IN HAMMER'S *VAMPIRE CIRCUS*.

ARTIST JOE SMITH'S
EYE-CATCHING POSTER
FOR HAMMER'S *THE
MUMMY*.

A FINE BELGIAN POSTER FOR
HAMMER'S *THE CURSE OF
THE WEREWOLF*.

THE GLORIOUS
AMERICAN POSTER TO
*HOUSE ON HAUNTED
HILL*, TODAY A GRADE-A
COLLECTIBLE.

THE INNOCENTS, QUITE POSSIBLY THE FINEST SUPERNATURAL FILM OF ALL.

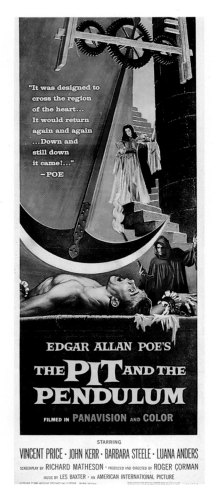

THE PIT AND THE PENDULUM, ONE OF THE MOST STYLISH OF ROGER CORMAN'S POE MOVIES.

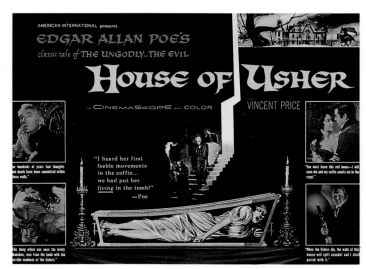

HOUSE OF USHER, THE MOVIE THAT LAUNCHED AIP'S LONG-RUNNING AND HIGHLY SUCCESSFUL POE SERIES.

AMERICAN INTERNATIONAL PRESENTS EDGAR ALLAN POE'S
THE PIT AND THE PENDULUM
IN PANAVISION AND COLOR

STARRING VINCENT PRICE · JOHN KERR · BARBARA STEELE · LUANA ANDERS · SCREENPLAY BY RICHARD MATHESON · PRODUCED AND DIRECTED BY ROGER CORMAN · MUSIC BY LES BAXTER

VINCENT PUTS THE SQUEEZE ON *THE PIT AND THE PENDULUM*'S LUSCIOUS-LOOKING BARBARA STEELE.

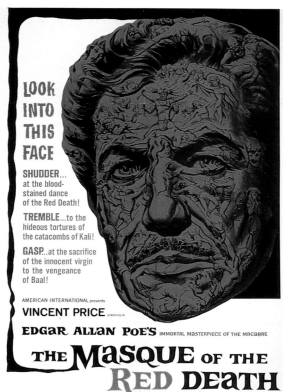

LOOK INTO THIS FACE

SHUDDER... at the blood-stained dance of the Red Death!

TREMBLE...to the hideous tortures of the catacombs of Kali!

GASP...at the sacrifice of the innocent virgin to the vengeance of Baal!

AMERICAN INTERNATIONAL presents
VINCENT PRICE STARRING IN
EDGAR ALLAN POE'S IMMORTAL MASTERPIECE OF THE MACABRE
THE MASQUE OF THE RED DEATH
in PATHÉCOLOR

Also Starring HAZEL COURT · JANE ASHER · Screenplay by CHARLES BEAUMONT and R. WRIGHT CAMPBELL · From a Story by EDGAR ALLAN POE · Produced and Directed by ROGER CORMAN

THE FACE OF EVIL: A FANCIFUL PORTRAIT OF VINCENT PRICE AS PROSPERO IN *THE MASQUE OF THE RED DEATH*.

"Evil things, in robes of sorrow, assailed the monarch's high estate." —POE

What was the terrifying thing in the PIT that wanted women?

AMERICAN INTERNATIONAL presents
EDGAR ALLAN POE'S
THE HAUNTED PALACE
in PATHECOLOR and PANAVISION

STARRING VINCENT PRICE · DEBRA PAGET · LON CHANEY
Produced and Directed by ROGER CORMAN · Screenplay by CHARLES BEAUMONT
Executive Producers JAMES H. NICHOLSON and SAMUEL Z. ARKOFF · AN AMERICAN INTERNATIONAL PICTURE

THE HAUNTED PALACE: A PASSABLE H. P. LOVECRAFT ADAPTATION SPUN INTO A "POE MOVIE" BY AIP.

ALBERT KALLIS'S
UNFORGETTABLE
POSTER FOR THE
RATHER MORE FORGET-
TABLE *THE UNDEAD*
(1957).

AN EXTRAORDINARY BELGIAN POSTER FOR THE ITALIAN
HORROR CLASSIC *BLACK SUNDAY*.

CURSE OF THE DEMON (1957),
A FINE AND LITERATE ADAPTA-
TION OF M. R. JAMES'S TALE
OF SUPERNATURAL REVENGE.

their material, Hammer proved adept at staying within the limits allowed by Britain's often-harsh censors (and it's worth remembering that most of the classic Universal horror films, which seem tapioca-bland today, were either drastically cut for English release or simply banned outright, often for years). Hinds's original plan for *Curse of the Werewolf* called for Richard Wordsworth's beggar character, Leon's real father, to be a werewolf himself, thus making Leon's affliction seem like a direct inheritance.

This plotline, however, fell afoul of a censor's mindless edict that sex and horror shouldn't be mixed—which was, of course, the key to the Hammer formula!—and the studio was told that either the rape or the werewolf angle must go. (Often, changes like these are made at the script approval stage, but Michael Carreras has indicated that the banned material was in fact filmed and cast aside.) In any case, this deletion doesn't harm the picture, and in fact probably improves it. To me, at least, the idea that Leon is the innocent victim of an inscrutable working of Fate, of more general "sins of the fathers," has a much greater resonance than the notion that he simply has some genetic predisposition to werewolvery.

There's one howling goof in Hinds's script that I point out for your amusement; it really doesn't affect the film a bit. Even so, it is strange that the opening narration should be delivered by Don Alfredo, who states that these events occurred "some two hundred years ago," and then proceeds to inject *himself* into the story! We can only assume that the don is recounting these events at the end of a very long retirement. (I suspect this gives us a small insight into just how quickly the script was thrown together.)

Nevertheless, the screenplay is mostly a fine piece of work, and one machine-tooled for Terence Fisher's talents. All the situations and character types Fisher loved so well are here— the aristocratic past, seen through a fine patina of

nostalgia; the rythms of village life, of church and roisterous taverns; a nasty, debased noble, the real villain of the piece; the "good" aristocrat, embodied by Don Alfredo; a foreground story of doomed romance, with an attractive and tragic pair of lovers. As usual in Hammer horror, there's also a unifying tension between objectified good and evil, here personified by and battling within one man. Hinds's story has a neatly circular construction, opening and closing with the pealing of church bells, and contains some rather perverse commentary on Christianity in the form of Leon's nativity.

Naturally, this framework has lent itself to critical noodling; one writer has a list of no less than eleven symbolic "antonyms" to be found in the story. But I prefer to remember *The Curse of the Werewolf* as just what it appears to be: a moving, involving horror tale, built on well-realized characters that earn our interest and our sympathy.

THE GORGON
Hammer, 1964 (U.S. release 1965)
P: Anthony Nelson-Keys
D: Terence Fisher
S: John Gilling; shooting script revised by Anthony Hinds
Starring Peter Cushing (*Dr. Namaroff*), Christopher Lee (*Professor Meister*), Barbara Shelley (*Carla Hoffman*), Richard Pasco (*Paul Heitz*), Michael Goodliffe (*Professor Heitz*), Patrick Troughton (*Inspector Kanof*), Jack Watson (*Ratoff*), Jeremy Longhurst (*Bruno Heitz*), Toni Gilpin (*Sacha Cass*), and Prudence Hyman (*the Gorgon*).

Nightwalkers rating:
💀💀💀

PRUDENCE HYMAN AS THE FAIRLY SILLY-LOOKING TITLE CHARACTER FROM TERENCE FISHER'S *THE GORGON*.

The Gorgon, an atmospheric, melancholy little film, reunited the three main talents behind the initial wave of Hammer horror film—actors Peter Cushing and Christopher Lee, and director Terence Fisher—for the first time since 1959's *The Mummy*.

In 1910, in the Ruritanian-style central European statelet of Vandorf, a beautiful artist's model, Sacha Cass, is killed in an encounter with a mysterious being. She's *literally* petrified, the seventh victim found turned to stone in five years. Her lover, artist Bruno Heitz, is found hanged, so the local police conspire with local medical man, Dr. Namaroff, to pin him with the crime. Namaroff, cold and sinister, clearly has a secret. Bruno's father, Professor Heitz, arrives to investigate, and discovers a conspiracy of fear and silence. One night, Heitz follows a mysterious trilling out of his home and up to Castle Borski, a haunted ruin on the outskirts of town. There he confronts the same shadowy creature that killed Sacha. Terrified, he stumbles back to his quarters, already in mid-petrification, and scrawls a note before he dies.

Bruno's brother, Paul, arrives in town to discover his father already dead, his body in the hands of the police. Reading the professor's note, he learns of his suspicion: that the real killer is Megaera, one of the gorgons of classical mythology, whose glance can turn their victims to stone. According to legend, Megaera had dwelled in the Vandorf area, and Heitz believed her spirit had entered some local person. Shortly after Paul's arrival, Dr. Namaroff sends his assistant, Carla Hoffman, to spy on him. However, Namaroff hadn't counted on what happens next: that Paul and the delicately beautiful Carla become attracted to one another. (Namaroff loves Carla, in his reptilian way.) One evening, Paul encounters the gorgon but he's saved by seeing its image reflected in a pool, rather than eye to eye. Even so, he's thrown into a coma for days, and awakens ashen and prematurely aged. Carla nurtures Paul back to health, and love blooms.

Next to arrive in Vandorf is Professor Meister, Paul's teacher and a friend of his father's. Meister is a forceful man who'd become concerned about Paul's absence. With the story laid before him, he throws himself into investigating the strange deaths. Meister learns that Carla arrived in the area an amnesiac, and still suffers from memory lapses with each full moon. The professor deduces that Carla is unknowingly possessed by Megaera, and that Namaroff is hiding her secret. Paul is too much in love to understand, but Carla begins to suspect the truth. She begs Paul to take her away, but he refuses to leave until his father's killer is found. Finally, in a moonlit confrontation at the castle, the protagonists meet for a final time. Paul comes to meet Carla, but Namaroff, heartbroken, is there to slay Megaera. Paul and Namaroff fight; Paul is knocked out, but Namaroff is gorgonized before he can strike. Paul also succumbs to the gorgon's gaze as Meister beheads her; and, dying, watches as Carla's features replace the gorgon's.

The screenplay by John Gilling, a talented Hammer writer and director, emphasizes the doomed love between Carla and Paul at the expense of the monster tale, a choice that was particularly congenial to Fisher's gentle romanticism. The screenplay was heavily rewritten by Anthony Hinds, and Gilling, never shy in interviews, once called the resulting film "abysmal," stating that Hinds's interference "murdered what might have been a very good movie." While this judgment seems too harsh, the script as filmed does feel like a patchwork. To cite just one example, we never learn who hanged Bruno or why. What's more important, the love story really isn't developed fully enough, although fine acting by Barbara Shelley and former Royal Shakespearean Richard Pasco goes a long way toward filling in the gaps. In particular, Pasco's measured, careful performance and magnificently resonant voice make him fitting company for Cushing and Lee.

Shelley wanted to play the gorgon herself, but the producer felt that the necessary makeup changes would add too much time to the film's shooting schedule, so the monster role went to another actress, Prudence Hyman. (Shelley, who would appear to be an excellent sport, even offered to play the part with real grass snakes in her hair.) Unfortunately, the gorgon makeup is a bland and clumsy rendition of the traditional character of myth, which is to say a woman in a nightgown with several large rubber snakes in her hair—not exactly a blood-curdling sight. (Special-effects master Ray Harryhausen created a considerably more effective gorgon in the 1981 film *Clash of the Titans*.)

As for the stars, there's an odd and refreshing role reversal; for a change, Cushing gets the sketchy, unrewarding role, although he ably conveys Namaroff's cold-fish nature. Lee is always more interesting when playing against type, and here he's clearly having a good time as the hero, blustering and using his physically imposing quality to memorable effect. Also worth noting is James Bernard's haunting score, which is unusually fine, subtler and more finely textured than most of his work for Hammer.

The Gorgon was a personal favorite of Terence Fisher's, and something of a comeback film; he hadn't made a movie for Hammer since the critical and box-office failure of *The Phantom of the Opera* two years before. Despite its effects problems and a lack of overt horror thrills, *The Gorgon* deserves credit as an ambitious attempt to create a new and different monster for the screen. In its best moments, *The Gorgon* weaves a rather sweet spell of wistfulness and regret that makes it one of Fisher's most noteworthy efforts.

FRED CLARK AS AN ENDEARING BUT SHORT-LIVED BARNUM TYPE, IN HAMMER'S SECOND MUMMY-FEST.

THE CURSE OF THE MUMMY'S TOMB

Hammer, 1964

P, D: Michael Carreras
S: Michael Carreras, writing as "Henry Younger"
Starring Terence Morgan (*Adam Beauchamp*), Fred Clark (*Alexander King*), Ronald Howard (*John Bray*), Jeanne Roland (*Annette Dubois*), George Pastell (*Hashmi Bey*), Jack Gwillim (*Sir Giles Dalrymple*), John Paul (*Inspector Mackenzie*), and Dickie Owen (*the Mummy*).

Nightwalkers rating:

Of all the traditional horror film menaces, mummies seem the most subject to the law of diminishing returns. Universal's too-long series provides one case in point, and here's another. Hammer's second foray into the mummy subgenre, *The Curse of the Mummy's Tomb*, is inferior in every way to the 1959 *Mummy*, although some decent performances and an occasional flash of imagination keep it from being a complete loss.

In 1900, an expedition to Egypt headed by Sir Giles Dalrymple (author's note: tee-hee) and bankrolled by a cartoonish American showman, Alexander King, has discovered the fabulous tomb of Ra Antef, son of a great pharoah. Also along on the expedition are the requisite beautiful woman, Annette Dubois, her colorless fiancé, John Bray, and an Egyptian scholar, Hashmi Bey. Dalrymple and Hashmi Bey want to give the find to the Egyptian government, but King has no intention of letting his loot go to "some stuffy museum in a one-camel town." Instead, he intends to turn the mummy into a spectacle that will educate the public "at ten cents a time." On the boat back to England, Annette meets a mystery man, Adam Beauchamp, who begins courting her while John seethes in the background. In a lengthy flashback, Annette tells Adam Ra Antef's legend. Ra, a saintly sort, was driven into exile by his unsavory brother Bi. Before being slain by his brother's agents, Ra was befriended by a nomadic people who gave him the Medallion of Life, which can revive the dead. Anne has inherited the medallion from her father, an archaeologist slain by bandits, but she doesn't know what it is. John borrows the piece to study it, but loses it to an unseen attacker.

In London, King busily prepares his spectacle, despite the warnings of Hashmi Bey, but the mummy turns up missing at the premiere. At this point, King may as well be wearing a large sign stating "WILL BE KILLED BY MUMMY." Soon, both King and Sir Giles are fatally manhandled by the reanimated Ra Antef. The mummy next attacks Adam, but is distracted by Annette. Adam addresses Ra Antef in ancient Egyptian as it leaves, telling the dimmest viewer that there's something different about this fellow. The mummy then visits John, who tries to trap the creature with the aid of Hashmi Bey and the police. Hashmi has a sudden crisis of conscience over his involvement in Ra Antef's disinterral, and begs to be "destroyed painfully"(!). Ra obliges, grinding the Egyptian's skull under his heel as if it were a cigar butt, while the police look on with an odd indifference.

Annette decides to elope with Adam, but is surprised to learn that he's somewhat older than she thought; about 3,700 years older, to be exact. For Adam is actually Bi, the mummy's own brother, cursed by their father to live forever unless he is slain by Ra's own hand. (He has an Egyptian temple installed in his basement.) It was Adam, of course, who stole the Medallion of Life, and who has the mummy. Adam/Bi has tired of his eternal existence, and his brother's discovery has shown him the way out. Now, having arranged the deaths of the despoilers of Ra's tomb—apparently rules are rules, Egyptian curse-wise—Adam wants his brother to slay both himself and Annette, so they can be together in the afterlife. John and the police crash in, having trailed the mummy to Adam's home. In the ensuing alarums and excursions, Annette escapes and Adam dies with his brother in the passages beneath his house.

As the credits indicate, *The Curse of the Mummy's Tomb* was *auteured* into existence almost single-handedly by Michael Carreras. At this time, Carreras had no formal connection with Hammer, which was being run by his father, but produced films for the company on an independent basis. The film, which was the lower half of a British double bill with Terence Fisher's infinitely superior *The Gorgon*, rarely rises above potboiler status. It's badly paced and often plodding, and the mummy makes a surprisingly late appearance, considering he's allegedly our center of interest.

The technical aspects also are iffy. Bernard Robinson's set designs are impeccable, as always, filled with the same sort of realistic Egyptian bric-a-brac he used to such good effect in *The Mummy* (and, given Hammer's perennial thriftiness, I assume much of it is recycled from the earlier film). On the other hand, the movie is indifferently and sometimes murkily filmed, not in Cinemascope, as many sources would have it, but in Techniscope, a cheaper process that produced a wide-screen image by cutting the conventional 35mm frame lengthwise into two, with a consequent loss in picture sharpness.

The performances are reasonably good, considering what the actors had to work with. Best of show goes to veteran American character actor Fred Clark—believe me, even if the name means nothing to you, you've seen this guy all your life—as the Barnumesque Alexander King. Clark usually played irascible blowhards of one stripe or another, but here he injects a twinkle into the role that makes him rather likeable. Terence Morgan's Adam Beauchamp is another standout, smoothly charming and charismatic in the best Fisher-villain style.

The most interesting thing about *The Curse of the Mummy's Tomb*, however, is Michael Carreras's script (the "Henry Younger" pen name was an in-joke on fellow-Hammerite Anthony Hinds's usual "John Elder" pseudonym). It's hardly a cinema milestone–it's overly talky and drags in places—but the screenplay does contain some mythic overtones that give it a certain interest. The Adam/Bi angle is an intriguing swipe from the legend of the Wandering Jew, doomed to live forever; the Medallion of Life seems like a borrowing from the legend of the Golem, who was animated by a magic amulet.

These moments, however, can't supress our impatience during the bandage-clad villain's inevitable shuffle-through. Ra Antef, as played by longtime Hammer stuntman Dickie Owen, isn't given the slightest chance to display any meaningful personality or emotion. There's not a flicker of the pathos that Karloff and Lee brought to their respective interpretations. The mummy here is reduced to the same status he held in the later Universal pictures—a slow-moving, mindless menace. And a rather dull one.

THE PLAGUE OF THE ZOMBIES
Hammer, 1966
P: Anthony Nelson-Keys
D: John Gilling
S: Peter Bryan; contributions by John Gilling
Starring Andre Morell (*Sir James Forbes*), Diana Clare (*Sylvia Forbes*), Brook Williams (*Dr. Peter Thompson*), Jacqueline Pearce (*Alice Thompson*), John Carson (*Clive Hamilton*), Alex Davion (*Denver*), and Michael Ripper (*Sgt. Swift*).

Nightwalkers Rating:

Movies about traditional zombies—that is, the voodoo-created versions, as opposed to the flesh-eating corpses of George Romero and his imitators—have always been rare. *Good* ones are even rarer; happily, Hammer's one stab in this direction turned out to be one of their better efforts. I feel fairly safe in saying it's also the only movie about Haitian magic to be set in Cornwall.

This unlikely but grim tale opens with a voodoo ceremony, complete with Haitian

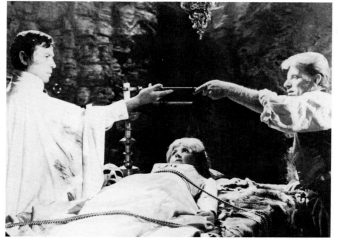

SINISTER RITUALS SOLVE A CORNISH LABOR SHORTAGE IN *THE PLAGUE OF THE ZOMBIES.*

drummers in cartoonish bone-through-nose regalia, and led by a masked, imposing white man of aristocratic bearing. Intercut scenes show that their efforts disturb the asleep of Alice Tompson, wife of Dr. Peter Tompson, physician to a small Cornish village whose inhabitants are succumbing, one by one, to a mysterious malady. Tompson's inability to cure or even diagnose their illness has driven him to the brink of despair. In desperation, Alice has written to her friend Sylvia Forbes, daughter of Sir James Forbes, Peter's professor and mentor. Sir James and Sylvia journey to Cornwall, to see if they can help.

Alice hides the effects of the magical assault she's undergoing from the others. She's evasive and coquettish in a way reminiscent of Dracula's victims. Soon she wanders off in a trance. Sylvia follows, but is kidnapped and threatened with thinly veiled rape by the hired goons of the local squire, Clive Hamilton. Hamilton appears, however, and after scattering his rabble, smoothly apologizes to Sylvia. Despite herself, she's intrigued by the squire, who is, ahem, an imposing man of aristocratic bearing (the film's mysteries aren't terribly hard to puzzle out). Meanwhile, Sir James and Peter decide to autopsy the victims of the plague, only to find their coffins *empty*. As Sylvia returns from Hamilton's house, a horrible, corpselike creature throws Alice's body at her feet.

Sir James continues his investigations, learning that Hamilton's wealth is another mystery, as the family's dangerous tin mines appar-

ently have lain empty since the local villagers refused to work in them. We also learn that Hamilton had spent some years in Haiti. (Remember what I said about this movie's mysteries.) Hamilton calls on Sylvia to express his condolences over Alice's death. Through an elaborate ruse, he manages to prick Sylvia's finger and secrete some of her blood in a small vial. That evening, Sir James and Peter, still seeking a candidate for autopsy, open poor Alice's coffin just in time to see her revive as a zombie. Sir James beheads the lifeless girl with a shovel as she staggers out of her grave.

At this point, an understandably horrified Peter passes out. An ensuing dream sequence is easily the most famous moment in *The Plague of the Zombies.* In an eerie scene lit in sickly greens, Peter finds himself in the cemetery and watches helplessly as the dead erupt from the earth around him, slowly writhing free of the soil, and surround him. Film writers who discuss the film seem required by law to praise this scene, which has a nightmarish quality unlike anything else in the Hammer corpus, and is marred only by some unconvincing zombie makeup. (It's difficult to believe that George Romero hadn't seen this scene prior to making *Night of the Living Dead*.)

Hamilton uses Sylvia's blood in a voodoo ritual, and she begins to fall under his spell, her wound bleeding in response just as Alice's had. Sir James, however, has by now pieced together the mystery, rather later than us; Hamilton is using Haitian black magic to recruit undead workers for his mines. The knight breaks into Hamilton's house and discovers voodoo dolls that control the zombies. When he casts them on a fire, the zombies in mines below the house begin to smoulder. Sir James plucks his daughter from an altar as the place erupts into flames.

The Plague of the Zombies was shot back to back on the same sets with *The Reptile*, another above-average Hammer horror also set in Cornwall (Hammer's production designer Bernard Robinson deserves special credit for brilliantly disguising this fact, by the way). Together, the two films (which some fans call the Cornwall Classics) represent the best-known and most respected work of director John Gilling, an occasionally interesting journeyman who began as a screenwriter and also directed extensively in British television.

THE WALKING DEAD CLAIM ANOTHER VICTIM (JACQUELINE PEARCE).

While the film's script falls pretty flat in some respects—it's built around "mysteries" that are crystal clear to any half-awake viewer—it's lively nonetheless, and deserves points for originality in the way it incorporates an unusual menace into Hammer's traditional period British settings. The script is also interesting for its vaguely leftish political undercurrents; the squire's decision to zombify the reluctant locals to keep his mines going certainly takes labor exploitation to its logical extreme. The original screenplay was written by Peter Bryan, a camera operator turned screenwriter who also wrote Hammer's *Hound of the Baskervilles*. No respecter of the Hammer legend, Gilling once stated that the scripts for both Cornwall films, "as usual, were very bad," and that he rewrote both extensively as he shot.

Of the players, Andre Morell is easily the most memorable, playing Sir James as a dash-it-all colonel type who is somehow both insufferable and endearing. It's a ripe and winning performance that teeters close to parody without falling over the edge, in an interestingly offbeat reinterpretation of Hammer's standard Champion of Good. John Carson as Hamilton is competently suave in his more conventional villain role. Diana Clare's Sylvia, however, is pretty and pretty wooden, although not distractingly so.

David Pirie has called *The Plague of the Zombies* one of Hammer's "most deeply pessimistic films," citing, for instance, Alice's disturbing and undeserved death (or, rather, deaths). It really doesn't play that way, though. While it's rather dull in spots, and a bit clumsy in its construction, *The Plague of the Zombies* is a refreshingly different horror film, and one of the most entertaining of its era.

THE REPTILE
Hammer, 1966
P: Anthony Nelson-Keys
D: John Gilling
S: Anthony Hinds, writing as "John Elder"
Starring Noel Willman (*Dr. Franklyn*), Jennifer Daniel (*Valerie Spalding*), Ray Barrett (*Harry Spalding*), Jacqueline Pearce (*Anna Franklyn*), Michael Ripper (*Tom Bailey*), John Laurie (*Mad Peter*), Charles Lloyd-Pack (*the Vicar*), Marne Maitland (*Malay servant*), David Baron, (*Charles Spalding*), and George Woodbridge (*Old Garnsey*).

Nightwalkers rating: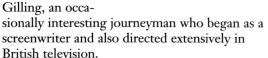

The second of John Gilling's Cornwall Classics dovetails nicely with *The Plague of the Zombies*, and not just because they were shot on the same sets. The two films share common themes, dense plotting, and a rather grim mood. However, *The Reptile* is interesting in its own right, with an offbeat and visually appealing *femme fatale* at its center.

In turn-of-the-century Cornwall, the superstitious villagers of Clagmore Heath are succumbing to a strange malady that began after a wealthy stranger moved into a nearby mansion (the comparison with *The Plague of the Zombies* is obvious). We learn right away that this Black Death is no disease, when Charles Spalding is attacked by a mysterious figure. His throat bitten, he foams at the mouth and turns a deep green(!) as he dies; village officials call it heart failure. Charles's brother and sister-in-law, Harry and Valerie Spalding, arrive in the village to claim the estate, and find the locals stand-off-ish: "They don't like strangers in these parts," explains the gruff innkeeper, Tom Bailey. While set-

ROY ASHTON'S BIZARRE SNAKE-GIRL MAKEUP, A HIGH-
LIGHT OF DIRECTOR JOHN GILLING'S *THE REPTILE.*

tling into Charles's cottage, the Spaldings meet the owner of the above-mentioned mansion, aloof and sad-seeming Dr. Franklyn, and a harmless lunatic called Mad Peter. Peter rambles unhelpfully about a "they" behind the village's troubles, and says that Charles was murdered; he returns shortly to die at their feet, his face dark green.

Valerie meets Franklyn's daughter, Anna, a young woman who leads an oddly restricted life under the watchful eyes of her father and a creepy Malay servant. At a dinner gathering reluctantly hosted by the reclusive Dr. Franklyn, the Spaldings learn that the doctor and his daughter traveled for years in Asia, studying "the primitive religions of the East." Anna breaks up the party by playing the sitar in an increasingly frantic and entranced fashion. Later, the servant offers her a kitten in a way that implies she's not just gonna *pet* it. People who haven't yet figured out that Anna is our monster should apply for admission to a Home for the Unobservant.

Harry teams up with Tom Bailey—both are former military men who've traveled widely in the East—and the two exhume Peter and Charles, finding that both bear the fang marks of a king cobra. Anna sends Harry a note asking for help. He sneaks into the mansion, but is attacked and bitten by a bizarre snake-woman. Valerie barely saves him with hasty first aid, then goes to the Franklyn mansion herself, still trying to help Anna. Meanwhile, Dr. Franklyn decides to kill his serpentine daughter, but finds only her *shed skin* (!!) in her four-poster. The snake girl is resting near a sulphurous hot spring which, for

some reason, lies in a cellar beneath the mansion (not, to the best of my knowledge, a common design feature in Cornish housing). The Malay attempts to protect her, but Franklyn tosses him into the sulphur pit.

Valerie arrives, and Franklyn tells all: While travelling in Borneo, he'd pried into the secrets of the Ourang Sancto, a cult of Snake People, who took revenge by changing his daughter into a were-reptile. In this condition, Anna stalks victims in the village, and sheds her skin each year (I *love* that touch), but remembers nothing when she reverts to human form. (As near as I can tell. The Malay, by the way, seems to have been a member of the Ourang Sancto, but this isn't clarified.) Meanwhile, the Anna-reptile revives and slays her father. Harry shows up to save Valerie, as the whole house goes up in flames (again, an ending quite reminiscent of *Plague of the Zombies*).

The Reptile originated as a story idea developed by scriptwriter Anthony Hinds. The plot is a bit too intricate and occasionally confusing, with several dangling loose ends. Like its sister film, it's structured as a mystery, although there's really no one else in the picture who could be the snake-thing *except* Anna. On the other hand, in Gilling's hands, *The Reptile* sustains its brooding atmosphere quite well. There's a satisfyingly tragic inevitability to Franklyn's death at the hands of the daughter he had inadvertently but grievously wronged. The performances are highlighted by Noel Willman's Dr. Franklyn, who effectively sketches the man's shame and sadness; and by Jacqueline Pearce as Anna, whose brief appearances in human form are impressively and seductively sensual. (Watch her writhe to the Malay's "snake-charming" keening.)

Ultimately, though, *The Reptile* is probably best remembered for its bizarre and original menace. If you've never seen the film, I realize you might find the idea of a snake-woman inherently risible, like an Armadillo Girl. However, this unlikely creature turns out to be one of Roy Ashton's finest makeups ever for Hammer; if her slit-eyed, reptilian countenance isn't entirely convincing, it's still disturbing. *The Reptile* was Roy Ashton's final picture for Hammer, ending an association that spanned some forty films. His work was always limited by tight budgets and shooting schedules, and the end results were decidedly uneven (see his atrocious monster for *Evil of Frankenstein*). But at his best, as seen here, Ashton the monster-maker could create ghoulish miracles.

THE MUMMIFIED GUARDIAN PREM STANDS BY HIS BOY KING KAR-TO-BEY, IN THE UNINSPIRED *THE MUMMY'S SHROUD*.

THE MUMMY'S SHROUD
Hammer, 1967
P: Anthony Nelson-Keys
D: John Gilling
S: John Gilling, from a story by "John Elder" (*Anthony Hinds*)
Starring John Phillips (*Stanley Preston*), Andre Morell (*Sir Basil Walden*), David Buck (*Paul Preston*), Elizabeth Sellars (*Barbara Preston*), Maggie Kimberley (*Claire*), Michael Ripper (*Longbarrow*), Tim Barrett (*Harry Newton*), Roger Delgado (*Hasmid Ali*), Catherine Lacey (*Haiti*), Eddie Powell (*Prem the mummy*), Dickie Owen (*Prem in flashback*), and Richard Warner (*Inspector Barrani*).

Nightwalkers rating: 💀½

This very, very tired film, which filled out the bottom of a double bill with the distinctly better *Frankenstein Created Woman*, was the last Hammer movie ever made at their old home at Bray studios. It is, alas, more of a whimper than a bang.

The late John Gilling once told *Little Shoppe of Horrors* that he accepted the *Mummy's Shroud* assignment—his last for Hammer—in part to escape the tedium of television work. Unfortunately, much of that tedium seems to have accompanied him onto the sets of this film, which has little on its mind other than recycling the plots of the first two Hammer mummy films (this time sticking a bit closer to the "Curse of King Tut" myth that inspired them all). Against this dearth of ideas, the film offers one or two imaginative touches, but it's a far cry from the Cornwall Classics that made Gilling's reputation among horror fans.

The Mummy's Shroud opens (inevitably, it seems) with a flashback to Egypt circa 2000 B.C. Through accompanying (uncredited) narration by Peter Cushing, we learn of Prem, faithful protector of Kar-to-Bey, a pharoah's son, who guards his charge after their expulsion from the kingdom following a palace coup. When the boy dies, Prem buries his body secretly in the desert. A few millennia later, in 1920, an expedition stumbles on Kar-to-Bey's tomb. The expedition is led by distinguished scientist Sir Basil Walden, and backed by yet another venal businessman, this time a pompous coward named Stanley Preston. Also familiar is the dire "death to all infidels" warning delivered by the tomb's Bedouin guardian, Hasmid Ali.

Kar-to-Bey's badly desiccated corpse is taken back to a Cairo museum, where—wouldn't you just know it—it is stored directly adjacent to the mummy of Prem, the boy's old guardian. Sir Basil's female assistant, Claire (our sex appeal for this outing, a prodigiously eyebrowed blonde whose looks are exotic verging on bizarre), has disquieting premonitions of impending doom. Preston, a nasty blowhard, grabs credit for Sir Basil's discovery. When the scientist falls ill following a snakebite, Preston bribes the authorities to have Sir Basil put away in an asylum, where he can't contradict the millionaire's self-aggrandizing account of the expedition.

Meanwhile, Hasmid has seized Kar-to-Bey's burial shroud, which bears "the words of life and death" that will resurrect the dead. Hasmid uses the cloth to bring Prem back and (do you really need this filled in?) expedition members start turning up dead—fifty minutes into this rather slow-moving picture. Sir Basil is the first to go, and as he's the only major character capable of generating any interest or sympathy, it's rather disappointing to see him exit the picture so early. Predictably, sniveling Preston gets his as well, as do some lesser lights. Finally, Claire somehow stops Prem cold with a second reading of mystic words of the shroud and, in the movie's one really memorable scene, the mummy literally *tears itself to bits*, pulling apart its own head and torso until nothing remains except its hands and a pile of dust. (This *is* nicely done.)

That's about it. The direction and cinematography are pretty dull. Moreover, although Bernard Robinson is credited with production design on *The Mummy's Shroud*, the movie is almost devoid of the richly ornamented *faux*-Egyptian touches he devised for the first two Hammer mummy films; *this* ancient Egypt is rather cheap and tatty-looking. The mummy is built like a linebacker—not precisely corpselike.

Andre Morell is typically competent in his too-brief role as Sir Basil; Elizabeth Sellars, as Preston's long-suffering wife, shows talent and conviction in a barely sketched-in part. What little affection attaches to this film is almost entirely due to the fact that it provided much-loved Hammer character actor Michael Ripper with one of his most substantial roles, as Preston's meek publicity agent. Ripper appeared in more than twenty Hammer films in all, usually for no more than a few moments in each, and nearly always managed to create distinctive and enjoyable characterizations. His role in *The Mummy's Shroud* is a typically polished turn.

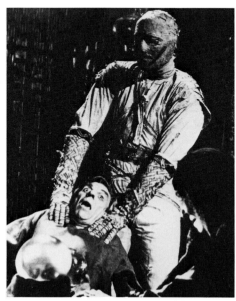

PREM MAKES SHORT WORK OF ANOTHER MISCELLANEOUS VICTIM IN *THE MUMMY'S SHROUD*.

Other than the performances, though, nothing really seems to rise above this movie's flat plain. It's not good and it's not really all that bad. It just sort of lies there.

BLOOD FROM THE MUMMY'S TOMB

Hammer, 1971
P: Howard Brandy
D: Seth Holt; substantial contributions by Michael Carreras
S: Christopher Wicking
Starring Andrew Keir (*Professor Julian Fuchs*), Valerie Leon (*Margaret Fuchs* and *Tera*), James Villiers (*Corbeck*), Hugh Burden (*Dandridge*), George Coulouris (*Berigan*), Mark Edwards (*Tod Browning*), Rosalie Crutchley (*Helen Dickerson*), and Aubrey Morris (*Dr. Putnam*).

Nightwalkers rating: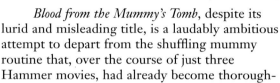

Blood from the Mummy's Tomb, despite its lurid and misleading title, is a laudably ambitious attempt to depart from the shuffling mummy routine that, over the course of just three Hammer movies, had already become thoroughly stale. Unfortunately, the movie is murkily plotted and confusing. At times, it engenders that maddening feeling one gets when watching a poorly dubbed foreign film; *something's* going on, all right, but it's sometimes difficult to tell just what. Oh, and strictly speaking, the film contains no mummies at all.

Blood from the Mummy's Tomb is based on Bram Stoker's late novel, *The Jewel of Seven Stars*, which concerns the possession of an archaeologist's daughter by the spirit of an ancient Egyptian witch-queen. The film opens with the standard dream-flashback to ancient Egypt, in which we see the living entombment of wicked (or, at any rate, unpopular) Queen Tera. As a part of the ritual, the priests sever one of her hands and throw it to a pack of wild dogs, who refuse it. The hand then crawls back into the tomb under its own power. Meanwhile, the priests departing Tera's tomb are all struck down by a sorcerous wind that somehow contrives to slit all their throats(!).

This puzzling flashback and others come to us courtesy of the dreams of Margaret Fuchs, an incredibly shapely brunette who's a dead ringer for Tera. Her father, the attentive viewer will eventually puzzle out, led an expedition some years before that discovered Tera's tomb, and brought her fresh-as-spring, uncorrupted body back to England. (The hand is stored separately.) The ensuing years have not been kind to the expedition's members; one is a scared mouse, while another resides in an asylum. Professor Fuchs, who keeps Tera in a fully equipped Egyptian temple in his basement, is none too well. All are haunted by a dark, ill-defined secret concerning Margaret's birth, which took place at the exact moment that the expedition entered the tomb. Margaret's mother died in labor, and the infant Margaret died temporarily, only to come back to life an instant later; in some way, Tera's spirit seems to have entered her.

Yet another expedition member, Corbeck, arrives on the scene. Corbeck is Evil, and Fuchs's deadly enemy. He says things like "The meek shan't inherit the earth; they wouldn't know what to do with it." Corbeck wants Tera to be reborn through Margaret (why?). Margaret's twenty-first birthday is approaching (so?), and Professor Fuchs presents her with Tera's ring, a walnut-sized red stone bearing the symbol of a constellation of seven stars. (We later learn that the constellation is rendered as it appears in the present, *not* in Tera's era; hence the ring announces the time of Tera' rebirth.) The ring is apparently intended to protect Margaret, but her

A REBORN QUEEN TERA FACES STIFF OPPOSITION IN *BLOOD FROM A MUMMY'S TOMB*.

possession by Tera begins only *after* she wears the ring, so what gives?

At any rate, Tera begins to manifest through Margaret more and more. With Corbeck, the possessed girl goes off to reclaim certain of Tera's artifacts from the other expedition members, because they are needed to complete Tera's physical resurrection (why?). These unfortunates are killed, each in turn, by that mysterious throat-cutting wind, as is Margaret's insipid boyfriend (a richly satisfying moment; I'd been waiting a long time to see one of Hammer's useless "love interests" get bumped off). Finally, the ceremony of Tera' rebirth begins. At the last minute, Margaret and her father regain their wills (how?) and manage to stab both Corbeck and the newly reborn Tera. Then, the roof falls in, literally (why?). Everyone is obliterated by falling masonry except Margaret, who awakens in a hospital swathed in bandages from head to foot, looking just like a mummy—which must have struck someone as irony. Or something.

The reason for the film's baffling scenario doubtless has something to do with the untimely death of its director, Seth Holt, three weeks into production. Holt was a talented if erratic filmmaker who began his career as a film cutter at Britain's legendary Ealing Studios. He edited classics including *The Lavender Hill Mob* and Olivier's *The Entertainer*. As a director, Holt made two of Hammer's most highly regarded Hitchcockian thrillers, *Scream of Fear* and *The Nanny*. Holt's death forced Michael Carreras, who had just returned to Hammer as its managing director, to step in and salvage the project. Carreras thought Christopher Wicking's script "very confusing"—something I have no trouble believing, given his other work (see *To the Devil—A Daughter*)—and, to make matters worse, Holt's completed footage was in a chaotic state. Many master sequences lacked intros and exits for the characters, and so forth. Carreras finished filming the script, completed pick-up shots for about three dozen scenes Holt had left incomplete, and patched the thing together in the editing room as best he could.

Blood from the Mummy's Tomb does have its admirers; if it's a mess, it's a stylish mess. Holt's preference for mood over visceral shocks is evident throughout the picture, and many sequences are deftly arranged. After one of those windy magical attacks, there's a neat swipe from Val Lewton's *Cat People*—the shadow of an Egyptian dog or jackal is seen slinking along a wall, suggesting without insisting that these attacks are carried out by some vengeful Egyptian spirit in animal form.

The performances are generally competent, but no better. Valerie Leon is yet another of the later Hammer's seemingly interchangeable glandular cases, apparently chosen for what Joe Bob Briggs would call "her tremendous talents." Andrew Keir, who was excellent in Hammer's science fiction classic *Five Million Years to Earth*, seems flat and uninspired as Professor Fuchs. (Peter Cushing was originally slated for the role, and had begun filming, but dropped out after his wife's death.)

In release, *Blood from the Mummy's Tomb* proved to be a commercial failure, probably as much as anything because it failed to deliver up the bandaged menace promised by its garish title. After this film, Hammer pulled the plug on the mummy series. It was probably the right decision. A final note: in 1980, *The Jewel of Seven Stars* was remade as an *Omen*-style A-picture called *The Awakening*, with Charlton Heston, of all people, and Susannah York. Against all odds, this ponderous and mean-spirited movie was considerably worse than Hammer's failed attempt.

❖ 6 ❖

THOSE WHO RETURN:

Ghost Stories

**YOU WANT TO KNOW / WHETHER I BELIEVE IN GHOSTS /
OF COURSE I DO NOT BELIEVE IN THEM / IF YOU HAD KNOWN /
AS MANY OF THEM AS I HAVE / YOU WOULD NOT /
BELIEVE IN THEM EITHER**

—DON MARQUIS, *ARCHY AND MEHITABEL*

ersonal experience suggests to me that a good third to a half of the population have their own ghost stories. I may have one myself, despite my being about as psychic as a Chia Pet. Several years ago, my wife and I were staying at the George and Pilgrims, an inn in Glastonbury in England's West Country that has operated without interruption since 1475. Despite its age, the inn is, you might say, only casually haunted. The hotel accountant told us that at one point during a low season she stayed a month in one of the George's reputedly haunted rooms, and each morning someone not of the visible persuasion

gently shook her awake. "I never had to set the alarm once," said this practical woman, who took the experience quite in stride.

We had stayed in another room, but received permission from the hotel to photograph this haunted chamber, as it was empty at the time. At about 9:30 on a gray morning, we were loading cameras in our room, and talking frivolously about photographing a ghost. Guy Lyon Playfair, a lucid writer on such matters, refers to a "funny you should say that" effect common enough among amateur spook-hunters, and I assume we encountered it. Quite suddenly, we both heard what certainly sounded like a loud human voice in our room with us. My wife, who was closer to it, thinks it emanated from a point roughly in the center of the room, five or so feet above the floor. It wasn't a clichéd ghostly moan, and if I had to spell it, I'd render it something like "mmyuuhh." Although we were positive of what we'd heard, we quickly stepped into the hall and established that no one else was on our floor of the hotel—something we already knew, really, as the upper floors of the George creak like ship timbers in a high wind when anyone moves about.

I tell this story only because it captures the random, uncertain quality of what I may as well call real hauntings. Fictional ghost stories of necessity generally lack this quality, attributing motives and sentiment to the spooks in question for the sake of a satisfying tale. You know: *Ah! So the old pirate's ghost lingers on to protect his treasure!* This sort of pat, storybook symmetry is all too predictable in fiction, and tends to make even the allegedly true ghost stories of Elliott O'Donnell and some other celebrated "ghost hunters" seem suspect. By contrast, the work of the greatest master of the ghost story in English, Montague Rhodes James, is filled with the untidiness and hair-raising ambiguity of genuine hauntings. James's characters usually are sensible people who, quite by accident, brush against horrifying and inexplicable events and then extricate themselves as quickly as possible, with or more often without a tidy explanation.

The best ghost films of the 1957–1976 Gothic wave beautifully capture M. R. James's ineffable sense of what some call High Strangeness. Films like *The Haunting, The Innocents,* and *Carnival of Souls* use small, disturbing events—the touch of a cold hand in the dark; an indistinct figure seen across a marsh; a face glimpsed outside a car window—to fuse fear with wonder, creating a very pure and unforgettable sort of horror.

VINCENT PRICE MODELS HIS REMARKABLY SILLY SKELETON-PUPPETRY APPARATUS.

HOUSE ON HAUNTED HILL
Allied Artists, 1958

P, D: William Castle
S: Robb White
Starring Vincent Price (*Frederick Loren*), Elisha Cook, Jr. (*Watson Pritchard*), Richard Long (*Lance Schroeder*), Carolyn Craig (*Nora Manning*), Carol Ohmart (*Annabelle Loren*), Alan Marshal (*Dr. David Trent*), and Julie Mitchum (*Ruth Bridgers*).

Nightwalkers rating: 💀💀½

Evaluating the supernatural movies of William Castle is a tough task for me, because my affection for them has precious little to do with their quality. On a Saturday afternoon sometime in the early 1960s, I was scared waterless by a television broadcast of *House on Haunted Hill*, and I can still remember that horror now, although I'm well aware it's basically a silly film. Consider my rating as splitting a difference in opinion between my inner child and my flinty-eyed adult persona.

The first thing that should be understood about William Castle's horror movies is that, at their best, they represent an innocent, preadolescent art, not unlike the comedy of Benny Hill or the painting of Grandma Moses. Taken on these terms, without reference to logic or your critical faculties, they can be quite entertaining. (This is not necessarily true of Castle's Columbia programmers, nor his "thrillers," which tend be inept, watery Hitchcock imitations.) Most of the shocks in *House on Haunted Hill* are of an elementary kind—sudden noises, an unexpected hand on the shoulder—but bubbling beneath these is a childlike and rather charming dread of ghosts that seems quite close to true horror. Castle clearly hoped your heart would beat faster at the mere mention of the word, as mine certainly did when I was six.

House on Haunted Hill opens with a chorus of moans and chilling laughter of the sort that kids expect ghosts to make. Out of darkness swims the disembodied head of Watson Pritchard, who tells the history of the thoroughly haunted house that will provide our setting. The house has seen seven strange murders over a century, including that of Pritchard's brother. Now Pritchard owns the place, which scares the bejeebers out of him. Next to introduce himself is Frederick Loren, an eccentric millionaire who has rented the house to throw a most unusual party. He's invited a small group, including Pritchard; a doctor, David Trent; Ruth Bridgers, a newspaper columnist; Nora Manning, a soon-to-be damsel in distress; and Lance Schroeder, a handsome test pilot—all of them strangers to each other, and all in need of cash. Loren will pay each guest ten thousand dollars to stay in the haunted house overnight. In the event of ghost-inflicted homicide, the money goes to their estates.

The guests arrive at a decidedly odd haunted house. (Castle shot exteriors for this supposed century-old manse, with its conventionally creepy Victorian interior, at Frank Lloyd Wright's Ennis House, a bizarre Egypto-Mayan edifice in the Hollywood Hills.) Loren greets them, along with his coldly beautiful wife Annabelle, who heartily despises him, and issues each guest a .45 auto in a tiny coffin (great party, huh?) Spooky happenings ensue. Nora is terrified by an old crone who glides across the cellar, as if on wheels in a clumsy red-herring ploy; she turns out to be the wife of the house's caretaker (which doesn't explain her wheels).

SPOOKY ATMOSPHERE LAID ON WITH A TROWEL, IN *HOUSE ON HAUNTED HILL*.

The cellar also features that indispensable convenience, a bubbling acid vat. Lance is locked in a closet and sapped, apparently by a ghost. Mysterious gusts of wind run through the house. Doors lock themselves. Nora finds a severed head in her suitcase, which disappears when she fetches witnesses.

Annabelle is found hung, at a height too precarious to suggest suicide. The dead woman then begins appearing to Nora, leading the others to wonder whether she's going mad. At this point, the movie shifts gears, and we learn that Annabelle *faked* her own death (how?) and that she's in cahoots with her lover, Dr. Trent (remember him?) They're scheming to drive Nora crazy with fright and then get her to shoot Frederick—a pretty shaky plot, if you ask me. Loren, in any case, is more than their match at scheming. He fakes his own death at Nora's hands, and then tosses Trent into the acid vat in the cellar. Then, for no reason that I can fathom, he uses an enormous rod-and-reel puppetry apparatus to convince Annabelle that his *own* skeleton is rising from the acid pool; the puppet then pushes her into the vat(!!!). Ghostly laughter rises as the remaining cast members mill around, and after so much fun, it seems uncharitable to point out that none of this makes a lick of sense.

In one way, of course, *House on Haunted Hill* is the kind of thing that ghost fans hate most: a cop-out tale in which the haunting is revealed to be someone's scheme. For the six-year-old in me, though, those eerie wails that open and close the picture belie that notion. When Pritchard looks at the acid vat in which Annabelle and her lover are dissolving, and says, "Now there are nine. There'll be more—many more…"—I *believed* that. The house is filling up with ghosts…At any rate, the movie is a wild ride that's often surprisingly effective, even today. Viewers still jump when that rolling crone makes her first appearance.

Castle's partner and scriptwriter, Robb White, probably deserves major credit for the film's effectiveness. White's writing displays a roguish, brittle wit; the Lorens' Marriage Made in Hell is nasty fun, and reminds me more than a little of the famed E. C. comics of a few years before. Vincent Price makes the most of White's work in a typically buttery performance, his tongue planted so far in his cheek it's in danger of coming out the other side. The other cast standout is Elisha Cook, Jr. as the mouselike Watson Pritchard. Cook built a fairly steady career out of his perpetually worried expression, and he certainly uses it to maximum effect here.

The crowds of kids that lined up around the block for *House on Haunted Hill* weren't there for the acting, though—they were there to experience Emergo. Emergo, one of Castle's most famous gimmicks, involved an oversized plastic skeleton that was supposed to "leap from the screen" during the climactic sequence in which Price manipulates the skeleton to terrify his treacherous wife. The skeleton was attached to a line running from the projectionist's booth to an unobtrusive box over the theater screen. If all went well, the projectionist was supposed to reel in the skeleton, which was stored in the box, so that it would sail over the audience's heads. This Rube Goldberg arrangement was less than perfect, however, and dumped the skeleton squarely on its initial Los Angeles test audience. Even when Emergo worked properly, young lads across America soon discovered that the big skeletons made really fine slingshot and BB-gun targets. Cinematic history became a little richer.

House on Haunted Hill isn't a classic by any means, but over the years it's provided a lot of innocent pleasure to a lot of people. Castle, who wasn't blind to his limitations as a filmmaker, would

be pleased to know that his work is still remembered fondly. As he once said to English writer John Brosnan, he made "cheap, *fun* films." Not a bad job, and not a bad legacy.

13 GHOSTS
Columbia, 1960
P, D: William Castle
S: Robb White
Starring Charles Herbert (*Cyrus Zorba*), Jo Morrow (*Hilda Zorba*), Martin Milner (*Benjamen Rush*), Rosemary DeCamp (*Medea Zorba*), Donald Woods (*Buck Zorba*), and Margaret Hamilton (*Elaine*).

Nightwalkers rating:

It's fashionable among knowledgeable fans to admire William Castle's *House on Haunted Hill* while despising his later spook movie, *13 Ghosts*. This may be due in part to the fact that Castle's partner, writer Robb White, was so dismissive of the film. White played a major role in Castle's best-known works, and has received much of the credit for their success. White called *13 Ghosts* his "least favorite," and his only fond memory of the film seems to have been the day that a circus lion, brought in to play a ghost(!), urinated copiously on the cast and crew.

But, folks, the two films are not that far apart. It's true that Vincent Price's plummy presence is sorely missed, and that *13 Ghosts* is marred by some clumsy and sophomoric attempts at humor; but if you enjoy the kiddie thrills of *House on Haunted Hill*, chances are that you'll get a little amusement out of this campfire story as well. Besides, any movie that comes equipped with a Ghost Viewer can't be a total loss.

Castle had followed *House on Haunted Hill* with a bizarre Vincent Price science fic-

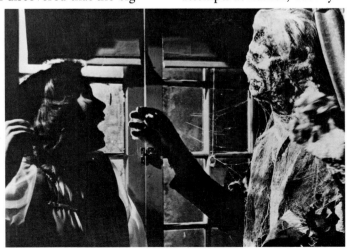

A SHOCKING MOMENT, MORE OR LESS, FROM WILLIAM CASTLE'S RATHER SILLY *13 GHOSTS*.

tion story, *The Tingler*, and one of his better-received killer-thrillers, a *Psycho*-clone called *Homicidal*. With *13 Ghosts*, Castle returned to supernatural themes. In doing so, he decided to forgo the cop-out denouement of *House on Haunted Hill* and dish up a baker's dozen of the real ectoplasmic article. According to Castle's autobiography, the idea for the film came to him during *Homicidal*'s European promotional tour. While driving through the French countryside, Castle and his wife passed a desolate, haunted-looking house. On a whim, Castle bought it. His intention was to have twenty million keys made as giveaways for a ghost picture, only one of which would bear the correct number indicating that its winner had won a "haunted" house in France. For some reason, this idea fell by the wayside; in its place was born Illusion-o, one of Castle's most endearing gimmicks.

Illusion-o allegedly required dozens of tests to perfect, but its basic concept is simple: The movie was shot in black and white, but the film's thirteen ghosts were tinted in red on the print. Each moviegoer was issued a ghost viewer containing clear strips of red and blue plastic. To see the ghosts clearly, you watched through the blue plastic, which would make them stand out in sharp relief. If, on the other hand, you found yourself overcome by stark terror, you could find easy relief simply by watching through the red strip—dubbed the ghost remover—which would obscure their images. I am sorry to report that most modern prints of the film, such as Ted Turner's television print, are printed in black and white only, meaning that the ghosts are always, but just barely, visible.

All this groundwork having been laid, we can now deal with the plot as an afterthought, which is pretty much how Castle approached it. A penniless paleontologist, Cyrus Zorba, is keeping his family about a half-step ahead of their creditors when he learns that his long-lost uncle, Plato Zorba, has died and left him a large, fully equipped mansion. Naturally, Cy wastes no time moving his wife, Hilda, daughter, Medea, and young son, Buck, into the house. (By the way, the Zorba family is as white-bread as they come, despite their strange monickers; the name "Buck Zorba" in particular has a melodious ring.) Soon, however, they discover a small problem: Plato, an avid student of the occult, developed a device to capture and collect ghosts,

and now *his* spirit has joined them in the house.

The film's official ghost roster reads as follows: 1. the clutching hands, 2. the floating head, 3. flaming skeleton, 4. screaming woman, 5. Emilio with cleaver in his hand; 6. his unfaithful wife, 7. her lover, 8. executioner and decapitated head, 9. hanging woman, 10. lion, 11. lion tamer without head, 12. Dr. Zorba, 13. ? I trust you find this enlightening. For the record, number ten is our incontinent friend who enlivened Robb White's day, Emilio appears to have been an excitable chef; and Plato Zorba himself comes in at number twelve. As for Number thirteen? Read on.

The ghosts cavort about with lots of moaning and gusts of mysterious wind, staging floor shows throughout the house; Emilio beheads his wife and her lover in a sort of spectral Punch-and-Judy mime, and so forth. Cy mutters things like "There's probably a simple explanation," until he discovers some of his uncle's effects—a book describing the ghosts, and an unwieldy set of goggles that make them visible. (From now on, he puts on his ghost viewers when you do.) The scary housekeeper who came with the place tells Cy that his uncle converted all his assets to ready cash before dying, which explains why Plato's oily young lawyer, Benjamen Rush, is constantly nosing about the place. (The housekeeper, played by Margaret Hamilton, Dorothy's nemesis in *The Wizard of Oz*, is repeatedly called "the witch" by Buck; someone seems to have thought this was a real knee-slapper.)

Buck discovers the horde of cash that has eluded lawyer Rush for months by sliding down a bannister and tripping a hidden switch. Rush quickly discovers the treasure as well, and plots to steal it all. We learn, through spectral intervention, that this rat killed Plato with a canopy bed whose cover descends at the touch of a button to smother its victims (no, really). He tries to kill Buck as well in the Bed of Death, but is foiled by Plato's ghost, who squishes him in there instead, leaving the family wealthy and making Rush (ta da) ghost number thirteen!

All right. It isn't *Battleship Potemkin*. I still think it's sort of amusing, and, as far as I'm concerned, the sight of Cy peering through his high-tech ghost viewers remains a classic image of fifties cinema.

THE INNOCENTS

20th Century–Fox, 1961
P, D: Jack Clayton
S: Truman Capote, William Archibald and John Mortimer; uncredited contributions by Jack Clayton
Starring Deborah Kerr (*Miss Giddens*), Meg Jenkins (*Mrs. Grose*), Michael Redgrave (*Uncle*), Martin Stephens (*Miles*), Pamela Franklin (*Flora*), Peter Wyngarde (*Peter Quint*), and Clytie Jessop (*Miss Jessel*).

Nightwalkers rating:

From the ridiculous to the sublime.

The Innocents opens with a small girl's voice, singing a wistful little ballad about lost love. Against blackness, we see a pair of hands clasped, in desperation or in prayer. A woman sobs, her face anguished. "All I want to do is save the children, not destroy them. More than anything, I love the children." This is not merely a classic of horror cinema; it's one of the most stylish, evocative movies ever made, and quite possibly the most faithful and effective literary adaptation in film history.

The Innocents is based on what is arguably the best-known ghost story in English, *The Turn of the Screw* by Henry James—still the one work by this rather difficult author that many people ever manage to read. This 1898 novel, which is brief and relatively free of James's often tortuous literary style, is a disquieting story of innocence corrupted (a favorite Jamesian theme) by what may or may not be a particularly ugly haunting.

In Victorian England, Miss Giddens is a young governess embarked

THE SHATTERING CLIMAX OF *THE INNOCENTS*: KERR WITH MARTIN STEPHENS.

on her first situation. Her employer is a wealthy and rather dashing London bachelor who's found himself saddled with an orphaned niece and nephew, Flora and Miles. The uncle (who is never named) freely admits he has "no place for them, mentally or emotionally," so, being the decent sort of cold bastard, he hires Miss Giddens to assume complete responsibility for their care and education at his distant country estate; a previous governess had died. Giddens is kind and quite pretty, but there's something nervous and birdlike about her, a lonely, dangerously vulnerable quality that signals trouble. She's obviously smitten by the uncle, and greatly flustered about it.

Miss Giddens is delighted to find that the estate is a lavish mansion, surrounded by gardens and a peaceful pond. (Exteriors for *The Innocents* were shot at Sheffield Park, a fine Tudor manor house in Sussex.) The first false note in this tranquility comes as soon as she arrives, when she hears a woman's voice calling Flora's name; the housekeeper, Mrs. Grose, didn't call out, and there's no one else about. Flora, a girl of ten or so, is much like the house, attractive and charming but somehow faintly sinister. Early on, she asks Giddens what happens to the souls of the "not so good"— "If I weren't [good], wouldn't the Lord just leave me here to walk around? Isn't that what happens to some people?"—a pretty significant portent. Another hint of the strange comes when Flora confidently tells Giddens and Mrs. Grose that Miles will be returning from school soon, even though it's the middle of the term. A few days later, her prophecy comes true; Miles has been expelled as "an injury to the others," an oddly indefinite phrase. He proves to be an angel-faced, precocious boy of about eleven, with a gift for flattery.

Miss Giddens begins seeing ghosts—or does she? The indistinct figure of a man stands atop the house's tower, obscured by shafts of hazy daylight. A miserable-looking woman stands motionless in a bank of reeds, watching Giddens and Flora from across the pond. During these encounters, all sound—all *life*—seems to drain away from Giddens, leaving her suspended in a silent, timeless moment. The governess suspects that the hauntings and the children's odd behavior are all part of the same mystery, of "something secretive and whispery and indecent" lurking in the house's shadowy corners. From Mrs. Grose, she learns that the former governess, Miss Jessel, had loved the house's valet, a cruel man named Quint. The two pursued a violent passion openly, in "rooms used by daylight, as if they were dark woods," *and* in front of the children, who were devoted to them. Then Quint was killed in a drunken accident, and Miss Jessel drowned herself in the pond, heartbroken. Giddens decides that these unhappy lovers are the ghosts she sees—and that they seek to revive their ugly affair *through the children*.

The distraught governess is sustained by her determination to root out and banish the evil in the house. She comes to believe that the children are conspiring, "talking horrors" behind her back, and the hauntings continue. She finds the sobbing specter of Miss Jessel seated at a desk in the house's schoolroom. The figure vanishes, and Giddens, with a look of shock and wonder, finds a tear on the desk. (Or was it only a drop of water? There's a flower vase nearby.) Later, a glowering, saturnine Quint watches her through a window…and, at bedtime one night, Miles (or Quint's restless spirit?) plants a frankly passionate kiss on Giddens's mouth. Convinced that the children are the key to the hauntings, the governess resolves to force them to admit the "truth" of their possession. In a shattering and, yes, *horrifying* confrontation, all these innocents pay a far higher price than they deserve.

Considering the universally high esteem in which James's *The Turn of the Screw* has always been held, it's a little surprising that the story wasn't filmed until 1961; but then, the sexual current revolving around the children is fairly explosive stuff, even today. In 1950, the novel was adapted for the stage with great success by playwright William Archibald, who first gave it the marvelously apt title of *The Innocents*. Various film projects based on the novel and play collapsed throughout the fifties, until English director Jack Clayton took it up in 1960. Clayton, an uneven but talented and fiercely independent director, had just had a major international hit in 1959 with *Room at the Top*, a gritty, realistic movie about class prejudice and social climbing in modern-day Britain. In part to confound his critics and admirers, who presumably expected to see him do more of the same, Clayton next turned to James's decidedly ungritty story, receiving a mediumish (at the time) $1 million budget from Twentieth Century–Fox.

The development of a suitable script proved to be a complex and time-consuming affair. According to film scholar Stephen Rebello (whose 1983 *Innocents* retrospective for *Cinefantastique* is probably the best study of the film), Fox purchased film rights for the play as well as the book, an arrangement that gave William Archibald first crack at the script. However, Clayton and Archibald failed to mesh, and Archibald left the project after producing little or nothing used in the final film. Clayton developed a new story treatment, and brought in John Mortimer, the British writer best known today for his "Rumpole of the Bailey" series, to work on the script for several weeks. Mortimer, in turn, suggested Truman Capote, whose ornate, slightly ghoulish touch proved perfect for the project. Clayton credits Capote with virtually the entire final shooting script, which is, in all, a masterpiece of sensitive and faithful adaptation.

To bring the script to life, Clayton assembled one of the finest casts ever to appear in a supernatural film. Michael Redgrave was chosen for the small but crucial role of the uncle, and he gives this basically nasty character a certain blunt honesty and sex appeal that makes Giddens's attraction understandable. (Clayton told Rebello that he could have had Cary Grant, no less, for the uncle, if he'd agreed to give Grant an additional scene at the end. Fidelity to the story won out, but the director was sorely tempted.) Fox insisted on Deborah Kerr as the governess, but Clayton can hardly have complained; as Miss Giddens, the nine-time Oscar nominee delivers one of the most finely nuanced performances of her career. The story's knife-edge balance between the psychological and the supernatural rests almost entirely with Kerr, and she maintains it beautifully, never letting our fundamental sympathy for the character entirely overwhelm our doubts about her.

Of course, there would have been no movie at all without the children, and both Pamela Franklin and Martin Stephens are phenomenal. Their performances are all the more extraordinary when one considers that neither was really aware of the film's story as it was being made. Clayton, fearful that the story might damage them psychologically, didn't give either child a script, and instead fed them each day's lines the night before. In particular, based on his work here and in 1960's chilling science fiction fable *The Village of the Damned*, Martin Stephens should certainly rank on any short list of the best child actors. He wasn't cute in the conventional sense, but he had a far rarer gift, a remarkable ability to generate menace through his angelic features, his strangely adult manner and aristocratic diction. Both of Stephens's horror-related roles are, in their way, as fine as any work done in the genre, not excepting Cushing or Karloff (yes, I mean that). Unsurprisingly, few parts suited for his unique talent came along, and Stephens later gave up on acting all together, and reportedly became an architect. I suspect it was more our loss than his.

Clayton worked closely with his cinematographer, Freddie Francis (whose own directorial efforts are discussed elsewhere in this volume) in developing a look that would convey the director's enthusiastically Freudian interpretation of the story. The rich visuals provide constant counterpoint to the story via a pictorial shorthand. Just before Giddens sees Quint for the first time, for example, she wanders, bemused, in a garden, and comes upon a half-forgotten marble cherub. As her eye lingers on the graceful carving, a fat, obscene-looking bug crawls from its mouth—as good a visual representation of the story's themes as I can imagine. This approach is arguably a little too "artsy" at times; Phil Hardy's *Encyclopedia of Horror Movies* grumps about Clayton's "penchant for images that are ever so pregnant with meaning." There's a repeated bit of business with falling rose petals, for instance, that almost seems to shout THIS IS A SYMBOL, BY GOD. For the most part, though, Freddie Francis's luminous black-and-white photography is so beautiful that we're absorbed by the imagery without fretting overmuch about its meta-content.

Francis told interviewer Wheeler Winston Dixon that Clayton gave him "a completely free hand photographically" on *The Innocents*, which allowed him to improvise and experiment. Francis's ingenuity would prove crucial on the shoot, as by his own admission Clayton simply forgot, until a very late date indeed, that the film was to be shot in widescreen Cinemascope. Early Cinemascope was limited and clumsy, and it simply hadn't yet been used to produce the kind of moody, intimate photography that Clayton had planned. To get the sort of Wellesian, deep-focus depth of field he wanted, for instance, the process demanded extraordinary amounts of illumination, so that a cozy, room-sized set might be bathed in as much as 250,000 watts of light. (You can imagine the steam bath the players were enjoying, in their stiff Victorian costumes.) Francis also devised special filters that allowed full illumination only in the center of the frame, leaving the margins of the image faintly dimmer and indistinct, increasing our uncertainty as to whether what we see there is real or imagined (the effect is all but lost on video).

Ultimately, any consideration of *The Innocents* must address the question of how successfully the movie version preserves the elegant ambiguity of James's story. The film constantly subverts our confidence in Giddens, distancing us from her viewpoint. Mrs. Grose, whom we half-expect to become an ally, instead clearly comes to question the governess's sanity. Some critics, particularly horror buffs, have charged the movie with stacking the deck in favor of neurosis. Leonard Wolf, for instance, feels that at the climax, Miss Gidden "is exposed…as certifiably and criminally insane." To which I would reply: lighten up. Nothing in *The Innocents* is that certain. Moreover, it seems to me that some overt focus on Giddens's mental state is needed to preserve the novel's intended uncertainty, to defeat our natural inclination to simply believe what we see: I mean, *of course* these are ghosts; we're seeing them with our own eyes, aren't we?

The Innocents contains several classic horror moments. My favorite comes fairly late in the film, when Giddens causes Flora to break down by insisting that she admit to seeing Jessel's ghost. As the governess berates the terrified child, we see Jessel, standing again at the pond's edge like a bone-china scarecrow, her indistinct features a rictus of grief. Flora dissolves into screaming fits, and is hustled away by Mrs. Grose. Giddens turns to watch them leave, looking both devastated and strangely elated. She turns back to look at the pond again, and every bit of our experience with clichéd filmmaking tells us that Jessel will be gone.

But she's not. Jessel still stands there, her face a yawning emptiness, staring silently at the new governess, soaked and unheeding in a sullen rain, and utterly inexplicable. It's an unforgettable moment, and as close to pure horror, as *I* define it, as anything in film.

"I DON'T BELONG IN THE WORLD": CANDACE HILLIGLOSS AND SIDNEY BERGER IN THE CULT CLASSIC *CARNIVAL OF SOULS*.

CARNIVAL OF SOULS
Harcourt Productions/Herts-Lion, 1962
P, D: Herk Harvey
S: John Clifford
Starring Candace Hilligloss (*Mary Henry*), Sidney Berger (*John Linden*), Frances Feist (*Landlady*), Herk Harvey ("*The Man*"), Stanley Leavitt (*Dr. Samuels*), and Art Ellison (*Minister*).

***Nightwalkers* rating:** 💀💀💀½

"I don't belong in the world...something separates me from other people."

Ah, yes, *Carnival of Souls*. Some controversy on this one. Is it a hauntingly poetic near-masterpiece of supernatural dread? Or is it a boring, amateurish piece of arty crap? Opinions are divided in my circle, at any rate, but I trust my rating shows where I stand. I think *Carnival of Souls* is one of the most unsettling and unforgettable of all modern horror movies.

Mary Henry, an aspiring church organist, is an odd, withdrawn young woman, nervous and not terribly friendly. She accepts a car ride from several other girls her age, only to be caught up in an impromptu drag race with some teenaged boys. The girls' auto loses control and plunges over the side of a bridge, and only Mary survives, finding herself muddied but intact on a sandbar in the river. A few days later, she leaves for a new position with a church in Salt Lake City. While driving to her new appointment, she passes a deserted pavilion near the Great Salt Lake. Once a bathing center and carnival, with fanciful Moorish domes and a boardwalk, the rotting hulk has been abandoned even by the receding waters of the lake. Mary feels strangely drawn to the ruin. Shortly after, she sees a leering, corpse-pale man watching her through the window of her *moving* car; the same figure then appears in her headlights, and disappears just as quickly.

Safely settled into a Salt Lake City boarding house, Mary attempts to settle into a routine, but the ruined pavilion, visible from her bedroom window, and the man both continue to haunt her. Fear forces her farther into her shell; her sole human contact is with a good-natured slob, John Linden, who also rooms in the house, and his clumsy attempts to seduce her do little to relieve her loneliness and alienation. One day, while trying on a dress in a department store, Mary becomes aware of an odd change in the atmosphere. All sound drains away from the scene except for her own footsteps, and the store's clerks and patrons can no longer see or hear her. Leaving the store, she walks in eerie silence through the town, like a living ghost. Even a jackhammer crew goes about its work without sound (this use of sound is reminiscent of Jack Clayton's *The Innocents*). In a park, the returning sounds of bird song and road noise announce that she's returned to "reality"—but, a few seconds later, she sees the man again.

On the verge of distraction, Mary tells her

story to a local physician, Dr. Samuels: "It was as though for a time I didn't exist…as though I had no place in the world." Later, while practicing in the church, she has a vision of the man rising out of the murky waters of Salt Lake, leading a procession of the dead, who perform a bizarre *danse macabre* in the pavilion's rotting ballroom. Mary tries to leave town, but develops car trouble. While waiting at a mechanic's shop, the silent "unreality" strikes again, along with another vision of the mysterious man. Mary wanders the streets once more, apparently invisible to all passersby. She boards a bus, only to find it occupied by the leering dead of her vision. In desperation, she returns to Dr. Samuels's office, but, in a classic shock sequence, finds You Know Who sitting in the doctor's chair—and then starts awake, to find herself still in the mechanic's shop.

Mary now seems to begin to understand and accept her fate. She travels alone to the pavilion. The corpses again rise from the waters, led by the mystery man, and repeat their dance of death. Mary finds herself dancing with them, then flees. The dead pursue her, careening wildly and silently amid the pilings beneath the old pavilion, until they catch her at last beside the lake shore….The next day, men from Salt Lake City find her abandoned car, and her footprints leading onto the sand beside the lake—where they stop, with no sign of Mary. In the final scene, the car from the film's beginning is dredged from the waters beneath the fatal bridge. Mary's body is in the car with the others. The dead have reclaimed their own.

Carnival of Souls was the brainchild of Herk Harvey, a Kansas-based producer and director of educational and "industrial" films— those unheralded shorts that still provide the nation's filmmakers with much of their bread and

MARY HENRY, REBORN FROM THE WATERS, IN AN ATMOSPHERIC MONTAGE FROM *CARNIVAL OF SOULS*.

butter. While working on assignment near Salt Lake City in June 1961, Harvey stumbled on the remains of a deserted lakeside pavilion called Saltair, once a 1940s tourist resort. The pavilion's atmosphere of lonely decay immediately impressed Harvey as a powerful asset for a horror movie. Upon returning to Kansas, Harvey recruited a local writer, John Clifford, to produce a script involving the pavilion and Harvey's basic image of dead bodies rising from the lake to pursue a victim.

Harvey and Clifford formed Harcourt Productions to bring the project to life, and solicited local backers to raise a total budget of less than thirty thousand dollars—a miserly sum even by 1961 standards. Harvey was able to make use of the production facilities and equipment of his "day-job" corporation, Centron of Lawrence, Kansas, which helped stretch the budget. The crew and some of the cast consisted of fellow Centron employees, including a talented cinematographer, Maurice Prather. A friend of Harvey's and then-head of the University of Kansas drama department, Sidney Berger, was cast as blowhard John Linden, and Berger in turn helped Harvey find an unknown New York actress, Candace Hilligloss, for the crucial role of Mary.

Filming proceeded over a trouble-free month in Lawrence and Salt Lake City, in an essentially improvisational fashion. The script was under constant revision throughout the shoot. For instance, the sequences in which Mary drops out of reality, which seem so vital a part of the finished film, were devised and added midway through production to fill out a dull stretch in the exposition. While shooting in the pavilion, the company found it could use its generators to revive the carnival's old lighting system for the first time in years; the ghostly lights reflecting across the lake were visible for miles, prompting a police investigation.

This sort of pinchpenny production is grueling, unforgiving work, and most filmmakers at this level are happy to pull in *any* sort of feature that halfway hangs together. Harvey's group accomplished considerably more. There are some obvious technical limitations and crudities; the first few minutes, for instance, seem to have been shot silent and (badly) overdubbed in post-production—a hallmark of poverty-row film-making (*The Creeping Terror* comes to mind).

Mostly, though, *Carnival of Souls* is amazingly assured, given its humble origins. It's a dreamy movie that takes time to generate its mood, an approach that some find either pretentious or dull. I don't. Prather's rhythmic, strangely hypnotic photography has a way of lingering on apparently ordinary objects and persons until a sinister quality seems to radiate from within them. A barely perceptible strangeness, a sense of something not right, suffuses the entire film, creating a palpable feeling of unease. Prather heightened this off-kilter effect by using deliberately contrasting film textures—a flat, grainy look for daylit exteriors, and muted, shadowy effects for interiors and the final confrontation with the spirits of the dead. This sequence, in which the dead rise from the lake and pursue Mary, combines beauty and menace in a way rarely seen in American film, echoing the best moments of Val Lewton's movies.

Some of the minor performances are uncertain and stiff, lending a campy flavor to a few scenes. A preacher's rant about "Sacrilege! Blasphemy!" grates a bit because it seems so disconcertingly amateur. But Candace Hilligloss's Mary, who carries the movie, perfectly mirrors its oddly off-center quality. Hilligloss studied method acting under its greatest proponent, Lee Strasberg, and reportedly found *Carnival of Souls* a fairly frustrating experience, precisely because Harvey didn't *want* her to understand her character's motivations. Instead, Mary drifts through the action, more than a little like a specter herself. As Harvey explains it, Mary was drawn as a thwarted individual who has never succeeded in truly living. Her stubborn spirit, desperate for more life, somehow rejects death—until being called back by whatever shadowy powers govern the realm beyond, as represented by the man (who was played by Harvey himself). Sidney Berger as John Linden, the movie's only other significant character, brings quite a bit more than required to a one-dimensional role. Linden as written is little more than a cartoon boob, but Berger (who now runs the University of Houston drama department) gives him an edgy anger that makes him considerably more interesting—like Ed Norton of "The Honeymooners" in an Elia Kazan film, say.

The storyline developed by Clifford and Harvey owes a lot to Ambrose Bierce's short story "An Occurrence at Owl Creek Bridge" (and, fittingly, director Robert Enrico's celebrated short adaptation of that story, *Incident at Owl Creek*, is one of the few horror films to rival *Carnival of Souls* in evoking the uneasy sense of a waking dream sliding into nightmare). It's the best sort of ghost story, entirely lacking the cloying romantic sensibility that undermines many efforts in this subgenre. Instead, the events are satisfyingly shuddery and inexplicable, yet seem to correspond to some sort of coherent dream logic that lies just beyond our comprehension.

Sadly, although Harvey and his talented company proved they had the chops to make a good movie, they were woefully ignorant about the distribution end of the business. Harcourt struck a deal with a newly formed distributor, Herts-Lion. The deal began to sour almost immediately when the distributor insisted on hacking about nine minutes out of the film for its initial release, obscuring some plot points and destroying much of the movie's poetic mood. After some months of unspectacular business, Herts-Lion folded without returning a penny in profits to Harcourt—the company's head had hastily decamped for Europe—leaving Harvey's investors high and dry. Worse news was to come; Harvey found that Herts-Lion had never paid Du-Arts Labs for striking the exhibition prints used in *Carnival of Soul*'s initial release. Ownership of the film reverted to Du-Arts, which sat on the original negative for years, and Harvey never made another feature.

A modestly happy ending of sorts did eventually come about. *Carnival of Souls* earned a subterranean following among horror buffs after the eventual release of the cut version to television. After a number of years, Harvey was able to purchase the original negative back from Du-Arts for a token amount, and in 1989 director and film buff Richard Haines persuaded a firm called Panorama Entertainment to restore and release an uncut version of *Carnival of Souls* to art theaters and video. The 1990 limited theatrical release garnered favorable attention from the likes of Siskel and Ebert and Leonard Maltin, vindicating Harvey's quirky vision at last. Today, rental prints of the restored version are readily available. You should see this movie.

THE HAUNTING
MGM, 1963

P, D: Robert Wise
S: Nelson Gidding; based on *The Haunting of Hill House* by Shirley Jackson
Starring Julie Harris (*Eleanor Vance*), Claire Bloom (*Theodora*), Richard Johnson (*Dr. Markway*), and Russ Tamblyn (*Luke Sannison*).

Nightwalkers rating: 💀 💀 💀 💀

"Hill House had stood for ninety years and might stand for ninety more....Silence lay steadily against the wood and stone of Hill House, and whatever walked there, walked alone."

These foreboding lines from Shirley Jackson's classic *The Haunting of Hill House* introduce Robert Wise's superb filmic adaptation, which easily ranks as one of the finest supernatural movies ever. Indiana native Wise will always be best remembered for *West Side Story* and *The Sound of Music*, but *The Haunting* harkens back to the beginning of his directing career, when he worked with legendary producer Val Lewton on films such as the Karloff horror classic *The Body Snatcher*. Certainly, *The Haunting* reflects Lewton's preference for suspense and atmosphere over visceral shocks, and the film's gorgeously moody black-and-white cinematography perfectly complements this approach.

Hill House was born bad. Built by a cold, unfeeling man, Hugh Crain, the house

was plagued by misfortune from its beginning. Both of Crain's wives died under mysterious circumstances. Crain's sad, withdrawn daughter Abigail grew up and grew old in the house's shadowy silences, dying one night while ringing for a paid companion who had abandoned her to meet a lover. The companion, too, met with an unhappy fate, hanging herself from the top of a spiral staircase. Since then, Hill House has acquired a reputation for haunting that attracts a psychic researcher, Dr. Markway, who sees it as an ideal proving ground for his investigations.

Markway assembles a small team to aid him. Eleanor Vance, or "Nell," is a neurotic spinster who, as a child, was the center of a poltergeist episode. Nell is fleeing a stifling home life; after eleven years of caring for a demanding, self-centered invalid mother, she's been sharing an apartment with a spiteful sister who holds her responsible for the mother's death. Also on Markway's expedition is a psychic, Theodora ("*just* Theodora"), a strong-willed and perceptive lesbian. Rounding out the little group is Luke Sannison, the obnoxious nephew of Hill House's current owners, who expects to inherit it. (Luke casually speculates about selling off the house's magnificent library at a quarter a book.) An odd and intriguing triangle quickly develops. Theo is clearly attracted to Nell, and her advances must have seemed a bit shocking to contemporary viewers. Nell barely notices Theo's interest, and rapidly falls in love with Markway; *he*, in turn, a married man, is oblivious to Nell's feelings.

The house begins its assault on the group's first night, with a traditional array of phenomena including a spectral chill and a pounding in the walls. (Virtually all of the film's spooky happenings are suggested through some remarkably evocative sound effects.) Soon, it becomes clear that whatever entities inhabit the house are mainly interested in Nell. Odd connections emerge. An eerie statue of Crain's family includes a figure of the young Abigail that looks remarkably like Nell. Theo uncovers a more disturbing parallel when she learns a secret of Nell's; she had failed to answer her mother's call on the night she died...just like Abigail Crain's companion. Nell's special relationship with the house and its ghostly inhabitants is underlined

JULIE HARRIS AND CLAIRE BLOOM IN AN EERIE MOMENT FROM ROBERT WISE'S *THE HAUNTING*.

when the group finds that *something* has written "help Eleanor come home" on one of the walls.

At least two subsequent scenes rank as high-water marks in modern horror. One night, while sharing a bedroom with Theo, Nell wakes to spectral voices and laughter, followed by more pounding in the walls. She feels Theo's cold hand, gripping her's like a vise, and finally, when the terror becomes too great, Nell screams— only to realize, when the lights come on, that she's been sleeping on the couch, while Theo's in bed across the room. *Who was holding Nell's hand?* And later, as the terrified group huddles in the house's library, a paranormal booming fills the room, and its massive wooden doors begin slowly to *bulge inward*, as if some enormous beast were straining against them.

The characterizations and character relationships in *The Haunting* are for the most part subtle and well-rounded. Markway is stalwart but a bit of a bore, given to impromptu lectures on the beliefs of the Montuzi bushmen and the like. Russ Tamblyn's hep-cat skeptic, Luke, is supposed to be irritating, of course, and succeeds a little too well. (He never actually uses the phrase "daddy-o," but he's certainly the type.) By contrast, Theo is attractive and sympathetic, It's characteristic of *The Haunting* that we're never quite sure whether Theo is genuinely psychic or simply a keen judge of human nature.

Ultimately, though, *The Haunting* belongs to Julie Harris's Nell, perhaps the most complex and deftly drawn character in supernatural film. Harris vividly captures Nell's frustration and fear, her profound loneliness, and her subconscious delight in being a center of attention at last— even if those attentions come from the invisible denizens of Hill House. As Nell's sanity crumbles, the house responds to her desperate need for acceptance in its own lethal way. Theo delivers the coda: "She had no place else to go. The house belongs to her now, too. Maybe she's happier." The vanquished survivors gather before the house, and we hear Nell's voice repeating the opening narration, ending with "We who walk here, walk alone." The black house has gained another permanent resident.

THE SKULL
Amicus, 1965

P: Milton Subotsky and Max J. Rosenberg
D: Freddie Francis
S: Milton Subotsky
Starring Peter Cushing (*Christopher Maitland*), Christopher Lee (*Sir Matthew Phillips*), Patrick Wymark (*Anthony Marco*), Jill Bennett (*Jane Maitland*), Nigel Green (*Police Inspector Wilson*), Maurice Good (*the phrenologist*), George Colouris (*Dr. Londe*), April Olrich (*his mistress*), Michael Gough (*auctioneer*), and Patrick Magee (*police surgeon*).

Nightwalkers rating: 💀💀💀

The Skull is Freddie Francis's best work as a director, and arguably the finest shocker made by Milton Subotsky's Amicus Productions. It's certainly one of the few Amicus movies to rival

Hammer's best in quality. This probably is due at least in part to the fact that so many Hammer alumni were present—Francis was joined in the film by Peter Cushing and Christopher Lee, as well as several other lesser lights of the Hammer universe. Nonetheless, the movie isn't simply an imitation. *The Skull* has some inventive and disturbing moments of psychological fear that make it unique among the films of its day.

The Skull is based on a short story, "The Skull of the Marquis de Sade," by Robert Bloch. Story and film both rely on the marquis's infamy to portray him as a sort of ultimate avatar of evil. (This is rather a grand claim for Donatien Alphonse Francois de Sade, a plump petty noble who never killed anyone, so far as we know, and spent a fair number of years in the clink on petty charges. His worst crimes seem to have been paddling the occasional servant girl and writing some of history's most boring pornography.)

The plot of this stylish horror tale is fairly straightforward. In a fog-bound stretch of early nineteenth-century France, a phrenologist—a student of the now-discredited science that sought to trace connections between human physiognomy and character—unearths de Sade's body and steals the skull for his studies. The phrenologist quickly comes to an uncomfortable end, as does his mistress; de Sade's skull is mysteriously capable of inciting innocent men to murder.

In present-day England, we meet Christopher Maitland and Sir Matthew Phillips, friends and rival collectors of occult artifacts and souvenirs of the bizarre—a mass murderer's dagger, books bound in human skin—knickknacks of that sort. Maitland is offered the skull by Anthony Marco, a weaselly chap who often provides the collector with outré objects on a no-questions-asked basis. Marco's possession of the skull is making him distinctly nervous; nevertheless, he demands an enormous price for it.

Maitland is skeptical at first, but his curiosity is piqued when Sir Matthew mentions that the skull once belonged to him, and that he believes it to be still inhabited by the demonic spirit that possessed de Sade. The skull was stolen from Sir Matthew shortly before, to his tremendous relief. He warns Maitland to stay away from this sinister bauble, but only succeeds in further interesting the collector. As his obsession increases, Maitland begins having hideous nightmares. Marco is found dead, his throat ripped. Maitland seizes the opportunity to steal the skull, and kills Marco's snooping landlord in the process. The skull-demon continues its work on Maitland, driving him to rub out Sir Matthew as well. The frenzied collector balks at killing his own wife to appease the demon's bloodlust, only to die in her place, his throat torn out like Marco's—apparently by the skull itself.

It's a tribute to the skill and conviction of *The Skull*'s execution that this unlikely scenario is often chilling and never laughable. There's a nice sequence, for instance, in which Cushing temporarily pulls free of the skull's influence and manages to drive a dagger into its eye socket. Leaving the room, he immediately discovers the same dagger thrust through *his own pillow*. Toward the end, the skull takes to flying about on its own. This effect is about as effective as can be expected from puppetry, but the wires show up pretty clearly in a few shots. Its passage through the house is interestingly marked by a kind of invisible wave of force that pushes framed pictures askew and, at one point, shatters a mirror.

Freddie Francis's direction of the film is

PETER CUSHING CONTEMPLATES A DEADLY SOUVENIR OF THE MARQUIS DE SADE, IN *THE SKULL*.

generally excellent, although the movie's pacing drags in places. As usual, the camerawork is fluid and interesting, with extensive use of gliding dolly shots and a skull's-eye-view gimmick. Francis mounted an oversized skull mockup on the front of an Aeroflex camera, and, while having himself wheeled about on rollerskates(!), personally shot a number of scenes from the skull's viewpoint, giving the viewer the sensation of peering out from the skull's bony recesses. It's a striking effect, blunted a bit by excessive repetition.

Francis's photographic style, which I admire very much, was prompted by a combination of practical and artistic concerns. The roaming camera tends to involve the viewer in the film more fully than the relatively static work of, say, Terence Fisher—"if you move your camera around…you feel you're not on a set, and the people aren't on a set. It becomes real," as Francis told interviewer Wheeler Dixon. Moreover, Francis's style was deliberately gauged to make it difficult for his producers to second-guess, recut, and reshape his movies after the fact—a common occurrence in low-budget filmmaking, and one that seems to have irritated Francis no end. To stymie this sort of interference, Francis liked to stage longish dolly shots incorporating various close-ups without a cut, rather than breaking the action up into individual shots that later could be reshuffled by an overeager producer.

Speaking of Milton Subotsky, he was precisely the sort of producer Francis had in mind when he developed this strategy; by his own admission, Subotsky *loved* messing about in the editing room. Subotsky once stated that Francis's footage simply didn't tell a story, and that he assembled the last four reels of *The Skull* in the editing booth in an entirely different way than Francis had envisioned, from "teeny trims and bits and pieces of film." Francis, in turn, has claimed this story is "absolute nonsense." (The

two men's various interviews contain florid expressions of mutual respect that make it seem clear that they loathed each other.) In my opinion, the finished print of *The Skull* makes Subotsky's story seem unlikely.

Subotsky's script, however, is more than competent, barring a few rough spots, such as one early scene in which Maitland and Marco spend several minutes telling each other things they would already know so that we can get up to speed. For the most part, though, it's a restrained and largely wordless exercise—Subotsky was intrigued with the idea of making an essentially silent horror film—and contains at least one bravura sequence: As Maitland falls under the de Sade-demon's influence, he has a terrifying nightmare (borrowed freely from Kafka's *The Trial*) in which he's kidnapped by police agents and forced to play Russian roulette before a silent, corrupt-looking judge. After the nightmare, all disturbing camera angles and violent color, comes to an end, he wakes up to find himself not in bed at home, but fully dressed and standing in Marco's apartment, *without any idea of how he's gotten there*. It's a truly scary and disorienting moment that is, quite simply, as good as anything being done in horror during the period.

THE LEGEND OF HELL HOUSE
20th Century–Fox, 1973
P: Albert Fennell and Norman T. Herman
D: John Hough
S: Richard Matheson
Starring Roddy McDowall (*Ben Fischer*), Pamela Franklin (*Florence Tanner*), Clive Revill (*Dr. Curtis Barrett*), Gayle Hunnicutt (*Ann Barrett*), Roland Culver (*Rudolph Deutsch*), and Peter Bowles (*Hanley*).

Nightwalkers rating:

Timing is everything. If *The Legend of Hell House* had been made a few years earlier than it was, today it might be more generally regarded as (at least) a minor classic of supernatural cinema. Unfortunately, it made its debut in the same season as *The Exorcist*, and has dwelled in that movie's shadow ever since, to the detriment of its own reputation; more on that later.

The Legend of Hell House concerns the Belasco mansion, dubbed "Hell House," site of a haunting so violent that the place is regarded as "the Mount Everest of haunted houses." The house's original owner, Emeric Belasco, was a twisted genius who lived out the fantasies of de Sade. In the 1920s, he led a band of disciples through a depraved course of sexual perversion and murder that left twenty-seven dead. A team of investigators has been hired by an eccentric millionaire to spend a week in the house and establish definitively whether the human personality can survive death. This isn't simply an academic exercise, as previous attempts to investigate the house resulted in *more* deaths and insanity.

The current team's de facto head is a dogmatic physicist, Dr. Barrett, who doesn't believe in spirits and assumes that the energies producing the haunting can be measured and dissipated. Barrett is reluctantly forced to work with a young medium, Florence Tanner, who believes Hell House to be a case of "controlled multiple haunting" produced by various spirits and dominated by the soul of Emeric Belasco, "like a general with his army." Along with Barrett's wife, the team is rounded out by another medium, Ben Fischer. As the sole survivor of a

HERE, KITTY: PAMELA FRANKLIN FACES AN UNWELCOME VISITOR IN THE SORELY UNDERRATED *LEGEND OF HELL HOUSE*.

disastrous 1953 investigation, he only wants to collect his money and get out in one piece.

The house quickly begins working on its visitors through a combination of fear and a rather slimy sexuality. Barrett is the subject of a vicious poltergeist attack, and narrowly escapes being killed by flying crockery and a falling chandelier. Barrett's wife is tormented by morbid sexual fantasies and, in sleepwalk trances, finds herself attempting to seduce Fischer. Florence is contacted by an entity claiming to be Daniel Belasco, Emeric's son, still trapped in the house by his evil father. Daniel makes thoroughly unspiritual advances on Florence and, in one unsettling sequence, apparently rapes her. The nastiness of the attacks accelerates as Barrett completes work on a machine designed to banish Hell House's hauntings once and for all, through a powerful countercharge of energy. His confidence, as you might guess, turns out to be misplaced, and Hell House claims more victims.

For the most part, this is a beautifully executed movie. Director John Hough, who also directed *Twins of Evil*, assembled a number of disturbing sequences. The poltergeist attack on Dr. Barrett is shocking and kinetic, the best thing of its kind on film. Belasco House is effectively claustrophobic and eerie, with set designs as opulent as anything Hammer ever mounted. And the tiny cast's performances are without exception excellent. Pamela Franklin (the child costar of *The Innocents*) in particular should be singled out for her portrayal of Florence Tanner, who combines steely determination with a powerful and fatally naive spirituality.

My biggest complaint (and the *only* reason I withhold a fourth skull) is that the ending revelation—which concerns Emeric Belasco's all-too-human ego—seems to me arbitrary and unconvincing. In this, however, the film merely repeats the only major flaw in the book on which it is based.

The Legend of Hell House began as a 1964 novel of that name by Richard Matheson. It was obviously inspired, at least in part, by Shirley Jackson's *The Haunting of Hill House*. But Matheson disliked the psychological, is-it-all-in-their-minds approach that Jackson's book took, and, as he said in a recent interview, resolved to write a "haunted house story where you damned well *know* it's haunted." Thirty years later, *The Legend of Hell House* is still violent, disturbing stuff. Filmed faithfully, it might receive an "X" rating (pardon, "NC-17") even in today's jaded climate.

The movie was the first and only independent production by James H. Nicholson, legendary cofounder of American International Pictures. (Nicholson left AIP in 1971, but his fledgling career as an independent was tragically cut short by brain cancer.) Nicholson's eye was still firmly fixed on teenaged and family markets, and he had no interest in making what is now called a "hard R." In scripting *The Legend of Hell House*, Matheson reshaped his novel into a 'PG' effort that left more to the viewer's imagination than his graphic prose had. What resulted was a subtle and unnerving film that scares without gross-out effects and gouts of Max Factor blood.

Nonetheless, in the wake of *The Exorcist*'s startling redefinition of what a horror film could be (and get away with), many fans and critics seemed to feel that *The Legend of Hell House* was Milquetoast stuff. *Cinefantastique*, for instance, held up *The Exorcist*'s graphic extremes as a model, and clucked disapprovingly that the movie "lacked the conviction and courage of the original source material." Similar sentiments have been echoed by a number of other serious students of horror.

Often cited, for instance, is Florence's rape scene. In the film, the scene's impact is carried entirely by Franklin's horrified reactions, and her giggling hysteria afterward. The book, on the other hand, describes her attacker as an apparition of a rotted corpse with a "leering smile." How much more horrifying it would have been, the film's critics seem to say, had we been presented with a fellow in a gooey latex suit cavorting atop Ms. Franklin, as per some recent gore-and-snore-fest like *Bride of the Reanimator*.

Yet twenty years of increasingly tedious diminishing returns from this approach surely have proven that the imagination is still the best special-effects shop going. And note also that many of the people who dislike *The Legend of Hell House* praise atmospheric pieces like Val Lewton's *Cat People* to the skies. Why this sort of subtlety and restraint should be judged commendable in one case, and cowardly in another, simply escapes me.

MYSTERY AND IMAGINATION

Edgar Allan Poe in Film

AN ENTHUSIASM FOR POE IS THE MARK OF A DECIDEDLY PRIMITIVE STAGE OF REFLECTION.

—HENRY JAMES

Edgar Allan Poe has been called our most prominent second-rate author, a judgment that may have some justice to it. Even the most disapproving give the man his due, of course; a perceptive if vicious critic, fine poet, creator of the detective story. Yet despite his entombment in a thousand Lit Trad courses throughout our nation, a trace of doubt seems to remain about this quizzical figure. He's still the one great American author that it's sort of okay to dislike.

Part of the problem is the sheer amount of sloppy, prolix writing to be found in Poe, which caused comment even in his own windy era. Plowing through a fat volume of his work, one is continually reminded that he was, after all, a magazine writer, paid by the word and perpetually in need of money. I can think of few authors of whom I would say this, but it's probably better to read a little of Poe's work than a lot. That handful of classic short stories that have been anthologized repeatedly really do capture the best qualities of the man's fiction, with a minimum of his stylistic excesses.

THE PROFESSIONALS: VINCENT, PETER LORRE, AND BASIL RATHBONE, STARS OF *TALES OF TERROR*.

Poe was by choice a profoundly limited writer in the sense that his horror work is devoted, with an extraordinary and singleminded concentration, to the few emotional effects that concerned him. (Poe also wrote a number of comic sketches, but it's a rare humor piece that can remain funny for more than a few decades, and Poe's *definitely* haven't survived as more than curiosa.) Even his best stories, such as "The Fall of the House of Usher," are virtually devoid of characterization, wit, or any apparent sense of insight or self-awareness. In the case of pieces like "Ligeia," they're often all but free of plot as well. Many stories are little more than monologues by inevitably nervous and neurotic narrators. Obsessive themes of Poe's, such as his horror of premature burial, are used repeatedly. Everything extraneous to the production of Poe's characteristic mix of fear, guilt, and regret is pared away.

Unsurprisingly, Poe has proven difficult to capture on film. A variety of directors, including Fellini and Vadim, have tackled Poe with indifferent results, but his ideal interpreter to date has proven to be Roger Corman, whose series of Poe-inspired horror films for American International represent his best directorial work. Corman had been an incredibly productive hack producer-director for only five years when he turned to Poe, and had already demonstrated a modest, quirky talent, but the Poe material seems to have fanned a spark of something like genius within him. The director had spent a few years in analysis prior to beginning the Poe series, and was imbibing Freud like an enthusiastic freshman as he made them. His earnest, unsubtle approach to the psychological underpinnings of Poe's stories—watch for lightly veiled incest subplots!—works surprisingly well, and comes as close as anyone has yet to realizing Poe's claustrophobic fever dreams on the screen.

HOUSE OF USHER
American International, 1960
P, D: Roger Corman
S: Richard Matheson
Starring Vincent Price (*Roderick Usher*), Mark Damon (*Philip Winthrop*), Myrna Fahey (*Madeline Usher*), and Harry Ellerbe (*Bristol*).

Nightwalkers rating: 💀💀💀

The movie that ushered in (sorry) the American portion of the Gothic renaissance feels a bit uncertain in places, rather like its trailblazing British counterpart, *The Curse of Frankenstein*. But *House of Usher* is in every way the better movie. It's elegant, drenched with atmosphere, and technically polished well beyond anything previously seen from Roger Corman or AIP.

The film is, of course, based on one of Edgar Allan Poe's most famous and successful stories, "The Fall of the House of Usher," a brief mood piece concerning the doom of an ancient and cursed family. The story is probably the best possible introduction to Poe, filled with hysteria and madness, and turning on his obsession with the grisly idea of premature burial. As is true of much of Poe's work, "House of Usher" is all overheated emotion, and virtually plotless; yet Richard Matheson's canny script remains remarkably faithful to the original, while expanding on its themes and making it all just a bit more grim.

VINCENT PRICE BEHIND THE SCENES OF AIP'S *HOUSE OF USHER.*

As *House of Usher* opens, dashing young Philip Winthrop makes his way through a blasted-looking New England wilderness to the ancient, sinister house of the Usher family; his fiancée is the fair Madeline Usher. Madeline and her brother, the disturbed and disturbing Roderick Usher, are the last of their line, and neither seems a good prospect for longevity. Madeline, recently returned from Boston, is wan and ill-looking, while Roderick suffers from an "acuity of the senses" that makes normal sound and any light above twilight dimness almost unbearable. Roderick is convinced that both he and his sister are dying; they're "like figures of fine glass…the slightest touch and we may shatter." Philip learns that "the Usher line is tainted," riddled with killers and madmen, and its descendants have been broken beneath the weight of generations of sin and insanity, until even their house and the surrounding landscape are steeped in evil.

Roderick loves Madeline desperately, in an unhealthy way, and resents Philip's presence. He forbids the young lovers to marry, for fear that their children would spread the Usher curse "like a malignant cancer." Philip, the manly sort, resolves to spirit Madeline out of the gloomy mansion, but before he can do so, she apparently dies. Only after she's been sealed in her crypt beneath the house does Philip learn that Madeline was prone to fits of catalepsy—a deathlike sleep. Philip dreams of Madeline trapped and screaming in her coffin (in a tinted, arty dream sequence that Corman would repeat in more than one subsequent Poe film). Finally Roderick admits the truth—he buried his own sister *alive*; with his heightened senses, he can even hear her struggles within her tomb. Too late to the rescue, Philip finds that Madeline, bloody and maddened, has clawed her way out. Madeline leaps on her brother, and the siblings, now both quite unhinged, struggle and die as the evil house bursts into flames around them. Philip departs as the rotted remnants of the House of Usher sink into a black tarn.

House of Usher was a remarkable leap forward in Roger Corman's directing career. Little in his earlier movies suggested he would be capable of this film's sustained interest and quality. In his autobiography, Corman says, "My own bias was for a moving camera," and if you read this book through, you'll see that I agree. The camera work in *House of Usher* is sinuous and evocative, featuring unusual, disorienting angles and extensive use of point-of-view shots. With his director of photography, Floyd Crosby, Corman devised complex and beautifully lit takes that send the camera stalking and gliding, pulling us relentlessly through the house's brooding corridors.

Filled with his newfound enthusiasm for Freud, Corman wanted to re-create "the world of the unconscious," and strove to give *House of Usher* an intentionally claustrophobic and unreal look. This effort led to one of Corman's most inspired off-the-cuff ideas. During the shoot, Corman heard about a brushfire in the Hollywood Hills. The next day, he grabbed a camera, a horse, and costar Mark Damon, and headed for the site of the fire, where he shot the opening, Philip's approach to the house, amid a surreally charred and ravaged landscape. Similarly, Corman was able to film spectacular shots of the burning "House of Usher" in part by torching a delapidated Orange County barn that he bought for fifty dollars. (Predictably, Corman reused this footage several more times; seasoned AIP fans can point out the barn's burning chicken coop in film after film.)

Just as important to the film's look was another member of Corman's team, art director Daniel Haller, who displayed the same sort of genius for atmosphere on the cheap as did Hammer's Bernard Robinson. Haller bought ornate stock sets from Universal for twenty-five hundred dollars—stuff they couldn't *possibly* build for that money—and borrowed existing sets from other studios. Special mention also should be made of Roderick Usher's wonderful paintings of his ancestors. These violent, almost cartoonlike portraits (by Burt Shoenberg) are wholly unforgettable, looking like a cross between the drawings of Edward Gorey and some hellish version of Charles Keane's enormous-eyed waifs.

Roderick Usher was Vincent Price's best role in years. He's the perfect embodiment of Poe's romantically morbid character, from whom "darkness…poured forth upon all objects…in one unceasing radiation of gloom." Price had made horror films before, but with this film he graduated to full-fledged genre stardom, ranked with (and typecast as much as) Karloff. Unfortunately, the rest of the tiny cast range from mediocre to worse. Mark Damon is particularly wooden; Matheson has remembered him "playing, I guess, at being a method actor, and before he went on the set he would run in place and huff and puff…" He's terrible. But when Vincent is on screen, you scarcely notice anyone else, anyway.

There would be more "AIPoe," as its fans would learn to call it—and soon.

THE PIT AND THE PENDULUM

American International, 1961
P, D: Roger Corman
S: Richard Matheson
Starring Vincent Price (*Nicholas Medina* and *Sebastian Medina*), John Kerr (*Francis Barnard*), Barbara Steele (*Elizabeth Medina*), Luana Anders (*Catherine Medina*), and Antony Carbone (*Dr. Charles Leon*).

Nightwalkers rating: 💀💀💀

Given AIP's success with *House of Usher*, it was inevitable that they ask Roger Corman to venture into Poe territory again. *The Pit and the Pendulum* proved to be a more flamboyant elaboration of the first film's plot and themes, with a classic over-the-top performance by Vincent Price and, with the possible exception of *Masque of the Red Death*, the most impressive visual elements of the entire Poe series.

Poe's "The Pit and the Pendulum" was a logical candidate for AIP's next adaptation, since it's one of the author's most famous tales and features a torture device that is both horrific and visually interesting. The story, alas, is unfilmable, consisting mainly of one long scene featuring the interior ruminations of one of Poe's unnamed, neurotic heroes. Richard Matheson solved this problem essentially by rewriting *House of Usher* and grafting "The Pit and the Pendulum" on as a climax.

Although it's set in 1540s Spain, the film opens much as did *House of Usher*, with a young man arriving at a mysterious, cobwebby house

VINCENT PRICE LOVES A FAITHLESS BARBARA STEELE ALL TOO MUCH IN *THE PIT AND THE PENDULUM*.

in search of a woman. Francis Barnard has come to the castle of Don Nicholas Medina to investigate the reported death of his sister, Elizabeth, the don's wife. Francis has a pugnacious, Jack Webb-style manner, and refuses to buy into Nicholas's rather feeble story that Elizabeth died from "something in her blood."

In conversations with Nicholas, his sister, Catherine, and doctor and family friend Charles Leon, Francis learns that life in Medina's castle had driven Elizabeth into a strange state of morbidity and fear. This doesn't seem too implausible, considering that Nicholas's late father, Sebastian Medina, was a leader of the Spanish Inquisition, and that "the blood of a thousand men and women" has been spilled in the dark crypts where Elizabeth was found mysteriously dead of fright. Nicholas's uncle and mother were adulterous lovers, and, as a child, he saw his mad father kill them both, the mother being immured alive behind a wall (a lift from Poe's "The Cask of Amontillado"), an experience that left Nicholas scarred for life.

Despite the nature of the Medina's household, Francis is unconvinced that mere "atmosphere" could kill his sister, and continues his investigations. Meanwhile, Nicholas is tormented by ghostly phenomena—Elizabeth's harpsichord playing itself one night, and so forth—that slowly convince him that his bride, like his mother, was buried while alive, and has returned to haunt him. Finally, Elizabeth rises from her tomb to confront him, so terrifying Nicholas that he slumps into apparent death, at which point (the old switcheroo!) Dr. Leon emerges from the shadows to embrace Elizabeth's "corpse"—and we learn that (as in the classic French thriller *Diabolique*) it's all been a plot to frighten Nicholas to death. Unfortunately for the scheming lovers, Nicholas isn't dead, but instead has been driven into homicidal dementia.

Frothing-mad Nicholas makes short work of Dr. Leon and traps Elizabeth in a handy iron maiden. And what, you say, about that pit and pendulum? Francis is strapped into the enormous contraption and spends several perspiration-filled moments watching the blade descend, until Catherine Medina (who spent most of the film threatening to become Francis's love interest) arrives with a brawny servant to the rescue. Nicholas takes the Big Dive into the pit and Francis is saved. As the survivors exit the torture chamber, Catherine swears the room will be sealed off for all time. They aren't aware that Elizabeth is *still alive*, mouth gagged, in the iron maiden below. The camera pulls in on her eyes, visible through a slit in the torture device, and wide with terror.

As I've already indicated, the first two thirds of *The Pit and the Pendulum* are almost a remake of *House of Usher*. Details major and minor are repeated, including the ancient house and its secrets, the weird family portraits, the premature burial, and so on. Corman's fascination with dime-store Freudian symbolism is still present; instead of the brother-sister incestuous subcurrents of *House of Usher*, we get the vaguely Oedipal notion of Nicholas becoming his father and killing his "mother"—weighty stuff, indeed (the Poesque clichés begin to wear thin). Nevertheless, in most respects *The Pit and the Pendulum* seems more successful and more entertaining than *House of Usher*, with a gaudy color and intensity the earlier film lacks.

Much of the film's success must be attributed to Vincent Price. Price's Nicholas Medina is a considerably more florid conception than his Roderick Usher, which was (for Price) almost underplayed. He's got a number of juicy and memorable Pricean lines—"Am I not the spawn of his depraved blood?" is my favorite—yet he rarely lapses into the hamminess he sometimes displayed when saddled with inferior scripts. His descent into madness, and his sadistic glee as Sebastian (in flashback), convey an impressive sense of physical menace that the courtly actor seldom achieved in later roles.

Barbara Steele is equally strong in her brief role as faithless Elizabeth. As in her Italian horror work (see *Black Sunday*) she displays an uncanny knack for projecting a sense of evil through facial expression and body language—which is just as well. In this, her first and most notable American horror movie, some bonehead at AIP saw fit to have her redubbed by another actress. Unfortunately, John Kerr, the second-billed star is simply not in the same league with Price and Steele, and instead is the film's greatest weakness. Kerr, most famous for a role in *Tea and Sympathy*, seems out of his depth; he marches through *The Pit and the Pendulum* with an unfailingly pouty look and little discernable talent.

The major impression *The Pit and the Pendulum* leaves, however, is of beautiful design and execution. Daniel Haller's art direction is particularly memorable, especially his enormous set for the pendulum chamber—decorated, as per Poe's description, with shuddery and colorful "figures of fiends in aspects of menace." Haller created the cavernous interiors of Medina's castle by literally gutting a soundstage, removing all catwalks and overhead lighting, and dressing the chamber all the way up to its roof. Haller's sets are well-matched with Floyd Crosby's camera-work, which pans and glides around the castle interiors with a fluid elegance reminiscent of Mario Bava's *Black Sunday*—and, as Bava's film was in a highly successful release as *The Pit and the Pendulum* was being made, I'm inclined to think the resemblance isn't accidental.

The pendulum itself, by the way, was a large, impressive mechanical prop, eighteen feet long and weighing more than a ton, and operated by four stagehands who swung it through a fifty-foot arc. Initially, it was fitted with a rubber blade, but this tended to catch on John Kerr's chest. Thereafter, a metallized blade was used for closeups. Kerr wore a steel band to protect his vitals. but by all accounts his look of sweaty anxiety during the sequence isn't just method acting.

The film was another major success for AIP, earning nearly $2 million in rentals (against production costs of $200,000, according to Corman) and winning warm notices. The numbers established that *House of Usher* hadn't been a fluke; Poe—as interpreted by AIP—was big box office.

THE PREMATURE BURIAL
America International, 1962

P, D: Roger Corman
S: Charles Beaumont and Ray Russell
Starring Ray Milland (*Guy Carrell*), Hazel Court (*Emily Gault*), Richard Ney (*Miles Archer*), Heather Angel (*Kate Carrell*), Alan Napier (*Dr. Gideon Gault*), John Dierkes (*Sweeney*), and Dick Miller (*Mole*).

Nightwalkers rating: 💀 ½

Three times definitely was *not* a charm in the case of Roger Corman's Poe movies. The third entry, *The Premature Burial*, marks the nadir of the director's efforts on the series (though some later, non-Corman AIPoes arguably are worse). A weak script and a cruelly bad bit of miscasting pretty much wreck its chances from the get-go. In addition, the repetition of themes and plot elements among the Poe entries has by now become more apparent and more annoying.

One such instance is used right away. Emily Gault arrives at a spooky, ancient house, looking for her fiancé, Guy Carrell, a promising medical student, who has vanished out of her life suddenly and mysteriously. Guy is neurotic and near-paralyzed with fear related to a family curse; his sinister sister, Kate, watches over him jealously. Barring some gender switching, this is almost identical to the setup of *House of Usher*, and close to *The Pit and the Pendulum* as well.

Guy's unfortunate obsession is a terror of premature burial (again, a plot element that figured prominently in the previous two films). Guy's life was forever shattered at the age of thirteen, when his father died. The man suffered from catalepsy, and Guy believes he was buried alive. Deceased family members are (as we've come to expect) tucked away in a basement crypt beneath the house, and Guy thinks he heard his father's "pitiful, desperate cry" from the tomb. Guy has spent the years since, dwelling on the terror of premature burial. His soliloquy is lifted directly from Poe's original: "Can you possibly conceive it? The unendurable oppression of the lungs, the stifling fumes of the damp earth, the rigid embrace of the coffin...." He's a lot of fun, all right; and he's convinced that the same fate awaits him. Nevertheless, Emily is grimly determined to marry him, and nudges him to the altar despite Kate's thinly veiled hostility.

The marriage does not prosper, as Guy's gloom alienates Emily. (There's an unintentionally amusing scene straight out of *The Addams Family*, in which Guy and Emily sit in the fogbound, malarial-looking swamp surrounding their house, the wind howling in their ears, and Guy asks her, "Aren't you happy here?") Soon, he hatches a lunatic plan to avoid his fate. He builds a special crypt with multiple escape hatches and loads it with provisions—the coffin even has escape tools mounted on its inner lid. Despite these precautions, he's still tormented by hallucinatory dreams in which his gadgets fail one by one, leaving him trapped in the tomb. Emily calls in Dr. Miles Archer, her old beau and a friend of Guy's, who warns her that Guy's obsession may trigger the seizure that he dreads. Miles and Emily decide that the only way to cure Guy is to exhume his father and prove that he wasn't actually buried alive. Unfortunately, the contorted corpse that falls out of the tomb seems to prove that he *was*. Guy snaps, and falls forward in the trance he had always dreaded. Emily's father, Dr. Gideon Gault, is on hand to pronounce Guy dead, and, in the movie's only effectively nightmarish sequence, the paralyzed man is prepared for the grave as we eavesdrop (via voiceover) on his terrified thoughts.

And so Guy is buried—along with any further attempts at logic or plausible plotting on *Premature Burial*'s part. Before he can expire, he's inadvertently rescued by a pair of grave robbers in the employ of Dr. Gault, who, it transpires, wants to experiment on his "late" son-in-law's body. Guy takes this unsentimental attitude poorly; he kills the grave robbers and the doctor, then stalks back home to find his bride. Guy buries her alive, for no apparent reason save madness. Miles tries to intercede and Guy starts to wallop him with a shovel; then Kate shoots her brother(!). Kate tells Miles that Emily had plotted to drive Guy mad, and had planted a ringer corpse in his father's tomb(!!). Kate had known all about the plot, but didn't tell Guy because she had no proof(!!!) None of which explains much of *anything*—like why Guy killed Emily when he had no knowledge of her scheme, or why Kate would kill her beloved brother to save a stranger, or...but you get the idea. It's a dumb climax at best.

The Premature Burial was a milestone in the occasionally stormy relations between AIP and its star producer/director, Roger Corman. At the time, Pathé American, one of Hollywood's biggest film laboratories, was dipping its toes into the film distribution business, and thought that a Roger Corman Poe

RAY MILLAND, MISCAST AS GLOOMY GUY CARRELL, IN CORMAN'S TIRED-SEEMING *THE PREMATURE BURIAL*.

picture would be a good bet—after all, the technical team was Corman's, and the Poe stories were in the public domain. Corman had become dissatisfied with his financial arrangements with American International, and Pathé offered him better terms. Moreover, Corman badly needed to make a deal with a distributor at this point; he'd just invested a lot of his own money in the only "serious" film of his career, *The Intruder*, a sincere, hard-hitting indictment of Southern racism, and Hollywood was treating it like an unwelcome object in the punchbowl, if you get my drift. (He never made this mistake again.) Pathé agreed to release *The Intruder* as part of a package deal including a Poe movie.

The only hitch was that Vincent Price would be unavailable, since he was under a personal contract with American International. (According to Corman's autobiography, AIP made the deal with Price precisely to prevent him from taking the series elsewhere.) Corman hired Ray Milland to fill in for Price as the doomed protagonist. On the first day of the shoot, however, AIP's Jim Nicholson and Sam Arkoff dropped by the set, sporting wide grins, and cheerfully informed Corman that they were partners again. Arkoff had phoned Pathé and reminded them that AIP was one of their lab's biggest customers—and that this arrangement might change if Pathé began copying the studio's most lucrative idea. Pathé hastily bowed out of the project, selling its interest in the film back to Nicholson and Arkoff. AIP patched things up with Corman after two months of negotiations,

essentially by honoring the terms of Pathé's deal. (*The Intruder*, by the way, was left to die without decent distribution.)

Corman used virtually the same crew as on the first two Poes; Daniel Haller's set designs and Floyd Crosby's photography are just as strong as ever. But, as I've already indicated, *The Premature Burial* was considerably less fortunate in its script. Corman hired screen veteran Charles Beaumont and Ray Russell, another gifted writer and, with Beaumont, a member of the little "school" of fantasy and horror authors that had coalesced around *Playboy*. While signing on for the screenplay, Beaumont and Russell reportedly forgot that Poe's "The Premature Burial" isn't even a story; it's an essay, which meant that the film plot had to be cobbled up entire. It's unclear just whose decision it was to recycle so much of the first two films for a third go-around, but there's little that's fresh or involving about this rehash. The incoherent and nonsensical ending is a worse problem; what the hell happened? Given the caliber of the screenwriters, it's tempting to speculate that some hamfisted script-doctoring was involved.

The Premature Burial's biggest problem, though, is the fact that the lead role clearly is suited for Vincent Price's flamboyant theatrics. Milland's more restrained, urbane style is all wrong for the part, making him seem simply cold and irritable, and often silly. Lines that should be delivered with Price's extravagant passion fall flat. Milland himself seems to sense how badly things are going; he muddles through the role, flaccid and embarrassed-looking. It's as bad a piece of miscasting as I've seen, and a complete waste of Milland's talent. (Corman got a considerably better performance out of Milland in his 1963 science fiction project, *X—The Man With the X-ray Eyes*.)

TALES OF TERROR
American International, 1962

P, D: Roger Corman
S: Richard Matheson
"Morella": Starring Vincent Price (*Locke*), Maggie Pierce (*Leonora*), Leona Gage (*Morella*). "The Black Cat": Starring Vincent Price (*Fortunato Lucresi*), Peter Lorre (*Montressor Herringbone*), Joyce Jameson (*Annabel Herringbone*). "The Facts in the Case of M. Valdemar": Starring Vincent Price (*Valdemar*), Basil Rathbone (*Carmichael*), Debra Paget (*Helene Valdemar*), and David Frankham (*Elliot James*).

Nightwalkers rating: 💀💀½

Tales of Terror is a marked improvement over the tedium of *The Premature Burial*, not least because it restores Vincent Price to his proper place at the center of AIP's Poe cycle. It's literally a mixed bag, an anthology movie made up of three stories of varying quality. As Roger Corman once told writer Ed Naha, "I was getting a bit tired of the Poe films by this time…I was exhausted. With *Tales of Terror*, we tried to do something a little different." Richard Matheson was brought back to the series to adapt four Poe pieces into three film vignettes (yes, that math is correct), each starring Price. Two of the tales at least succeed in breaking out of the series formula, and one is a comedic gem that would serve as inspiration for Corman's near-classic horror comedy *The Raven*.

The least of the stories comes first: "Morella" is yet another tale of dark obsessions and family secrets, this time with an overtly supernatural twist. It's intermittently effective, but numbingly reminiscent of the previous Poe

A TRILOGY OF SHOCK AND HORROR!

TALES OF TERROR in COLOR

…and there was an oozing liquid putrescence all that remained of Mr. Valdemar." POE

"I had walled the black monster up within the tomb." POE

ROGER CORMAN · RICHARD MATHESON · JAMES H. NICHOLSON · SAMUEL Z. ARKOFF · AMERICAN INTERNATIONAL

entries (as well as the greatly superior follow-up, *The Tomb of Ligeia*). In a crumbling New England mansion, its rooms impossibly thick with cobwebs and roaming tarantulas(!), lives an embittered old man, Locke. Locke's beloved wife, Morella, died in childbirth twenty-six years before, swearing vengeance on the baby. In the intervening years, Locke has kept the daughter, Leonora, away at boarding schools. Now she's caught some conveniently fatal disease (she *looks* healthy enough) and has returned to spend her last few months with the father she never knew. Alas, she finds that Locke is hardly the warmest of parents; she also discovers that her demented dad has kept Morella's mummified corpse in his bedroom. No points for guessing that Morella's vengeful spirit catches up with her erstwhile family (be sure to look for the flaming chicken coop from *House of Usher* in the final blaze).

Very much better is "The Black Cat," Matheson's comic reshuffling both of the title story and Poe's "The Cask of Amontillado." The story concerns a drunken lout (Peter Lorre) with the improbable monicker of Montressor Herringbone. His attractive and long-suffering wife, Annabel, begins an affair with a foppish wine connoisseur, Fortunato Lucresi (Vincent again), which sets Montressor's stewed brains boiling with thoughts of revenge. Montressor contrives to murder both Annabel and Fortunato, entombing them behind a cellar wall, but his crime is discovered when it emerges that Montressor had drunkenly walled his wife's detested cat in with them; its angry yowls alert two snooping policemen. This slight tale provides a vehicle for both Lorre and Price to display considerable and rarely seen gifts for comedy. Price's mincing Fortunato sends up his own flamboyant image quite effectively, providing a welcome breath of fresh air after all these

Mystery and Imagination: Edgar Allan Poe in Film

neurasthenic antiheroes. Lorre is just as good as the titanically smashed Montressor, who communicates in Popeye-style non sequiturs and muttered asides. Note the hurt-puppy quality with which he responds to the imprisoned Fortunato's pleas: "Haven't I convinced you of my sincerity yet? I'm genuinely dedicated to your destruction."

The final story, "The Facts in the Case of M. Valdemar" returns *Tales of Terror* to a serious vein, with one of Poe's more interesting minor tales, and one refreshingly free of mouldering mansions and depressives (although Matheson has tarted it up with a love angle missing in the original). Valdemar (Vincent), an elderly gentleman of great dignity and good will, is dying. His last days have been eased by a reptilian mesmerist, Carmichael (Basil Rathbone), whose hypnotic suggestions have eliminated much of Valdemar's pain. In return, Carmichael asks only to be allowed to conduct an intriguing experiment: he wants to hypnotize Valdemar *at the point of death*. Valdemar agrees, over the opposition of his wife, Helene, and his doctor. The ensuing experiment holds Valdemar in state of half-life, his mind alive and his body dead but suspended in time; his disembodied voice reverberates in the air, begging for release, an eerie broadcast from the Beyond. Carmichael, however, has no intention of freeing Valdemar unless Helene agrees to marry him. At last the affronted dead man rises, rotting and dissolving into goo, and carries the hypnotist back with him to the shadowlands.

Critical response to *Tales of Terror* was muted. Like Corman, many reviewers seemed tired of the Poe series; *The New York Times* called it "absurd and trashy," which seems overly harsh. The movie did $1.5 million in its initial release, results that were down a bit from earlier AIPoes but still plenty healthy enough to keep the series going.

Over the long run, however, *Tales of Terror* proved to be rather influential. For one thing, the movie seems to have paved the way for a resurgence of anthology horror pictures, a format that hadn't gotten much exercise since 1945's classic, *Dead of Night*. Possibly this was due in part to the fact that effective horror anthologies are hard to pull off; it's difficult to sustain that fragile, "horrific" spirit over the abrupt and repeated shifts in tone necessitated by the format. Nonetheless, within a few years after *Tales of Terror*, anthologies were popping up all over, including Amicus Productions' seemingly endless series (*Dr. Terror's House of Horrors, Asylum*, and others) and one-offs such as Mario Bava's 1963 compilation, *Black Sabbath*.

More important, *Tales of Terror* initiated the popular rediscovery of an earlier generation of horror stars. AIP co-head Jim Nicholson made a point of courting Lorre and Rathbone for this movie; Boris Karloff would soon begin working for the company as well. The easy oversimplification is "aging stars fallen on hard times"—definitely an exaggeration in the case of Karloff, who was frenetically active in television and elsewhere throughout the fifties and early sixties—but it is true that their likes fell into disfavor at the studios during the era of naturalistic "mumblers" like Brando and James Dean. By the time of *Tales of Terror*, Lorre was grossly overweight and ill, and Rathbone was, by some accounts, quite bitter over the decline of his often-brilliant career (ahead lay tripe like 1967's *Hillbilly in a Haunted House*). Even in their final years, however, these consummate pros possessed a style and effortless grace not often seen on the screen today.

Price once reminisced about those days in *Cinefantastique*: "All of us spoke with trained accents…we were different in our approach to acting—[and] if you wanted to stay in the business, you bloody well went into costume pictures." The ultimate success of *Tales of Terror* was that it inspired AIP and its imitators to give the established horror personalities of the thirties and forties—Lorre and Rathbone, Karloff, Lon Chaney, Jr., and others—a last burst of stardom, or a reasonable facsimile thereof, before a new audience.

THE MASQUE OF THE RED DEATH
American International, 1964
P, D: Roger Corman
S: Charles Beaumont and R. Wright Campbell
Starring Vincent Price (*Prince Prospero*), Hazel Court (*Juliana*), Jane Asher (*Francesca*), David Weston (*Gino*), Patrick Magee (*Alfredo*), Nigel Green (*Ludovico*), Skip Martin (*Hop Toad*), and John Westbrook (*the Red Death*).

Nightwalkers rating: 💀💀💀💀

The Masque of the Red Death is one of the high-water marks of modern Gothic cinema. No polished, mannered gem like *Curse of the Demon* or *The Haunting*, it's ambitious, original, uneven, sometimes pretentious, occasionally sloppy, and ultimately brilliant.

Throughout the early 1960s, AIP dabbled in coproducing films shot in Europe, particularly England and Italy. Pleased with the cost-effectiveness of European work, the company's managers decided to move the Poe series to England for *The Masque of the Red Death*. Upon arriving at Elstree Studios, Corman was delighted to find and use ornate sets from *Becket* and other expensive costume epics, which give his film an exceptionally sumptuous look. More important, *The Masque of the Red Death* was graced with an unusually thoughtful screenplay by fantasist Charles Beaumont and Corman's friend R. Wright Campbell. The resulting film owes less to Poe than to the somber imagery of Bergman's *The Seventh Seal*, which Corman greatly admired.

The script employs two Poe tales as its starting point, the title story and Poe's brief vengeance tale, "Hop-Frog." Set in a surreal, mist-shrouded medieval Italy, *The Masque of the Red Death* opens as a mysterious stranger in scarlet robes confronts an elderly peasant woman. He produces a white rose, which turns blood-red in his hand, and gives it to the woman, telling her to return to her village and announce that the day of their deliverance is at hand. The doomed peasants take hope, for their village is sorely oppressed by Prince Prospero, a vicious sadist.

Prospero and his troops enter the village and, emboldened by the stranger's message, two peasants insult the prince. The two—a youth, Gino, and an older man, Ludovico—are condemned on the spot, but are saved by the pleas of a peasant maiden, Francesca, who is Gino's lover and Ludovico's daughter. Prospero is intrigued by Francesca's beauty and innocence. Prospero's henchman, Duke Alfredo, says, "Can such eyes ever have known sin?" Prospero responds, with a sigh of satisfaction, "They will, Alfredo, they will." The peasant woman who received the sign is found mottled with the ghastly blood-blemishes of the Red Death, a virulent plague. Prospero seizes Francesca and her menfolk as prisoners, and orders his soldiers to burn the village to the ground. Its "deliverance" has arrived.

Safe in his fortress, Prospero's obsession with Francesca grows, for she is "a true Christian believer," whose strength of faith rivals his own in Satan. Gino and Ludovico are imprisoned, while Francesca is ensconced in Prospero's depraved court, much to the dismay of the his jealous favorite, Juliana. The prince's court is filled with debauched aristocrats who perfectly reflect Prospero's disgust for humanity. "Continue with your merrymaking. Act according to your desires," he tells them—a classic devil's invitation. Meanwhile, the Red Death ravages the countryside. Prospero has refugees and late-comers of all ranks killed by his archers, although, on a characteristic whim, he orders one small girl from the village spared. The "Hop-Frog" subplot intrudes; a dwarf entertainer, Hop Toad, loves a beautiful midget dancer, Esmerelda. After she is treated with casual cruelty by Duke Alfredo, Hop Toad swears revenge. The cunning dwarf ingratiates himself with Alfredo by suggesting a novel stunt for the prince's upcoming masked ball—the duke will dress as an ape, in a costume of the dwarf's devising, while Hop Toad plays his keeper.

Juliana, hoping to eliminate her rival, tries to help Francesca and her men escape to the plague-ridden wasteland outside, but Prospero discovers the plan and foils it, then forces Gino and Ludovico to play a form of Russian roulette with five daggers, one of them poisoned. Ludovico attempts to stab Prospero, who runs him through. The prince then banishes Gino from the castle, to certain death from plague; but Gino meets the mysterious stranger in red, who tells him to wait for Francesca to join him. Juliana tries to win back Prospero's heart by consecrating herself to Satan's service, only to be bloodily slain by the prince's hunting falcon.

The masked ball begins. Hop Toad leads in Duke Alfredo, dressed in ape garb, and claims his revenge by burning him to death in front of the assembled company. Prospero, amused by the scene, orders Hop Toad rewarded for the "entertainment." The prince then notices that one of the costumed revelers is wearing robes entirely of red, a color forbidden due to its association with the plague. He pursues and confronts the masked figure, who he assumes to be some sort of Satanic emissary. But the Red Death is unimpressed by Prospero's faith: "Death has no master. Each man creates his own heaven, his own hell." The Red Death moves among the revelers, spreading disease with every swirl of his cloak; the dying nobles arc and twirl in a surreal Dance of Death before collapsing at Prospero's feet. The dying prince seizes the Red Death's mask and sees that Death's face is *his own*, looking back at him dispassionately.

The film ends with a disturbing and austerely beautiful scene. The Red Death sits on the hilltop where we first met him, playing cards with the little girl whom Prospero spared from his archers. Through the mists, other colorful figures appear—a Green Death, a Yellow Death, and more, each the attendant spirit of some deadly plague. The Deaths greet each other and recount their night's work; a hundred thousand dead in China, and so forth. The Red Death says that six have been spared from his efforts: Gino and Francesca, Hop Toad and Esmerelda, the little girl and an old man. The Deaths disperse, leaving behind the chaos of existence, in which any justice seems random and meaningless.

The Masque of the Red Death is often described as "the best-looking" of the Poe films, and it's easy to see why. Those gorgeous leftover sets, as well as other interiors designed by Robert Jones and Colin Southcott, are lyrically photographed by Nicolas Roeg, an accomplished British cinematographer who went on to become a well-respected director in his own right (*Don't Look Now*, *The Man Who Fell to Earth* and others). Prospero's chambers, each decorated (as in Poe's story) in a single brilliant hue, as well as the enigmatic Deaths, are filmed with a sinister opulence; the movie only rarely lapses into the faintly cheesy television-ish look that mars some Corman efforts. Corman's direction is tauter than usual, and keeps the story moving briskly, avoiding the somewhat funereal pacing of some earlier entries in the series.

Prospero proved to be one of Vincent Price's most memorable roles. He plays the character with a silky menace and, thankfully, without a hint of tongue in cheek. It's a nice break from the shuddering, timorous heroes of the previous Poe movies. The film's other performances are uniformly excellent with the exception of Jane Asher's, whose Francesca is

convincingly vapid. The movie features brief but graceful turns by familiar faces such as Patrick Magee and Nigel Green, and Poe veteran Hazel Court is particularly good as Prospero's cast-aside mistress, in what proved to be her last film role (save for a bit part in the third *Omen* film in 1981). Court, who was pregnant during filming, retired after the movie was completed and began what became a thriving career as a sculptor.

Above all, the film's script is a marvel, weakened only by the arbitrary insertion of "Hop-Frog"; these sequences could be excised completely from the film without affecting the main story line, and seem added only to increase the running time. Nevertheless, the dialogue is consistently literate and thought-provoking, although it occasionally lapses into pseudo-profundity—it's easier to *ask* these rather familiar philosophical questions than it is to *answer* them, after all. Still, movies generally do such a wretchedly poor job of dealing with ideas, as opposed to emotions, that I find it exciting when one even tries to do so.

Prospero is fascinatingly complex, and rather sad for all his evil. The prince sees that "the world lives in pain and despair." He cannot believe in a God who would create such a sewer, and people it with men and women he regards as little better than vermin. "If there was a God, he is long since dead. Someone—or something—rules in his place," and for Prospero, that something is manifestly Satan, the god of "reality and truth." He's detached and almost gentle, demonstrating little interest in Francesca's body. Instead, it's her mind and soul he wishes to seduce. He is, in his way, painfully honest and sincerely committed to his philosophy. At one point, he remarks that "I'm not corrupting...I'm instructing."

The Masque of the Red Death received generally excellent reviews, although predictably a few critics thought that this "mere" horror movie was overreaching. Box-office receipts were rather tepid, possibly because the film rocketed over the heads of AIP's usual teen audience. In the years since, however, the movie's reputation has only grown. *Cinefantastique* put it rather well: "Had [*Masque*] been shot in a foreign language and subtitled, it would probably still play at art and revival houses today."

THE TOMB OF LIGEIA
American International, 1964

P, D: Roger Corman
S: Robert Towne
Starring Vincent Price (*Verden Fell*), Elizabeth Shepherd (*Lady Rowena Trevanion* and *Ligeia*), John Westbrook (*Christopher Gough*), Oliver Johnston (*Kenrick*), Derek Francis (*Lord Trevanion*), and Richard Vernon (*Dr. Vivian*).

Nightwalkers rating: 💀💀💀½

The Tomb of Ligeia ended Roger Corman's Poe series on a satisfyingly high note. Corman fans differ over whether *The Masque of the Red Death* or *The Tomb of Ligeia* is the more accomplished film. I lean to the former, but prefer to simply rank these two very different pictures as the director's best work. Considered together, they're all the more impressive for being polar opposites. The opulent colors and overtly surreal character of *The Masque of the Red Death* make it the splashier of the pair, but *The Tomb of Ligeia*, with its bleak, almost monotone palette and chilly emotional climate, is just as unforgettable.

Poe's "Ligeia" is a slight if famous piece, and nearly plotless; its unnamed, overwrought narrator tells of his maddening love for his first wife, Ligeia, and her eventual illness and death. Grief-stricken, he moves from the Continent to England and marries Lady Rowena Trevanion, only to watch her sicken as well, of a mysterious malady. Rowena apparently dies, then revives; but now has (or is it only his fevered imagination?) the face and form of his lost Ligeia. Corman and screenwriter Robert Towne brilliantly expanded on the themes of this brief story to create perhaps the most literate and subtle Poe film to date.

In 1821, Verden Fell buries his beloved Ligeia in a crypt on the grounds of his ancestral home, a manor house built amid the ruins of an ancient abbey. Ligeia, a sultry brunette, was a strange woman who insisted that she would return from the grave by sheer force of will. Fell is tormented by her memory, half-terrified, half-hoping she'll keep her promise. A mysterious black cat (who has wandered in from a different Poe story) installs itself near Ligeia's crypt. The gloomy Fell, who is intense in the same sense that the Pacific Ocean is damp, meets and wins the heart of Rowena, a vibrant young blonde who resembles Ligeia (as well she should, since they're played by the same actress). The black cat, which seems to act as Ligeia's surrogate, attacks Rowena, and later attempts to lure her to her death in a bell tower.

Soon afterward, Verden and Rowena marry, and on their honeymoon he cheers up sufficiently to seem more or less human. On returning to the grim manor house, however, he quickly slips back into his pattern of moody obsession, and disappears for hours each night. Rowena receives signs of her dead rival's displeasure; in one memorably chilling scene, she hears sounds in her bedroom one night, and after lighting a lamp discovers her own hairbrush covered with black hairs—Ligeia's color. Later, while entertaining guests, Verden discusses his interest in the then-new science of hypnotism, and demonstrates it on Rowena; while in a trance, she begins speaking in Ligeia's voice, telling him "I will *always* be your wife."

Rowena, skirting the edge of madness, discovers the ghastly reason for her husband's nocturnal disappearances. Before dying, Ligeia had thoroughly hypnotized her doting husband, convincing him that she would not and could not die. Obedient to her will, Fell has unearthed Ligeia's body and now keeps it in a secret bridal chamber in the bowels of the house, where he visits her each night, literally entranced. The necrophilic nature of these visits is blatant. Rowena discovers Fell ris-

VINCENT'S VERDUN FELL SINKS INTO DANGEROUS MADNESS IN *THE TOMB OF LIGEIA*.

ing from a bed in which Ligeia's improbably well-preserved corpse lies, limbs open in the classic love-doll position. Verden, sanity snapped, is attacked by the demonic cat and in his dying struggles manages, as you may have guessed, to set his house ablaze. (Shots from the *House of Usher* fire, including the burning chicken coop, are trotted out once again.) Rowena is rescued, but something about her enigmatic expression suggests that *Ligeia* may hide behind those eyes.

The *Tomb of Ligeia* was the first and only of Corman's Poe pictures to feature real locations, which open the film up quite a bit and alleviate some of the oppressively stagebound, repetitious feeling of the earlier entries. Exteriors were filmed at a ruined twelfth-century monastery and adjacent sixteenth-century manor house that Corman found after a manic weekend of rent-car driving, either in Norfolk or East Anglia (accounts vary). Interiors were shot at Shepperton studios near London, as Corman couldn't get permission to shoot inside the manor house. This was just as well. As the cast and crew readied the sets for the fire sequence, someone lit a cigarette and the entire stage burst into flames prematurely. Price managed to pull his costar out of harm's way, but both apparently were in real danger. (Quoth Corman: "I didn't even get it on film.")

Corman has said that he intended to make Ligeia part horror and part love story, and this balance is nicely struck in the script by Robert Towne (best known today as the screenwriter of *Chinatown* and *The Last Detail*). It's very nearly a masterwork, darkly intelligent and kinky, in a somber sort of way. A number of questions are raised and never answered. Fell's hypnotic trance doesn't explain the hairs in Rowena's brush, or her possession by Ligeia while under hypnosis. Even so, this ambiguity is also faithful to the spirit of Poe's story, whose mad and drug-addled narrator is never sure whether what he perceives is reality or illusion.

Towne was unhappy with the casting of Price in the lead role, which he felt should go to a younger actor (he'd envisioned Richard Chamberlain). Nevertheless, Price's performance in the film is one of his best. Price's Verden Fell is a visually arresting conception, dapper in (dyed) jet-black hair, funereal garb, stovepipe hat, and dark granny glasses. (As at least one person has noted, he looks like a photographic negative of white-haired Roderick Usher.) More important, Price is unusually restrained and effective, making his character seem pitiable, not villainous; his dark obsession is oddly reminiscent of Jimmy Stewart's in Hitchcock's *Vertigo*. As Rowena, Elizabeth Shepherd is interestingly unbeautiful, with a kind and intelligent face. Yet she's quite different as Ligeia, in a way that goes beyond hair color; the first time I saw *Ligeia*, I didn't realize the two characters were played by the same woman until the credits.

The *Tomb of Ligeia* was Vincent Price's favorite of the series, the one he felt came closest to capturing the claustrophobic beauty of Poe's prose. Many critics agreed, giving Corman the kind of praise many more "respectable" directors can only dream about. The critic for the London *Times*, seat of high-church culture in Britain, was moved to call *The Tomb of Ligeia* "a film which could without absurdity be spoken of in the same breath as Cocteau's *Orphee*."

❧ 8 ❧

OUT OF SPACE AND TIME

"Cosmic" Horror

THE OLDEST AND STRONGEST EMOTION OF MANKIND IS FEAR, AND THE OLDEST AND STRONGEST KIND OF FEAR IS FEAR OF THE UNKNOWN.

—H. P. LOVECRAFT

There has never yet been a first-rate film based on the work of H. P. Lovecraft, who was, in the estimation of many, the greatest American master of horror fiction. The following selections chronicle some interesting attempts, including a pair of films that are not directly based on Lovecraft but that owe something to the peculiar type of Gothic horror he invented.

Howard Phillips Lovecraft may or may not have been "his own most fantastic creation," as Vincent Starrett once dubbed him, but he did accomplish the not inconsiderable feat of making his predecessor and only rival in American letters, Edgar Allan Poe, seem relatively normal and well-adjusted. Lovecraft was born into a proud New England family of steadily declining means; after his father died insane, he was raised by a mentally unstable mother who kept her child virtually cloistered from the outside world until her own commitment to an asylum, well after he reached adulthood. He was strange, withdrawn man, dogged by ill health and poverty, and haunted throughout his life by vivid nightmares of cyclopean beings and nonhuman civilizations. Lovecraft identified so intensely with the eighteenth century—with its literature and with its architectural remnants in his beloved Providence, Rhode Island—that he

PETER CUSHING FLINCHES FROM THE DEADLY PAW OF *THE CREEPING FLESH*'S SHISH KANG.

essentially became a mental inhabitant of that era, even adopting its characteristic literary style and spellings. In his obsession with antiquity and his absolute rejection of the present, Lovecraft was perhaps the purest Gothic personality since Horace Walpole. He enjoyed a very modest success in the pulp magazines of the twenties and thirties before dying, virtually unknown, in 1937, at the age of forty-seven.

In the intervening years, Lovecraft's reputation has grown prodigiously, first in Europe and then in the land of his birth. The casual reader may find his work off-putting. His pseudo-antique prose is always lucid, but it's also adjective-laden, florid, convoluted—everything writers have been taught to avoid since Hemingway. Moreover, his story construction is usually pretty weak, with endings telegraphed well in advance, and an irritating overreliance on *a final horrifying revelation in italics*. But Lovecraft has won lasting fame not for his style, but for his concepts, which amount to nothing less than a complete cosmology, a self-contained Gothic universe. In the place of stale ghosts, vampires and the like, Lovecraft created a pantheon of beings he called Great Old Ones. They were the vast, incomprehensible creatures of his nightmares, as powerful and remote as gods, who once ruled our planet and who someday will again; who left behind enormous ruins in remote desert wastes and hidden polar valleys; who lie in wait, in ocean depths and deep space and hidden dimensions, to be summoned forth by mad or foolish humans who stumble upon the right gateways. Many of his stories are set in and around crumbling, "shadow-haunted" Arkham, a New England hamlet with an unusual number of otherworldly menaces lurking nearby.

Lovecraft's universe, dubbed "the Cthulhu Mythos" after one of his dark gods, has proven enormously influential to modern horror, and a number of other authors have chosen to write directly in its tradition. There's even a movement in modern ritual magic dedicated to the proposition that Lovecraft's dreams were mediumistic in nature, and that the entities of his stories actually exist in some space-time adjacent to ours (sleep tight, America). Lovecraft's tales involve a certain degree of mayhem, but their real power springs from a purely intellectual horror, which may explain why film, so good with emotions, so very bad with ideas, hasn't yet done him justice. His vision is the most pro-

foundly pessimistic position to be found in all of literature, a horror that makes the evisceration fantasies of Stephen King seem like episodes of "Gilligan's Island." In Lovecraft's world, everything we think we know—love and hate, good and evil, heaven and hell—is a pathetic fiction. The Great Old Ones are reality.

THE HAUNTED PALACE
American International, 1964
P, D: Roger Corman
S: Charles Beaumont
Starring Vincent Price (*Joseph Curwen* and *Charles Dexter Ward*), Debra Paget (*Ann Ward*), Lon Chaney, Jr. (*Simon Orne*), John Derkes (*Jacob West*), Leo Gordon (*Ezra Weeden*), Elisha Cook, Jr. (*Peter Smith*), and Frank Maxwell (*Marinus Willett*).

Nightwalkers rating: 💀💀½

There's a certain delicious irony in the fact that one of the better filmic adaptations of H. P. Lovecraft's work was promoted as "Edgar Allan Poe's *The Haunted Palace*," although I doubt Lovecraft would have savored the jest much.

The Haunted Palace is based, not on Poe's poem, but on one of Lovecraft's longest stories, "The Case of Charles Dexter Ward." Lovecraft completed this novella about the sorcerous resurrection of the dead in 1928 but, being the aggressive go-getter he was, never even got around to typing it up before his death in 1937. (Four years later, his friends August Derleth and Donald Wandrei saw the story into print.) Only tangentially a part of the "Cthulhu" cycle—it's set in Arkham, with stray references to his cosmic deities—"The Case of Charles Dexter Ward" is nonetheless one of Lovecraft's most colorful and atmospheric tales. At least in outline, Roger Corman's *Haunted Palace* follows its literary original more closely than most Lovecraft adaptations, although it takes abundant liberties and loses much of that fragile Lovecraftian eeriness.

In 1765, the fed-up residents of Arkham interrupt the magical rituals of a local wizard, Joseph Curwen, and burn him at the stake. As the flames reach him, Curwen promises to rise from the dead and curses the villagers and their descendants. One hundred and ten years later, Curwen's great-great-grandson, Charles Dexter

Ward, arrives in Arkham to claim his ancestor's strange castle as an inheritance. Ward and his beautiful wife, Ann, find the inhabitants of the doomed-seeming village to be a superstitious, unfriendly lot, still living in dread of the curse. Some Arkhamites are bizarrely mutated, missing eye sockets and other accessories.

The castle, however (transported from Europe, stone by stone), is comfortable enough, maintained by a caretaker named Simon Orne. Charles becomes fascinated with a mantel painting of Curwen, who exactly resembles him, and rapidly falls under the dead wizard's spell. Curwen takes over his descendant's body and identity, and begins his experiments again with the help of Simon (who's 150 years old and he's been waiting patiently for Curwen all these years, presumably dusting occasionally). His goal: to breed human women with the extradimensional Elder Gods(!).

Curwen/Charles revives his long-dead mistress from her coffin-dust (a vague nod toward the necromantic themes that play a far larger part in Lovecraft's tale), and begins murdering the descendants of his persecutors, one by one. This provokes the villagers once again to seize torches and burst into the castle, just in time to prevent Ann's ritual violation by an Elder God, who looks like a four-armed Creature from the Black Lagoon. Finally, Charles seems to reclaim his body, but a typically bleak Corman ending reveals that the dead wizard is still in charge.

Corman conceived his Lovecraft film as *The Haunted Village* while he was finishing *The Premature Burial*. While in development, the film went through a series of casting changes; Ray Milland and Hazel Court from *The Premature Burial*, slated to play Charles and Ann, were replaced by Vincent Price and Debra Paget, while Lon Chaney, Jr. stepped into the role of Simon when Boris Karloff became too ill to participate. American International then insisted on the title change, over Corman's protests, to cash in on the success of the director's Poe series.

The Haunted Palace lacks the energy and verve of the best Poe flicks; it's a little too slow-moving and stately. Even so, it's involving and good-looking, with some excellent, moody photographic work by Floyd Crosby. An exceptionally fine, brooding score by Ronald Stein also contributes to the film's effectiveness. The cast is studded with journeyman actors you'll recognize from any number of television Westerns, none of whom really stand out with the possible exception of perennially worried-looking Elisha Cook, Jr. More interesting is Lon Chaney, Jr., by this time deep, deep into the bottle, who still turns in a creditable performance as Simon. (With the exception of 1964's *Witchcraft*, this was Chaney's last quality genre movie; some *amazing* dreck followed.) Debra Paget, an extraordinarily lovely actress, invests the sketchy and fairly thankless role of Ann with some genuine human concern.

Unsurprisingly, though, *The Haunted Palace* is first and last a Vincent Price vehicle, and he was in fine shape for it. Listen to him wrap that ermine voice around this line: "I'll not have my fill of revenge…till they have felt, as I have, the kiss of fire on their bare flesh!" Few actors can even *recite* dialogue like that with a straight face, much less make it sing. Price could.

DIE, MONSTER, DIE!
American International, 1965
P: Pat Green
D: Daniel Haller
S: Jerry Sohl
Starring Boris Karloff (*Nahum Whitley*), Nick Adams (*Stephen Reinhart*), Freda Jackson (*Letitia Whitley*), Suzan Farmer (*Susan Whitley*), and Terence DeMarney (*Merwyn*).

Nightwalkers rating:

Well, I'm glad Lovecraft didn't live to see *this* one. *Die, Monster, Die!*, a film about as frightening as *The Care Bears Movie*, is a trenchant reminder of just how bad AIP products *not* directed by Roger Corman can be.

Die, Monster, Die! is a tedious adaptation of a famous H. P. Lovecraft tale, "The Colour Out of Space." Set (of course) in Lovecraft's haunted New England, the novelette tells the story of Nahum Gardner and his family, an affable farming clan whose lives are horribly changed after a mysterious meteorite buries itself in their land. Vegetation grows in disturbing, unnatural ways, glowing with an eerie phosphorescence of an indescribable color. Wildlife and farm animals, too, begin to succumb to the unearthly pestilence, mutating and ultimately crumbling while alive. Soon the rot begins to affect the hapless Gardner family as well. It's one of Lovecraft's best stories, restrained and effective, with a minimum of his usual purplish prose.

Die, Monster, Die! retains this basic plot and the marvelously Lovecraftian name "Nahum," but transplants the setting to England and adds an Ancient-Family-with-Dark-Secret storyline that seems lifted from one of Corman's Poe pictures. The story opens as Stephen Reinhart, a middle-aged-looking American college student, arrives in Arkham, a fearful and unfriendly

A MELTY-FACED FREDA JACKSON MENACES NICK ADAMS IN THE EMINENTLY FORGETTABLE *DIE, MONSTER, DIE!*

English hamlet. He's there to visit his best girl from college, Susan Witley, but quickly learns that the Witleys are both loathed and feared by their neighbors. The Witleys turn out to live in an exceedingly haunted-looking manor house, surrounded by a weirdly desolate matte-painting wilderness apparently the size of, say, Japan. Susan herself is sunny and vapid in the Marilyn Munster role.

Steve meets her father, wheelchair-bound scientist Nahum Whitley, and her mysteriously ill mother Letitia, who never leaves her curtained bed. Nahum is clearly unhappy with Steve's arrival; he has mysterious doings under way in a padlocked greenhouse and a dungeon-like cellar. Letitia, on the other hand, begs Steve to take Susan away. Our hero, suspicious, snoops around the house, which is filled with bizarre statuary and books with titles like *The Cult of the Outer Ones*. We learn that Nahum's father, Corbin Witley, was a much-feared demon worshipper who horrified the area and died under mysterious circumstances. (Despite the director's fondness for ominous zoom-ins on Corbin's portrait, this information has no relevance whatever to the subsequent plot.) Ultimately, Steve discovers Nahum's secret: he's discovered a green-glowing meteorite on his property, whose radiation causes plants and animals to grow strangely.

His greenhouse contains basketball-sized tomatoes and large part-lizard, part-turkey creatures in cages.

Letitia turns out to be mutating due to the meteorite's radiation, her face covered with green cottage cheese. She goes mad and attacks Steve, who whomps her with a candelabrum. Letitia then runs out of steam and dissolves, unconvincingly. A subsequent overexposure to the green meteor makes Nahum go all melty-faced in minutes. Steven grabs several medieval war implements off the wall and manages to do the aged scientist no damage at all. Nahum makes a grab for his daughter but stumbles off a second-floor landing. As he hits the floor, it bursts into flame, God knows why.

Die, Monster, Die! is a sad example of the sorts of things Boris Karloff found himself doing in the later 1960s. (His next film would be *Ghost in the Invisible Bikini*, which is actually a hell of a lot more fun than this thing.) During this shoot, he was recovering from a nearly fatal bout of pneumonia, contracted while filming AIP's *Black Sabbath* in Italy in 1963. Saddled with permanent lung damage, he was forced to perform with a minimum of movement for several years. Karloff still managed to do everything he could with the part. Even from a wheelchair, he's magnificently sinister, doing his best to rescue Jerry Sohl's lame dialogue with that unforgettable, antique-velvet voice. English actress Freda Jackson does nearly as well with the smaller role of Letitia Witley. By contrast, Nick Adams fills the role of Steve Reinhart like caulking compound. A strangely ferret-faced actor, Adams could be reasonably effective in supporting roles—he even received an Academy Award nomination for his work in 1963's *Twilight of Honor*—but failed to catch fire as a leading man; his spotty career was cut short by a fatal drug overdose in 1968.

As for the major culprits behind the camera: Daniel Haller began directing after a successful career as an art director that included his beautiful work on Roger Corman's Poe pictures. As a director, he worked primarily in television, which doubtless proved congenial to his flat, unimaginative style. Screenwriter Jerry Sohl was also a science fiction author who is remembered today, if at all, for mediocre science fiction novels like *Point Ultimate* and *The Altered Ego*. His script for *Die, Monster, Die!*, however, doesn't really come up to mediocrity.

THE CURSE OF THE CRIMSON ALTAR

(Initial U.S. release title: *The Crimson Cult*)
Tigon British/American International Pictures, 1968 (U.S. release, 1970)
P: Louis M. Heyward
D: Vernon Sewell
S: Mervyn Haisman and Henry Lincoln; additional material by Gerry Levy
Starring Boris Karloff (*Professor Marshe*), Christopher Lee (*J.D. Morley*), Mark Eden (*Robert Manning*), Barbara Steele (*Lavinia Morley*), Michael Gough (*Elder*), Virginia Wetherell (*Eve*), and Denys Peek (*Peter Manning*).

***Nightwalkers* rating:**

The Curse of the Crimson Altar is a crashing disappointment. It's often dismissed as a simple no-hoper, but it's actually something worse, a competent-seeming movie that betrays a promising buildup and disintegrates into the lamest sort of tripe.

The film is based, without credit and in the loosest way possible, on a 1932 Lovecraft novelette, "The Dreams in the Witch House." The tale concerns a typically Lovecraftian seeker after things forbidden, a college student who inhabits the former lodgings of a seventeenth-century witch. The witch and her demon familiar begin appearing to him in increasingly vivid dreams, luring him to other-dimensional realms; eventually these dream-world experiences spill over into the student's waking life.

The Curse of the Crimson Altar opens with a satanic ceremony presided over by a magnificent-looking Barbara Steele as the Black Witch, Lavinia Morley, resplendent in green body paint and ram's horn headdress. With the aid of an amusingly clad assortment of flunkies, she forces Peter Manning, a travelling antique dealer, to sign his name in a satanic ledger, sacrificing his soul to the Devil, or something to that effect. Some days later, Peter's brother, Robert, begins looking for him. Peter's last message was written from Cragston Lodge in Greymarsh, a village that was the Manning family's ancestral home. The squire of Cragston, J. D. Morley, denies any knowledge of Peter, but Robert decides to investigate anyway. Robert arrives in Greymarsh on Witch's Night, a village celebration commemorating the burning of the Black Witch (yes, the same one) hundreds of years before. (A handful of scenes nicely contrast the prosaic reality of twentieth-century life with hints of darker pagan survival, and are easily the most effective elements in the picture.)

At Cragston Lodge, Robert meets Squire Morley, an affable fellow who invites him to stay for awhile. Robert does so, and soon avails himself of Morley's beautiful daughter, Eve, in some mildly racy groping. Cragston Lodge is a creepy sort of place; as Robert remarks to Eve, "It's as if Boris Karloff's going to pop up any moment…"; seeing as he shortly *does*, this seems an overly cutesy gag. Karloff plays local supernatural scholar and red herring Professor Marshe, who briefs Robert on the legend of the Black Witch and the deadly curse she laid on her tormentors' families—a curse that has struck again and again throughout the centuries since her death. Robert learns that a Manning was Lavinia's chief accuser(!). Also contributing to the muddle is Elder (Michael Gough), a senile servant who pops up periodically to issue mysterious warnings.

Meanwhile, Robert suffers through a horrifying series of dreams in which Lavinia and her crew attempt to force him to sign the Devil's book, just as his brother had. Robert becomes convinced that the dreams are recollections of real events and, upon searching his room, finds a secret passage leading to the chamber in which the "nightmares" took place. The jig being nearly up, Morley ties up our hero and prepares to sacrifice Eve to Satan, only to be stopped at the last instant by Professor Marshe to the rescue. Cragston Lodge begins to burn. As the assembled cast watches from below, Morley appears on the roof and, as the flames lick ever closer, *changes into Lavinia before our very eyes.*

That's right—Christopher Lee is actually Barbara Steele. An unexpected ending, you'll agree. Actually, to fully convey the offensive stupidity of this idea, I should emphasize that the film cheats outrageously. Lee gives no hint or clue of villainy at all until the last few minutes, leaving me to wonder whether the Lee-to-Steele transformation wasn't a last-minute punt on someone's part. The bizarre revelation irritates because it seems so utterly arbitrary; why not Karloff as Lavinia? Or Eve, the daughter? Or the butler? Or the family dog?

Perhaps the most interesting bit of trivia concerning *The Curse of the Crimson Altar* is that Tigon, taking a page from Hammer's book, shot the film in a genuine country mansion—Grimsdyke House, the Middlesex home of Sir William Gilbert of Gilbert and Sullivan fame. The production was able to rent Grimsdyke House for a week's shooting for less than what a single day's studio space would have cost. What's particularly interesting about this is that Grimsdyke, a marvelously atmospheric setting, is also one of the more famous of England's reputedly haunted houses. (I've been in a few of these, and believe me, you wouldn't laugh quite so hard if you were alone at midnight with weak flashlight batteries.)

As for the performances, it's unfortunate that Karloff, Lee, and Steele are never given a scene together, but the bizarre plot twist of course made that impossible. Lee is unusually low-key and restrained—which makes the eventual revelation all the harder to swallow. Barbara Steele, who has said of *The Curse of the Crimson Altar* that "I just flew in and did that to pay the rent," is used simply for marquee value and her striking looks; her brief appearances as Lavinia

Barbara Steele's arresting appearance in *Curse of the Crimson Altar*, **one of the movie's few interesting features.**

call for little in the way of acting. This was Steele's last starring part in a horror film, and it's difficult to resist speculating that the dispiriting nature of the role and the movie itself didn't play at least some part in her decision to swear off genre films.

Sadly, a permanent retirement lay ahead for Boris Karloff. Always the quintessential professional, he gives his all as Professor Marshe; a *New York Times* review noted, "Karloff acts with a quiet lucidity of such great beauty that it is a refreshment to hear him speak old claptrap." The old trouper was eighty, confined to a wheelchair, and suffering from a collapsed lung, but these trifles didn't keep him from shooting night scenes outdoors for the film in a freezing rain, which led to double pneumonia. Incredibly, he recovered sufficiently to appear in *four* Mexican horror films (in scenes shot rapidly, back to back) and several American television shows before succumbing to respiratory disease in February 1969. "I intend to die with my boots and my greasepaint on," he once said—and he did.

THE DUNWICH HORROR
American International, 1969
P: James H. Nicholson and Samuel Z. Arkoff
D: Daniel Haller
S: Curtis Lee Hanson, Henry Rosenbaum, and Ronald Silkosky.
Starring Dean Stockwell (*Wilbur Whateley*), Sandra Dee (*Nancy Wagner*), Ed Begley (*Professor Armitage*), Lloyd Bochner (*Dr. Cory*), Sam Jaffe (*Old Whateley*), Joanne Moore Jordan (*Lavinia Whateley*), Donna Baccala (*Elizabeth Hamilton*) and Talia Coppola (*Cora*).

Nightwalkers rating:

Daniel Haller's second stab at adapting Lovecraft to film is a distinct improvement over *Die, Monster, Die!*, but at best it's a pallid rendition of what is often considered Lovecraft's best story.

"The Dunwich Horror," sold to the April 1929 issue of *Weird Tales* for the princely sum of $240, is a cornerstone of the Cthulhu Mythos; it's an imaginative and grimly effective novelette that shows off the most memorable feature of Lovecraft's work—that sense of a universe of ancient, monolithic evil glinting through the cracks in commonplace "reality." Set near haunted Arkham, it concerns horrendous twins fathered by a mysterious dark force and born to Lavinia Whateley, half-crazed daughter of an old wizard. One, Wilbur, is destined to become a sorcerer in his own right; the other is a mysterious, deadly creature kept locked away, who "look[s] more like the father," in Lovecraft's memorable phrase. Lovecraft sketches in the truly horrifying events that follow with a restraint and subtlety fully worthy of M. R. James, and for once his narrator isn't tongue-tied in the face of otherworldly evil; instead of his usual unnameable, indescribable menace, we get a good look at at least one of these boogers.

Haller's *Dunwich Horror* opens with Lavinia's birth pangs, attended by robed, cultish-looking figures, and then jumps forward some years. Wilbur Whateley, now grown, asks Professor Armitage of Miskatonic University to borrow the school's priceless copy of the *Necronomicon*, the text that "unlocks the gate to another dimension," that of Lovecraft's Great Old Ones. Whateley isn't the eight-foot, mutated monstrosity of Lovecraft's story; instead, he's a slight, intense-looking young fellow with a hypnotic gaze. Even so, Armitage understandably refuses his odd request. Wilbur's trip isn't wasted, however. He charms a young librarian, Nancy, into accompanying him back to his home

SANDRA DEE PLAYS A STUPOR CONVINCINGLY IN A BIZARRE RITUAL FROM *THE DUNWICH HORROR.*

in Arkham, where he lives with his intensely creepy grandfather. Once there, he sabotages her car and feeds her potion-laced tea. Later, they go on picnics.

Wilbur and his grandpa share the house with a mysterious something locked in a room at the top of the house. The movie cuts repeatedly to the locked door, rattling beneath heavy blows. Nancy begins having strange nightmares of orgiastic ceremonies involving seminude savages and lots of body paint (the first of several unfortunate bows to sixtiesness in *Dunwich Horror*). Meanwhile, Professor Armitage and a friend of Nancy's, Elizabeth Hamilton, fail to persuade Nancy to leave the Whateley's. By now she's thoroughly drugged and under Wilbur's spell. He takes her to a Stonehenge-like ruin on a mountaintop, the Devil's Hopyard—a magnificently eerie setting straight from Lovecraft's story, which reminds you of Haller's fine art direction on the Corman Poe films—and has sex with her on an ancient altar, in a hallucinogenic sequence that seems inspired by, or lifted from, *Rosemary's Baby*.

Meanwhile, while sneaking around the Whateley's house, Elizabeth inadvertently releases Wilbur's inhuman "brother" from his attic prison, and is promptly devoured. The creature is seen briefly in a flash of tentacles, but mostly is represented by flashing strobes and breathing noises (to be fair, Lovecraft's original beastie is usually invisible as well). The extradimensional what-is-it begins ravaging the local countryside, killing at random, while Wilbur snatches the university's copy of the *Necronomicon*, which he needs to open the portal that will bring Elder Gods to earth. Armitage confronts the wizard in a final, magical showdown, which is somewhat muddled. Wilbur is struck by lightning, apparently to tidy up the plot. His alien sibling appears and disappears. A coda reveals that Nancy is carrying Wilbur's child; Whateley's line continues.

Roger Corman served as executive producer on *Dunwich Horror*, and according to Corman scholar Mark Thomas McGee, preproduction was troubled, with numerous script rewrites. Even after a usable screenplay was developed, the Motion Picture Association of America threatened to give the film and "X" rating based on its review of the finished script, both for its sporadic nudity (milk-mild by modern standards) and for a scene calling for Sandra Dee to "undulate sexually," whatever that might mean. The movie as filmed does follow the story moderately closely, even including the novelette's chilling (and largely irrelevant) episodes concerning demonic whippoorwills that gather to catch the escaping souls of dying Whateleys. However, while many of the story's events are incorporated, the film ultimately seems to be little more than a garden-variety black magic story; once again, that ineffable Lovecraftian quality is largely absent.

A bewildering variety of actors were considered for the key role of Wilbur, from James Caan to Fabian(!). Eventually, the part went to former child actor Dean Stockwell. The flaccid script gives Stockwell little opportunity to display his considerable talents, and he looks faintly stoned throughout the film—not an impossible scenario, given the actor and the times. Nevertheless, he does bring a certain burning intensity to the role. Sandra Dee proves she can play a drugged stupor well enough. Veteran character actor Ed Begley is reliably good as Armitage; equally venerable Sam Jaffe, as Wilbur's grandfather, is given almost nothing to do, and sports a set of alarming glued-on eyebrows that look like caterpillars.

Haller's direction is no more than adequate and, other than the atmospheric scenes in the Devil's Hopyard, displays an odd lack of visual flair, considering his previous experience in art direction. And a final note, in passing: Few film scores are so bad that I find them distracting, but Les Baxter's music for *The Dunwich Horror* is one of them. It's an under-orchestrated, canned-sounding score that would seem far more appropriate in one of those interminable "Lady Chatterly" breast-o-ramas Cinemax runs after midnight.

HORROR EXPRESS
Granada Films–Benmar Productions, 1972
P: Bernard Gordon
D: Eugenio Martin
S: Eugenio Martin and Arnaud D'Usseau
Starring Christopher Lee (*Professor Alexander Saxton*), Peter Cushing (*Dr. Wells*), Telly Savalas (*Captain Kazan*), Silvia Tortosa (*Countess Irina Petrovski*), Alberto de Mendoza (*Pujardov*), Jorge Rigaud (*Count Petrovski*), Julio Pena (*Inspector Mirov*), Alice Reinhart (*Miss Jones*), Angel Del Pozo (*Yevtushenko*), and Helga Liné (*Natasha*).

Nightwalkers rating: ½

Horror Express, a *very* strange Spanish horror film, is most accurately described as a giddy combination of *Murder on the Orient Express* and *It! The Terror from Beyond Space*, the admirable little fifties science fiction thriller that served as a semiacknowledged model for *Alien*. Sounds weird, and so it is; *Horror Express* mixes a Lovecraftian premise with a lot of amusing balderdash, and vintage performances by Messrs. Cushing and Lee, imported to add class to the proceedings.

The thin but engaging idea behind this movie is an ancient, cosmic evil from the depths of space and time, a concept very much in Lovecraft's line. The entity in question is a formless, parasitic energy-being that can inhabit and possess living things, animal

THE DREAM TEAM: CUSHING AND LEE ATTEMPT TO UNRAVEL THE MONSTROUS SECRET OF THE *HORROR EXPRESS.*

or human. Marooned at our planet's dawn by its space-faring fellows, the thing has spent the last few billion years possessing trilobites, dinosaurs, and whatnot, patiently waiting for some form of earthly life to develop the technology and resources it needs to resume its voyage. (Why an energy-being would need this stuff is an unexplored question.) About two million years ago, the alien jumped into an apelike dawn man, only to be trapped in glacial ice.

In 1906, along comes English scientist Alexander Saxton, who chips the fossil out of the ice and boxes it up for shipment. The professor proposes to ship his mysterious prize across the vast wastes of Eurasia via the Trans-Siberia Express. Joining Saxton on board are a friendly scientific rival from home, Dr. Wells, and an assortment of colorful passengers including a count and countess, a police inspector and a fanatical, Rasputin-style monk. (There's also a gorgeous spy who makes not one bit of difference to the plot.) Of course, the "specimen," after thawing, quickly escapes—rather expertly picking the lock on its crate—and proves to have the ability to absorb men's thoughts with a destructive blast from its glowing red eyes. This process is fatal, as it boils the victims' eyeballs and smooths out the wrinkles in their brains, leaving the organs looking like large poached eggs. (*Really.*)

The alien-apeman is gunned down, but the entity quickly jumps into the body of another passenger, and continues stalking its victims one by one. As the train plunges on through the Siberian night, a plucky but rapidly dwindling band of survivors tries to discover who among them is harboring the eye-boiling monster. (This aspect is extremely reminiscent of John W. Campbell's classic science fiction novella, "Who Goes There?".) But wait, there's more. Saxton and Wells perform an impromptu autopsy on the apeman and discover that his eyeball fluid contains microscopic pictures of the alien's billion-year memories—tiny snapshots of a pterodactyl and a brontosaur, and a view of the earth from space! And then, as if the situation weren't complicated enough, we learn that the creature can also revive its own dead victims and direct them like a pop-eyed zombie army! Who will live? Who will die? What the hell is going on?

Yes, it's a weird *paella* of a script, all right. Still, director/screenwriter Eugenio Martin

demonstrates a blithe audacity, as does the production itself. *Horror Express* was born when producer Bernard Gordon acquired two model trains used in *Nicholas and Alexandra*, and decided to build another film around them. (They *are* great models.) The production, one of the first to be filmed at Madrid's Studio 70, relied almost entirely on the train models and two small railroad-car sets, redressed as needed to portray a succession of car interiors. This strategy allowed Martin to give the film a surprisingly polished look on what was probably a negligible budget.

The movie suffers from what one might call the "Sergio Leone effect"—just as an all-Italian Western can be disconcerting, the sight of all these swarthy Spaniards playing Russians eventually becomes a bit, ah, tittersome. An ill-chosen, Morricone-style soundtrack featuring lots of whistling adds to the vaguely spaghetti Western atmosphere, as does the dubbing (I must admit that I share the typical American distaste for dubbed dialogue). But in all, *Horror Express* works fairly well, given its premise. The action is fast paced and suspenseful; even the creature's signature death-stare is fairly unsettling, although it looks like a cheap enough effect (penlights behind painted Ping-Pong ball halves, perhaps?).

Best of all, Christopher Lee and Peter Cushing are in top form. In an interview with John Brosnan, Cushing remembered the shoot as an extremely happy one, and the two veteran players do appear to be having a fine time. Lee does his best pompous martinet, while Cushing relaxes into one of his humorous eccentrics, with some arch dialogue. Note his shocked reaction when someone proposes that he or Lee might be the monster: "Monster? We're British, you know!"

THE CREEPING FLESH
Tigon British/World Film Services, 1972
P: Michael Redbourn
D: Freddie Francis
S: Peter Spenceley and Jonathan Rumbold
Starring Christopher Lee (*Dr. James Hildern*), Peter Cushing (*Professor Emmanuel Hildern*), Lorna Heilbron (*Penelope Hildern*), and Jenny Runacre (*Emmanuel's wife*).

Nightwalkers rating: 💀💀½

Evil is a contagious disease, spread by alien blood corpuscles. That's the bizarre premise behind *The Creeping Flesh*, an incoherent but stylish horror film with science-fiction overtones that sports a highly unusual cosmic menace.

The Creeping Flesh opens in late Victorian days with an anguished Professor Emmanuel Hildern telling his story to an attentive doctor. Flashing back, a younger, more composed professor returns to his home after a scientific expedition to New Guinea. In a chest is his prize: a large humanoid but distinctly nonhuman skeleton, found in rock strata predating modern man. (Although it's never directly mentioned, it's tempting to assume the creature is extraterrestrial.) While preparing to clean the skeleton, the professor discovers that a splash of water on a severed finger bone makes it grow new flesh and blood.

In an amazingly convoluted series of deductions (strap in and try to follow this) the professor concludes from this peculiar event that the creature is "Shish Kang," an "Evil One" of ancient New Guinean superstition who will return to earth "when the sky gods weep"—rain, get it? Furthermore, upon examining the monster's blood, he learns that its tentacled corpuscles quickly attack and overwhelm normal cells. This leads Heldern to conclude that these tainted corpuscles are the root cause of all evil in the world(!). He further resolves to invent a vaccine that will free mankind from evil forever(!!).

This is of more than passing interest to Professor Hildern, whose personal life spurs much of the ensuing drama. The professor was once married to a beautiful and unfaithful dance-hall entertainer who died insane; he's terrified that his daughter, Penelope, will inherit her mother's malady. (The film treats evil, insan-

CHRISTOPHER LEE AS DR. JAMES HILDERN IN FREDDIE FRANCIS'S *THE CREEPING FLESH.*

ity, and sexual license as interchangeable, which does mesh nicely with the period's attitudes.) Acting rather more quickly than the scientific method dictates, he prepares a vaccine of monster blood, tests it on a monkey, and then injects his daughter with the substance. It becomes apparent that the professor should have watched that monkey just a *leetle* bit longer, as it abruptly keels over, apparently from a surfeit of raw evil. Penelope succumbs to the influence coursing through her veins and, like her mother before her, begins dancing badly and flirting in low taverns; eventually she kills a would-be rapist (an action that doesn't seem all that evil, by the way).

Meanwhile, the professor's ambitious and unscrupulous brother, Dr. James Hildern, learns of Emmanuel's discovery and snatches the skeleton, hoping to use it in his own research into insanity. While making his getaway, the doctor's coach is caught in a storm, and the downpour revives Shish Kang. The monster returns to confront its discoverer. Flashing forward again, it emerges that both the professor and Penelope have been incarcerated in a mental institution run by brother James; Professor Hildern's desperate, mad-sounding warnings about the Evil One are ignored by the staff. In a final revelation meant to shock, it emerges that the professor has lost a finger to Shish Kang, who presumably removed it in a spirit of tit for tat over its own lost digit.

Well! Screenwriters Peter Spenceley and Jonathan Rumbold seem to have been trying for something different, and they certainly succeeded. In some respects, the writing is fairly weak; there's a lot of clumsy expository dialogue in which characters stand around telling each other things they would already know. Dr. James

Hildern is given little development, beyond requiring Lee to be rather flatly unpleasant. (It's such a nothing role for Lee that it's faintly surprising to see that he's billed above Cushing, which rarely happened in their dual careers). By contrast, Cushing's Emmanuel Hildern is interestingly obsessive and fear-ridden, giving him considerably more depth. Lorna Heilbron, an exceptionally beautiful woman, ably plays Penelope's descent into madness (or evil, or whatever).

From a technical standpoint, *Creeping Flesh* is more than usually uneven. Freddie Francis's direction is nimble and nicely paced, but his penchant for offbeat camera work is taken to occasionally hilarious extremes, such as a point-of-view shot from *inside* the reanimated Shish Kang's head, looking out through the gooey eyeholes as if the monster's noggin were an empty jack-o'-lantern (it's a sillier reprise of the famous shot Francis employed in *The Skull*). Sets and costumes are excellent, but the monster effects, by Hammer alumnus Roy Ashton, are weak. Shish Kang is an unimpressive bogey-man that seems cobbled up from soft wax.

The Creeping Flesh received surprisingly warm reviews, considering the times and the type of film it was, and now has a minor-league cult following. Having read such sentiments for quite awhile before finally seeing the film, I was initially disappointed by the preposterous story line. However, in their recent work on Peter Cushing, writers Deborah del Vecchio and Tom Johnson interestingly point out that the story does gel beautifully, if you assume that Cushing's character is insane from the beginning! It's all there, if you look—the surreal nature of his theories; his obsession with his dead wife (he's forbidden his daughter to speak of her); his reckless decision to vaccinate his daughter against evil before she's shown any signs of madness. You could even speculate that perhaps the professor has been in that cell all along, and Shish Kang is just one more element of his mania. I doubt it's an interpretation intended by the movie's makers, but it does give *Creeping Flesh* an interesting added dimension of ambiguity.

9

SPELLS AND PHILTRES

IN THIS BOOK IT IS WRITTEN...OF SPIRITS AND CONJURATIONS;
OF GODS, SPHERES, PLANES, AND MANY OTHER THINGS WHICH
MAY OR MAY NOT EXIST. IT IS IMMATERIAL WHETHER THEY
EXIST OR NOT. BY DOING CERTAIN THINGS CERTAIN RESULTS
FOLLOW....

—ALEISTER CROWLEY, *MAGICK IN THEORY AND PRACTICE*

Our final type of Nightwalker includes those who traffic with powers of evil, witches and sorcerors.

The history of magic and witchcraft is as old as mankind; possibly somewhat older, in fact, as there are interesting indications that the Neanderthals practiced religio-magical rites as well. The popular understanding of magic today is premised on the ideas that, first, it's devoted primarily to showy displays of power, of mastery over the external world, and second, that it doesn't work. A modest study of the subject indicates that both ideas are at least cartoonishly oversimplified.

If magic were only a matter of self-delusion, you would expect it to show more imagination in an unlimited variety of rituals, beliefs,

and practices. Instead, scholars of magic have observed a remarkable unanimity of method and purpose among the world's magical systems, beneath the surface details. The *real* purpose of magic, as practiced for countless millennia by all peoples, seems to be to "complete the partial mind," as Yeats said; to shake ourselves out of the dull trance that passes as waking consciousness for most of us. Magic serves to galvanize the will, to focus and crystallize human energies toward a goal. And it does seem to bring with it power that can be felt by others, and which can serve either good or evil.

Most modern witches like to claim a direct link (which may be more poetic than factual) with a more or less benign form of nature worship existing in Europe for thousands of years, a faith that went underground during dark centuries of brutal persecution that murdered uncounted hundreds of thousands in the name of God. Nevertheless, the winners write the history books and set the tone, and witchcraft in horror movies still is most often portrayed in unrelentingly negative terms, although a few films such as *Burn, Witch, Burn!* do interestingly suggest an ongoing struggle between practitioners of white and black forms of the Old Faith.

The most interesting magician of the last few centuries unquestionably was Aleister Crowley, the Englishman who devoted his life to sifting, codifying and revitalizing the major systems of ritual magic. Crowley, who died in 1947, was one of his era's most fascinating figures. Robert Anton Wilson, a formidable writer on occult matters, has described Crowley as "a mountain climber, a hunter, an explorer, a bad poet, a prankster, a great poet, a novelist, a high initiate of yoga and magick, something of a first-class amateur scientist, and a chess master...." And a con man, an exhibitionist and an occasional sadist; and a man of power. Yet Crowley's tabloid image as "the world's wickedest man" still largely defines him to the public, and as such he provides the model for the villain in two of the Gothic renaissance's finest films, *Curse of the Demon* and *The Devil's Bride*. The demon-worshipping Father Rayner of Hammer's last horror, *To the Devil—A Daughter*, seems mutedly Crowleyan as well.

Crowley's Satanist reputation obscures a much more complex and fascinating character, yet this profoundly contrary man did little to dispel such smears. Quite the opposite, according to Wilson, "It is emphatically not true that his reputation as Satanist and Black Magician was spread entirely by his enemies; he collaborated gleefully in blackening his own character."

CURSE OF THE DEMON
(United Kingdom title: *Night of the Demon*)
Columbia, 1957
P: Hal E. Chester
D: Jacques Tourneur
S: Charles Bennett and Hal E. Chester
Starring Dana Andrews (*Dr. John Holden*), Peggy Cummins (*Joanna Harrington*), and Niall MacGinnis (*Dr. Julian Karswell*).

Nightwalkers rating:

With its rare combination of magisterial direction, strong performances, and literate, subtle screenwriting, *Curse of the Demon* ranks among the finest horror films ever made. The film is an adaptation of "Casting the Runes," by M. R. James, master of the English ghost story. Both story and film concern a curse cast by a vindictive magician, modeled on English sorcerer and all-around bad boy Aleister Crowley.

The film opens with a visit by terrified Professor Harrington (Maurice Denham) to Lufford Hall, English country home of Dr. Julian Karswell. Harrington has led a scientific exposé of Karswell's "devil cult"; now the would-be debunker pleads with Karswell to call off an unearthly pursuer. Karswell, urbane and cooly polite, not unreasonably responds, "You involved me in a public scandal. You said, 'Do your worst.' That's precisely what I did." Harrington, turned away, is subsequently killed by a wolf-headed demon.

Shortly afterward, Dr. John Holden, prominent American psychologist and fierce skeptic of the occult, arrives in London to participate in the Karswell investigation. During a brief meeting in the British Museum, Karswell manages to slip Holden a parchment marked with

THE DOG-FACED HELL BEAST OF THE OTHERWISE SUBTLE AND UNDERSTATED *CURSE OF THE DEMON*.

runic symbols—the same vehicle he used to kill Harrington. The parchment, we learn, is what bankers call a bearer instrument; whoever holds it is doomed to die on an appointed day (three days hence, in Holden's case) unless he can pass it on to a willing recipient.

The rest of *Curse of the Demon* concerns the steps

CURSE OF THE DEMON'S KARSWELL EXAMINES A TAILORING PROBLEM CAUSED BY HIS FELINE FAMILIAR.

by which arch-skeptic Holden becomes aware of the doom overtaking him and begins to fight for his life. Holden, tremendously stubborn, is initially inclined to ignore various portents—the feeling of coldness, an eerie tune drifting through his mind—but when the demon begins manifesting itself, he's frightened into belief. Holden enters into an alliance and a romance with Joanna Harrington, the unfortunate professor's daughter, and soon the couple begin a cat-and-mouse game with Karswell, attempting to ward off the runic curse by reversing it on the wizard. And if this plot description seems skimpy, well…this is one I really would hate to ruin for the neophyte.

Screenwriter Charles Bennett, a former collaborator of Alfred Hitchcock's, acquired the rights to the original M. R. James story in hopes of directing it himself, but joined forces with producer Hal Chester when he failed to win financial backing. Chester, in turn, assigned directing duties to Jacques Tourneur. Tourneur, a careful craftsman with a special talent for suspense, was nearing the end of a fruitful career that included the famed Val Lewton productions of *Cat People* and *I Walked with a Zombie* as well as the film noir classic *Out of the Past*. Tourneur had scant talent for or interest in action per se; instead, he had a far rarer and more delicate gift, one for evoking moods and for atmosphere. This is a movie of little epiphanies; like Carroll Reed's *The Third Man*, *Curse of the Demon* repays repeated viewings with a number of subtle and richly textured scenes that are, in their quiet

way, as perfect as any in the movies.

Typically memorable is Holden's first visit to Lufford Hall. He finds Karswell, demonist and murderer, entertaining local orphans as a clown, "Dr. Bobo the Magnificent." Karswell is genuinely fond of children, and seems almost affable with the man he's cursed, giving him a chance to recant. Holden's jeering disbelief goads the wizard into summoning up a cyclone—an impressive effect Tourneur was rightly proud of, created with strapped-down airplanes—sending everyone fleeing for shelter. "I didn't know you had cyclones in England," says the bewildered psychologist. "We don't. You could probably use a drink," responds the imperturbable Karswell. A later scene, in which Holden breaks into the hall only to be attacked by a demon "familiar" in the shape of a panther, is beautifully constructed and quite tense.

One famous controversy inevitably arising in any discussion of *Curse of the Demon* is producer Hal Chester's decision to include a "monster" in the picture—basically simple puppetry—rather than leaving the demon in the viewer's imagination, as Tourneur wished. To me, the demon's brief appearances at the film's beginning and end seem no worse than most special effects of the day. They're unfortunate but hardly a fatal flaw.

Compared to Dana Andrews's beautifully rounded performance in *The Best Years of Our Lives* for instance, his "Holden" seems rather flat and unappealing in his rote disbelief. Even so, Andrews's growing horror as he slowly begins to accept the incredible is quite effective. In any case, he's overshadowed by Niall MacGinnis as Karswell. MacGinnis (perhaps best known as Zeus in Ray Harryhausen's fantasy classic *Jason and the Argonauts*), a classic example of that characteristically English type, the Obscure but Brilliant Character Actor, plays Karswell with a basic decency and thoughtfulness that makes his embrace of evil seem all the more tragic.

When I think of *Curse of the Demon*, I always remember the lovely speech, written by Bennett, that Karswell gives as he walks in the woods with Holden just before the cyclone hits: "Where does imagination end and reality begin? What is this twilight—this half-world of the mind that you profess to know so much about?" This statement, like the film itself, seems to catch a fundamental truth about the nature of real magic.

THE UNDEAD
American International, 1957
P, D: Roger Corman
S: Charles B. Griffith and Mark Hanna
Starring Pamela Duncan (*Diana Love* and *Helene*), Richard Garland (*Pendragon*), Allison Hayes (*Livia*), Val Dufour (*Dr. Quintus Ratcliff*), Mel Welles (*Smolkin*), Dorothy Neumann (*Meg Maud*), Billy Barty (*the Imp*), Bruno Ve Sota (*Scroop*), Aaron Saxon (*Gobbo*), Richard Devon (*Satan*), and Dick Miller (*a leper*).

Nightwalkers rating: 💀💀💀—but wait, hear me out

With *The Undead*, I'm exercising my prerogative to shoehorn a film into this book that may or may not belong here. Certainly, "Gothic horror" seems rather too grand a label for this gloriously goofy ten-day, $70,000 quickie, shot in a converted grocery store on Sunset Boulevard. Nonetheless, it's important to the history of the Gothic renaissance, simply because this sort-of horror movie was Roger Corman's first stab at the themes he would develop with infinitely more success in AIP's Poe series. Never forget, however, that there are *two* Roger Cormans—the lightning-fast, "death-before-retakes" schlockmeister of *She Gods of Shark Reef* and *Attack of the Crab Monsters*, and the critics' darling of the sixties, the *auteur* of *Masque of the Red Death*. *The Undead* is emphatically the work of the former. Even so, despite its wretched production values and general air of incompetence, the thing displays a nonstop energy that makes it a hell of a lot of fun to watch.

The Undead was inspired by the odd fifties best-seller *The Search for Bridey Murphy*, an allegedly true account of a Colorado woman who, under hypnosis, produced extensive recollections of a previous life in eighteenth-century Ireland. *The Search for Bridey Murphy* was the first mass-market work to introduce the concept of past-life regression to a (briefly) fascinated American public. Corman thought a film based on this idea would pack audiences in. So, by the way, did the makers of *The She Creature*, *I Was a Teenage Werewolf* and *I've Lived Before*, all of which were lifted from *The Search for Bridey Murphy*. Corman's entry was originally called *The Trance of Diana Love*, but public interest in reincarnation had waned by the time shooting began, so the resourceful director changed the title and pumped up the horror elements.

The Undead concerns a past-life regression experiment conducted by Dr. Quintus Ratcliff on a hardened hooker named Diana Love (Don't you *adore* these names?). Quintus gestures hypnotically like Mandrake the Magician—"There's no end to my hand…it's like riding a tiny roller coaster…"—and Diana is transported back through the centuries to the Middle Ages, and a life as an innocent young girl named Helene. Helene has been unjustly accused of witchcraft, and is slated for execution. Somehow, however, Diana's spirit can communicate with her past-life counterpart (an idea that makes hash out of any reincarnation scheme I can think of) and helps her escape from her captors.

Helene takes refuge with a kindly gravedigger and village idiot, Smolkin. In one mildly horrific scene, part of Helene's escape involves being sealed in a coffin, under its resident corpse. Smolkin communicates almost entirely via morbid nursery rhymes, such as "Hey diddle diddle, the rat and the fiddle, the corpse jumped over the tomb." (He's got reams of this stuff.) Smolkin delivers Helene to the protection of Meg Maud, a kind-hearted, low-rent Margaret Hamilton, the only witch in the area who hasn't sold her soul to the devil. Those who have are led by Livia, a sultry and well-constructed witch who loves Helene's suitor, the knight Pendragon. Livia has framed Helene in hopes of winning his heart (am I going too fast?). Livia's a powerful witch, able to transform herself into a cat, an iguana(!), and a bat (although, on closer examination, it's not a bat—it's the flying Venusian creature first featured in the thrifty Mr. Corman's *It Conquered the World*).

Meanwhile, Dr. Ratcliff is afraid that his experiment will change history, with potentially catastrophic results. Ratcliff resolves to enter Diana's past to directly observe events as they unfold, via a none-too-well explained technique he learned from "certain priests in Nepal" (which he pronounces "nipple," by the way). Ratcliffe successfully plops down in the Middle Ages, nude like that fellow in *The Terminator* save for his wristwatch, which he later (after he has obtained pants) uses to convince Livia that he's a sorcerer.

A witches' sabbath ensues, attended by a fey-looking Satan. Dr. Ratcliff explains to Helene that, if she doesn't go through with her fated execution, all of her future selves will never be born (huh?). The souls of Diana and her other incarnations ring in, begging her via voiceover to let them all live. Persuaded, Helene goes cheerfully to her execution; in the present, Diana awakens, having gained Helene's purity and spiritual grace, and resolves to change her life. Dr. Ratcliff, however, is trapped in the past, and the Devil has a good laugh at his expense. Ahem.

As weird as this movie is, it could have been weirder. Charles Griffith's original script rendered the dialogue for all the past settings in strict iambic pentameter, the verse form often favored by Shakespeare and Milton. According to Griffith, Corman loved the idea at first, but got cold feet at the last minute and had the whole thing rewritten into regular English, more or less. Griffith wasn't the only disappointed participant; in interviews, cast members Mel Welles and Bruno Ve Sota recalled nearly choking to death while shooting the picture. Corman was disinclined to shell out for a fog machine, and instead gave the tiny grocery-store soundstage an appropriately mysterious look by lighting cre-osote smudgepots.

The cast, heavily salted with Corman regulars, manfully uphold the script (although Pamela Duncan, in the crucial dual role of Diana/Helene,

is rather stiff). Particularly noteworthy is the beautiful and sadly underappreciated Allison Hayes, who will always be best remembered as the oversized *femme fatale* of *Attack of the Fifty Foot Woman*.

I hardly know how to rate *The Undead*. Most of the horror films of the fifties and sixties, including Corman's later work, took themselves rather seriously. At worst, they tended to slide into boring mediocrity. *The Undead* is something else again. It's not horrifying, to say the least, nor is it by any stretch of the imagination a good movie in the conventional sense. But it possesses the saving grace of virtually all of Roger Corman's work: not a frame of it is dull.

HORROR HOTEL
(United Kingdom title: *City of the Dead*)
Vulcan/Amicus, 1960 (U.S. release, 1961)
P: Donald Taylor and (uncredited) Milton Subotsky
D: John Moxey
S: George Baxt (substantial contributions by Milton Subotsky)
Starring Christopher Lee (*Professor Alan Driscoll*), Dennis Lotis (*Richard Barlow*), Betta St. John (*Patricia Russell*), Patricia Jessel (*Elizabeth Selwyn* and *Mrs. Newless*), Venetia Stevenson (*Nan Barlow*), Tom Naylor (*Bill Maitland*), Valentine Dyall (*Jethro Keane*), Ann Beach (*Lottie*), and Norman MacOwen (*Reverend Russell*).

Nightwalkers rating:

IMMORTAL WITCHES READY A RELUCTANT SACRIFICE IN AMICUS'S FIRST SCARE SHOW, *HORROR HOTEL*.

Judged on purely visual terms, *Horror Hotel* is easily one of the most atmospheric horror films ever made. This dank, shadowy, fog-shrouded, every-face-lit-from-below movie (there isn't a sun-lit shot in the entire film) makes *The Seventh Seal* seem like *The Blue Lagoon*. The movie attached to this creepy cinematography, however, is uneven and problematic. *Horror Hotel* meanders along that thin and uncomfortable line separating the exaggerated emotions and perspectives of Expressionism from flat-out silliness, demonstrating flashes of near-brilliance and capital-D Dumb in about equal measure.

Horror Hotel opens in 1692, in the tiny Massachusetts hamlet of Whitewood, a clump of black huts dimly visible through rolling fog-machine mists. Elizabeth Selwyn is to be burned at the stake for witchcraft and ritual murder. The villagers, a snarling, pinched-looking lot straight out of a Bruegel painting, scream for Elizabeth's blood. Her paramour, Jethro Keane, offers up a whispered prayer to Lucifer. As Elizabeth is tied to the stake, the already black sky darkens further; then, suddenly—we learn that this sequence is a lecture being delivered by an intense, dangerous-looking college professor, Alan Driscoll.

At Driscoll's encouragement, a student, Nan Barlow, decides to travel to modern-day Whitewood to research a term paper on witchcraft. She does so over the protests of her brother, scientist Richard Barlow, and her boyfriend, Bill Maitland, both of whom consider her studies to be "fairy-tale mumbo-jumbo" (thus dismissing the entire field of anthropology). Nan drives to Whitewood, pausing to pick up a hitchhiker who materializes out of the fog. This man bears a distinct resemblance to Jethro Keane, as seen in the preamble. He tells her that "time stands still" in Whitewood, then *disappears* from the car when she arrives in the village! Nan, oddly unbothered by this event, locates the Raven's Inn, right next to a graveyard from which unhealthy-looking vapors boil.

Inside the inn, which is filled with shadows as thick and black as slate shingles, Nan is greeted, barely, by the forbidding innkeeper, Mrs. Newless. Mrs. Newless bears a distinct resemblance to Elizabeth Selwyn (try sounding her name backwards). Nan settles into her room then explores the town in a beautifully filmed sequence; the other inhabitants of Whitewood drift like wraiths through the fog, always pausing to stare silently at her. Upon visiting the town's old church, she finds it locked and inhabited only by old, blind Reverend Russell, who tells her that evil rules in Whitewood, and warns her to leave. (A nervous type, which Nan obviously is not, might be forgiven for concluding that this

community is, ah, troubled.) She also meets the sole normal-seeming person in town, the reverend's granddaughter Patricia, who's recently arrived to run the local bookstore.

Nan learns from an old book that Elizabeth Selwyn had marked a girl for sacrifice by taking a personal object of hers "to summon her through," leaving a dead bird and a sprig of woodbine in its place; the terrible deed took place on Candlemas Eve, February 1. Then, Nan finds that she's misplaced her locket, discovers a dead bird and sprig of woodbine in her bureau drawer, and—hey! whaddya know! It's February the first! Even Nan, who so far has displayed the intelligence of a jar full of marbles, begins to get worried—rather too late, however, to avoid being taken to a subterranean altar and ruthlessly killed by a robed and hooded circle of worshippers that includes Selwyn/Newless and Professor Driscoll! Yes, forty-five minutes into *Horror Hotel*—well over halfway through—the woman we'd assumed was our protagonist gets her ticket punched. Despite the occasional silliness of the preceding events, it's a potent and effective shock, which takes a similar gambit in *Psycho* a lot farther.

A few weeks later, Bill and Richard are naturally getting worried; their fears are not alleviated when Patricia comes to town with Nan's locket, which was slipped to her by Mrs. Newless's fearful, mute servant, Lottie (later killed for her indiscretion). In Whitewood, Reverend Russell tells Richard that the townspeople have a centuries-old pact with the Devil, giving them eternal life in exchange for the annual sacrifice of a girl on each of two holidays—Candlemas, and the "witch's Sabbath," which is (natch) *tonight*. The local witch folk have pencilled in Patricia for the festivities, and the pattern of dead bird and woodbine is repeated. The final confrontation occurs in the festering graveyard. Bullets have no effect on the immortal witches, but the shadow of a cross wielded by Bill causes them to burst into flames.

Horror Hotel is something of a landmark, since it was the first horror movie made by the newly born film company Amicus, soon to become Hammer's only serious rival as a successful and prolific maker of British-made genre films. The script was based on a story by Amicus cofounder Milton Subotsky, who (according to him) also made substantial, uncredited contributions to the shooting script by George Baxt.

Subotsky, who seems to have been a thoughtful and ferociously well-read man, reportedly found even Hammer's violence distasteful—he once told writer John Brosnan, "Sometimes I envy their bad taste but I just can't do that sort of thing." (Lord knows what he thought of *Dawn of the Dead*).

At any rate, Subotsky strongly favored a more mannered and subtle approach, and it's certainly reflected in this film, which some adherents consider to be one of the few serious rivals to Val Lewton's marvelously atmospheric work of the 1940s. The monochrome camerawork, by Desmond Dickinson, belies its forty-five-thousand-pound budget; the movie's look is nothing less than exquisite, with shadows as substantial as beefsteak, never-ending fogs that seem almost corporeal, and unforgettably grotesque faces worthy of Fellini. As more than one writer has pointed out, the rotting ambience of Whitewood seems very close indeed to H. P. Lovecraft's universe. Baxt and Subotsky also manage to pull off some effective and memorable moments of psychological horror, such as the Vanishing Hitchhiker riff. There's another nice *frisson* when Nan prepares to join the other guests of the hotel at a dance in a room adjoining hers; we hear the party's music and voices, but when she opens her door, the party room is vacant and silent.

This said, there's no getting around the fact that *Horror Hotel*'s story simply strains too hard for its effects. The various sinister developments are laid on with a trowel, as I trust my description makes clear, so thickly that any believable motivations, particularly on Nan's part, simply go out the window. The movie's impact is further blunted by its inadequate score, a small-ensemble (and undoubtedly cheap) affair that involves electric guitars and flutes, and occasionally underlines tense moments with laughably inappropriate bursts of low-grade jazz.

BLACK SUNDAY (1960), DIRECTOR MARIO BAVA'S EXTRAORDINARY TRIUMPH OF GOTHIC ATMOSPHERE.

Performances range from competent to excellent. Lee's role calls for pretty standard villainy of the kind he could have delivered by mail. The British cast acquits itself well with American accents, although those of Bill and Richard seem to fade in and out.

It's hard to know how much of *Horror Hotel*'s strengths and failings to attribute to its director, John Moxey. Subotsky, a hands-on producer if ever one lived, was always dismissive concerning the importance of the director's role, and I'm inclined to agree with him—in the case of movies produced by Subotsky. On the other hand, while Moxey rarely returned to horror in feature films, in 1972 he directed the television-movie blockbuster *The Night Stalker*, probably the finest television horror tale ever.

BLACK SUNDAY
(Italian title: *La Maschera del Demonio*)
Galatea-Jolly, 1960 (U.S. release: American International, 1961)
P: Massimo DeRita (American version produced by Lou Rusoff)
D: Mario Bava (American version directed by Lee Kresel)
S: Ennio de Concini and Mario Serandrei
Starring Barbara Steele (*Princess Asa Vaida* and *Princess Katia Vaida*), John Richardson (*Dr. Andreas Gorobec*), Andrea Checchi (*Dr. Thomas Kruvajan*), Ivo Garrani (*Prince Vaida*), Arturo Domenici (*Javutich*), and Enrico Olivieri (*Constantin*).

Nightwalkers rating:
💀💀💀💀

The United States print of *Black Sunday* begins with an amusing warning from American-International Pictures, announcing that the producers feel "a moral obligation" to warn us that the movie should be seen only by "persons with mature minds." (Unfortunately, I wasn't able to obtain that sort of help for this book, so I had to tackle it myself.) The movie that follows very nearly lived up to its hype. British censors prevented its release in the United Kingdom for nearly eight years, and several other countries banned it outright as well.

Today, however, *Black Sunday* is remembered not for its shocks but for its luminous black-and-white photography and incredibly rich atmosphere. Critics are overly fond of the phrase "visual poetry," but it's hard to avoid it in the case of this movie, which may be the best-looking horror film ever made, *not* including the Universal classics of the 1930s.

Black Sunday opens in a haunted corner of early seventeenth-century Moldavia, at the execution of a high priestess of Satan, Princess Asa Vaida, and her lover and servant, Javutich. Sentenced to die by her own brother, Asa promises to return to "torment and destroy" the succeeding members of the House of Vaida. She's killed in a particularly horrid manner; a metallic Mask of Satan, lined with sharp spikes, is hammered on to her strikingly beautiful face. The locals then attempt to burn her body, but are unable to do so when the heavens open up and drown the flames—a scene deliberately, and perversely, reminiscent of the legend of Christ's Passion. Two centuries later, a middle-aged doctor, Thomas Kruvajan, and his younger assistant, Andreas Gorobec, are travelling through the same area on their way to a medical conference. Kruvajan bribes the coach driver to take a little-used forest road, which travels near the crypt in which Asa was entombed. The coach breaks down near a fog-shrouded castle (not some matte painting, but the genuine article, a magnificent pile near Rome belonging to Italy's ancient Massimo clan).

"THE GIRL WHOSE EYELIDS CAN SNARL": THE INIMITABLE BARBARA STEELE IN *BLACK SUNDAY*.

While they watch the driver repair his vehicle, the doctors hear odd noises nearby and investigate. They discover that the wailing sound comes from a broken pipe organ in a ruined crypt, the place where Princess Asa was ultimately entombed. (The use of sound in this sequence, as throughout the film, is impressively subtle and effective.) Poking around, Kruvajan and Gorobec discover Asa's sarcophagus, which features a glass window positioned so that, if Asa were to revive, the sight of a stone cross above the tomb might stop her progress. A large bat attacks Krujavan, who, while flailing with his cane to defend himself, shatters Asa's window, destroys the cross, and drips a bit of his own blood into the tomb. Exiting the crypt, they meet one of the adjacent castle's inhabitants—Princess Katia of the House of Vaida, direct descendant of (and look-alike for) Asa. Dr. Gorobec obviously has a thing for Katia. In the tomb below, Asa's corpse is seething with unholy energies; new eyes bubble up in her skull like poached eggs, alarming and dislodging a nest of scorpions.

In the castle, Katia's father, Prince Vaida, is filled with foreboding. It's Black Sunday, two centuries to the day since his dark ancestor's death, the day on which legend says that the dead may walk the earth; and the wind is howling about his castle in a most disconcerting way. Meanwhile, in a storm-swept cemetery, Asa's servant Javutich claws his way out of his grave. Prince Vaida falls in a fit, and his family sends for one of the doctors Katia had met. However, Javutich is already one step ahead, rustling up a carriage and picking up Dr. Kruvajan, whom he delivers to Asa's crypt. Kruvajan is vampirized by the revived sorceress. The doctor, now in league with Asa, visits the castle and in turn quenches his thirst on the prince.

Meanwhile, Gorobec has become alarmed at his friend's mysterious absence and goes to the castle himself, where, in company with a savvy, Van Helsing-like priest, he discovers a network of secret passages connecting the castle with Asa's tomb. The pair soon discover Kruvajan in Javutich's empty grave. The priest shows us that, in this universe, vampires are killed with a stake through the *eye*, not the heart. After dark, Javutich seizes Katia and delivers her to Asa, who wants her blood to gain the vitality to survive until the next Black Sunday, a century hence. Gorobec and a torch-wielding mob, hastily organized by the priest, arrive at the tomb just in time; they very nearly stake Katia rather than Asa, until the providential sight of a cross at Katia's neck makes the proper course of action clear.

This brooding masterpiece made two substantial reputations, those of director Mario Bava and horror actress *par excellence* Barbara Steele. Bava entered directing after a long apprenticeship as a camera operator and, later, a director of photography, and always remained strongly concerned with the visual components of his films, serving as director of photography as well as director on *Black Sunday*. He was never better than in this film, which uses low-angle shots, fog-machine mists and what the British Film Institute once called "Bava's restlessly prowling camera" to create an unforgettable Land of Always-Night, a surreal wasteland nearly devoid of sun and life.

Black Sunday is almost alone among the movies of its era in employing the Expressionist look and sensibility of Universal's horror work. Hammer films, by contrast, seem almost documentary in their use of lush but prosaic settings and costumes. Moreover, the British censors had a point; *Black Sunday* contains scenes of almost nightmarish intensity—as when Gorobec mistakes Asa for Katia, and the witch's robes part to reveal rotted flesh beneath her gorgeous face. In this combination of the poetic and the terrifying, the movie seems to mark a blending of, or a transition between, two very different eras in film history.

As memorable as Bava's contributions was the performance of Barbara Steele, the only actress to achieve true, Karloff-style horror stardom. Steele, an Englishwoman of Irish descent, began her career in repertory theater and was signed as a starlet-in-training with Britain's J. Arthur Rank Organization. Steele moved to Hollywood when her contract was sold to Fox. According to her, she spent two years "sitting on the beach waiting to be called," an experience that left her "completely demoralized." Disgusted, she walked off the set of an Elvis Presley movie and moved to Italy, where *Black Sunday* made her an overnight star.

A good deal of Barbara Steele's magic lies in her appearance, and by this I do not refer to her beauty; beautiful women have been five-a-dollar in the movie business since Edison's days. Steele's is an undeniably *strange* face, with a broad dome of a forehead, emerald eyes compelling and almost too large, her mouth and chiseled cheekbones sensual yet oddly mannish. As Italian director Riccardo Freda rather famously said, "There are times, in certain conditions of light…when her face assumes a cast that doesn't appear to be quite human." Her appearance seems all the more significant in light of the fact that, to English-language audiences, her performances are essentially silent. Nearly all of her Italian horror roles, as well as her small part in AIP's *The Pit and the Pendulum*, were redubbed with other women's voices for United States and British release.

Although she made nine more horror films by 1966, Steele has always been a reluctant scream queen, far prouder of her small but interesting role in Fellini's *8½*. In interviews, she often expresses a fondness for "real" situations and emotions—ironic considering the degree to which she has become an icon rather than an actress. As film scholar David J. Hogan said, "Steele became a symbol, a personification of unpleasant emotion. Her remarkable face doomed her; she watched as her directors had all the fun." In 1980, Steele remarked, "I'm always playing these stylized roles, full of tension…but most of these roles are destructive and negative. I've had to force myself to play them." Steele withdrew from the screen in the later 1960s, thereafter choosing appear in only a handful of small but showy roles in films as diverse as *Pretty Baby* and *Piranha*. In 1991, however, she returned briefly to horror by playing Dr. Julia Hoffman in the short-lived revival of the Gothic television series "Dark Shadows."

Unlike many of the movies in this book, *Black Sunday* has been recognized as a classic almost from the day of its release, receiving respectful attention even from mainstream critics; *Time* praised its "brilliant intuitions of the spectral." The movie's reputation is especially impressive considering that, objectively speaking, there's absolutely nothing new or unique in the film's content; its basic setup was old even for its time, even trite. But *Black Sunday*'s stark beauty and authority make it seem as fresh and original today as it did three decades ago.

BURN, WITCH, BURN
(United Kingdom title: *Night of the Eagle*)
Independent Artists/American International Pictures, 1962
P: Albert Fennell
D: Sidney Hayers
S: Charles Beaumont, Richard Matheson and George Baxt
Starring Janet Blair (*Tansey Taylor*), Peter Wyngarde (*Norman Taylor*), Margaret Johnston (*Flora Carr*), Colin Gordon (*Lindsay Carr*), Anthony Nichols (*Harvey Sawtelle*), and Kathleen Byron (*Evelyn Sawtelle*).

***Nightwalkers* rating:** 💀💀💀½

"I do *not* believe." This arrogant declaration opens *Burn, Witch, Burn*, a subtle tale of witchcraft and black magic, beautifully scripted by two of the best modern fantasy authors.

Burn, Witch, Burn is based on Fritz Leiber's much-admired 1943 horror novel *Conjure Wife*, which science fiction author and prickly critic Damon Knight once called "easily the most frightening and…the most thoroughly convincing of all modern horror stories." The entertaining conceit underlining both book and movie is that all women are witches—the *bona fide* spell-casting kind—and that men are basically just too dumb and too wrapped up in their own affairs to notice! (I see some of you nodding.) A pompous academic who believes he's a self-made success discovers his wife's magical efforts to defend and advance his career, and forces her to abandon this "superstition"; disasters quickly follow, as he's literally cursed by a circle of jealous faculty wives.

In *Burn, Witch, Burn*, the skeptic in question is Professor Norman Taylor, professor of sociology at Hempnell Medical College in England. (The juxtaposition of this quiet campus setting with a series of increasingly chilling

events provides one of the film's many pleasing textures.) Taylor is a bitter enemy of superstition who has made the opening statement his credo—"four words necessary to destroy the power of the supernatural," as he says. The sociologist, who is handsome and popular with his students, is on a fast track for advancement at the small, cliquish college—much to the irritation of his colleagues' wives. At a deadly dull card party at Norman's house, tension between the rival wives fairly crackles in the air, while the husbands are completely oblivious. Later, while Norman prepares groggily for bed, his wife, Tansy, frantically searches the room until she finds a hex talisman hidden by Flora, her main rival.

After establishing the rhythm of Tansy's eerie double life, the plot sprints forward. Norman discovers a good-luck charm that Tansy has pinned into his coat pocket. Angered, he searches the house and finds a good many baubles of the witch's trade. Apparently feeling his ego is on the line, Norman forces Tansy to burn all her charms, to her evident horror. Within a day, the couple's life begins to crumble under an onslaught of apparent bad luck and coincidence. A pretty student of Norman's becomes hysterical and accuses him of rape; her jealous boyfriend threatens violence. That evening, a malign and invisible entity snuffles and snarls at their door.

Tansy realizes just how serious their predicament is. She performs a ritual in which she offers to die in her husband's place, and leaves for their seaside cottage, presumably to wait for the end. Norman pursues her, his skepticism by now fairly ragged. Near hysterics, he improvises a ritual of his own to summon her back from death, in a marvelously spooky graveyard crypt. By love or by chance, his clumsy attempt at magic works, calling Tansy back from a languorous walk into the ocean. This sequence is the real climax of the film; in the film's most unforgettable scene, Tansy appears at the crypt like Ophelia, pale and mad, dripping wet from the sea. Norman now has a fuller understanding of superstition—and of his love for his wife.

The remainder of the film is a slight comedown from the subtlety and polish of its first two thirds. Suffice it to say that Norman is finally attacked by a stone eagle, a gargoyle brought to life by Flora's magic, and that her spell is turned back on her in a fairly arbitrary way. It's an adequate closer, I suppose, but by this point the film has telegraphed its own punch with about forty too many lingering close-ups of the stone eagle, each delivered with a nudge from William Alwyn's over-insistent soundtrack. (In the same way, the British title, *Night of the Eagle*, is rather too much of a giveaway of what's really a fairly minor plot point.) The final scenes redeem the film in a neatly symmetrical moment: Norman,

TANSY (JANET BLAIR) CASTS SPELLS TO SAVE HER HUSBAND (PETER WYNGARDE) IN *BURN, WITCH, BURN*.

Artists. Matheson is notoriously hard to please concerning the execution of his scripts, but he's had nothing but praise for this movie. (Incidentally, according to him the eagle sequence wasn't *in* the script, but was added later.)

One last criticism: the movie is a trace unfortunate in the choice of leads. Janet Blair is effective in the crucial scenes, but she seems miscast. There's a farmer's-daughter, June Cleaver whole-

fleeing for his life from the spectral eagle, takes refuge in his own classroom, his proud declaration, "I do not believe," still visible on the chalkboard—and, as he cringes against the wall, we see he's inadvertently erased the "not" from the board.

The director of *Burn, Witch, Burn*, Sidney Hayer, was an interesting but minor journeyman whose best work was done for television; he's remembered, a bit, for seven episodes of the 1960s British spy-fantasy series, "The Avengers." *Burn, Witch, Burn* is by far his best film, so much so that it's tempting to attribute more of the movie's success to its screenwriters Richard Matheson and Charles Beaumont. (The script credits have been a subject of controversy; mystery novelist George Baxt has claimed extensive involvement, while Matheson maintains that Baxt's "contribution" was minimal to nonexistent.)

Matheson and Beaumont, both associated with American International at the time, decided to do the script on speculation, despite the fact that film rights to the book were held by Universal (which had already made an inferior version called *Weird Woman* in 1944). AIP was sufficiently pleased with the script to acquire the rights from Universal and finance an English-based co-production with Britain's Independent

someness to her that's wrong for Tansy, who should be a more exotic creature. Peter Wyngarde's Norman is better, but plays it a bit too thick and tyrannical to win our sympathy. (There's a hilarious story that Wyngarde, well-built and proud of it, insisted on wearing such skin-tight trousers that the director was forced to frame him almost entirely from the waist up, like Elvis on Ed Sullivan's show.)

THE DEVIL'S BRIDE
(United Kingdom title: *The Devil Rides Out*)
Hammer, 1967 (U.S. release 1968)
P: Anthony Nelson-Keys
D: Terence Fisher
S: Richard Matheson; based on *The Devil Rides Out* by Dennis Wheatley
Starring Christopher Lee (*Duc Nicholas De Richlieu*), Charles Gray (*Mocata*), Leon Greene (*Rex Van Ryn*), Nike Arrighi (*Tanith*), Patrick Mower (*Simon Aron*), Paul Eddington (*Richard Eaton*), and Sarah Lawson (*Marie Eaton*).

Nightwalkers Rating:

The Devil's Bride may well be the finest Hammer movie of all, showcasing the studio's classic strengths while avoiding the formula-bound tiredness that mars so much of its product.

The film's dead-serious and informed treatment of ritual magic reflect its origins as a 1934 best-seller, *The Devil Rides Out*, by Dennis Wheatley, one of the century's most popular writers of supernatural fiction. Wheatley was a deeply interested believer in the supernatural, and an acquaintance of then-famous "ghost-hunter" Harry Price, magician Aleister Crowley, and occult scholar Montague Summers, among others. Wheatley shared Summers's explicitly Christian interpretation of occult phenomena, and his works often feature conflict between black and white magic. Predictably, a thinly veiled Crowley figures prominently in *The Devil's Bride*, in his familiar if erroneous role as master Satanist; the villain's definition of magic—"causing change to occur by means of one's will"—is almost word for word a dictum of Crowley's.

Wheatley's beliefs meshed well with the Hammer universe of perpetual war between the forces of good and evil. In *The Devil's Bride*, the implacable foe of evil—the "Van Helsing"—is the Duc de Richlieu. The duke and his friend, manly, not terribly bright Rex Van Ryn, are sworn to protect the adult son of a mutual comrade from the Great War. (The film is set in a nicely realized 1920s rural England of manor houses and vintage motorcars.) The feckless son, Simon Aron, has become entangled in a satanic coven run by the charming but sinister Mocata. For once in a Hammer movie, the innocent corrupted by evil is male; Simon's relations with Mocata have a distinctly homoerotic undertone.

Richlieu and Van Ryn begin to battle for their ward's soul, literally kidnapping him from a coven meeting. Mocata has formidable powers, though, and soon lures Simon back. His friends trace him through a girl named Tanith, who is also in thrall to the cult. Soon Rex has fallen for this delicate beauty, and seeks to save her as well.

THE PROTAGONISTS OF *THE DEVIL'S BRIDE* AWAIT A MAGICAL ASSAULT WITHIN THEIR PROTECTIVE CIRCLE.

The ensuing magical war includes a satanic sabbath, led by Old Nick himself in goat-god guise, and a terror-filled night in a magic circle, from which Richlieu pits his white arts against demonic attacks and a visit from the Angel of Death itself. (Richlieu's defenses during the siege include garbled fragments of actual magical ceremony, including the invocation of the four archangels.) The film climaxes with the terrible "Su-Sama ritual," a Doctor-Strangesque showstopper that literally alters the fabric of time itself while dispatching the villainous Mocata and his followers.

The Devil's Bride has its weaknesses, but they're hardly fatal flaws. Director Terence Fisher himself pointed out that the love angle between Tanith and Rex seems superficial; they fall in love mostly to provide an additional emotional dynamic. A "satanic orgy" is weak-tea stuff, though it's probably about as much as the era's censors were likely to accept. More crippling are the film's generally poor special effects. The Angel of Death and a demon played by a poorly matted giant tarantula are particularly unimpressive. In all, though, the film's thoughtfulness and energy more than outweigh a few clumsy visuals.

The Devil's Bride's many graces include Richard Matheson's script, which is several cuts above most Hammer efforts. Wheatley himself considered it to be the best filmic adaptation of his work. Bernard Robinson's production design is typically opulent, and, most important, the lead performances are superb. Charles Gray's suave and epicene Mocata perfectly embodies what Fisher called "the attractiveness of evil." His stern opponent, Richlieu, is probably Christopher Lee's finest role for Hammer, confirming for me that Lee makes a more interesting hero than villain.

Richard Matheson has called the rest of the cast "almost atrocious," and Leon Greene's jutting-jawed Rex does indeed come across as a second-rate Rod Taylor. (Furthermore, his entire role was redubbed by another actor, Patrick Allen.) However, the charge is baseless in the case of Nike Arrighi, whose gentle, waiflike quality is exactly right for the role of Tanith, and a welcome change from Hammer's usual crop of busty Nordic bimbos. Sarah Lawson as Marie Eaton, a friend of Richlieu, is equally fine. Note that, aside from the Duke, the greatest strength of character in *The Devil's Bride* is demonstrated by women, another nice change from the misogyny underlying much of Hammer's work.

As always, Fisher avoids flashy camera work and complex narrative structures in favor of straightforward story-telling. Fisher's control of his material is most evident in the film's most famous scene, in which Mocata calls on Richlieu's allies, the Eatons. During an outwardly polite conversation with Marie Eaton, Mocata slowly places the woman under his mental control. His gradual dominance is suggested in a crisply edited series of shots that counterpoint the magician's soothing drone with his growing hold over Marie and the house's other occupants. It's a deft and quintessentially Fisherian sequence; the charming, mannered Mocata insinuates evil into an innocent household like a plague bacillus.

In *The Devil's Bride*, as in his other films, Fisher seems fundamentally uninterested in the supernatural; the magic circles and crucifixes are simply game tokens. Fisher's real concern lies in character and its consequences—the "charm of evil" versus the higher love, demonstrated in the single-minded, Old Testament righteousness of his heroes. Richlieu, like Van Helsing, is stern, unyielding and rather frightening, anything but charming. Fisher heroes are not

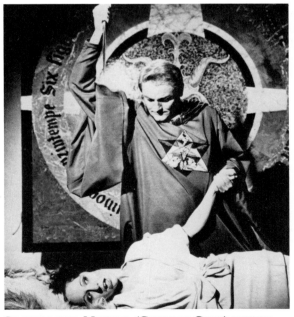

SUAVELY EVIL MOCATA (CHARLES GREY) OFFERS UP *THE DEVIL'S BRIDE*, NIKE ARRIGHI, TO THE DARK ONE.

dreamy-eyed mystics, but calculating, rational technicians who see a job to be done and do it without fanfare...rather like Fisher himself, by all accounts. If he wasn't the *auteur* some imagine him to be, Terence Fisher nonetheless gave us some of the finest genre films of the century.

TO THE DEVIL— A DAUGHTER
Hammer, 1976
P: Roy Skeggs
D: Peter Sykes
S: Christopher Wicking
Starring Richard Widmark (*John Verney*), Christopher Lee (*Father Michael Rayner*), Honor Blackman (*Anna*), Denholm Elliot (*Henry Beddows*), Michael Goodliffe (*George de Grasse*), Natassja Kinski (*Catherine Beddows*), Eva Maria Meineke (*Eveline de Grasse*), Anthony Valentine (*David*), Derek Francis (*Bishop*), and Isabella Telezynska (*Margaret*).

Nightwalkers rating: 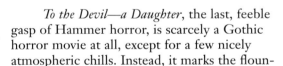 ½

To the Devil—a Daughter, the last, feeble gasp of Hammer horror, is scarcely a Gothic horror movie at all, except for a few nicely atmospheric chills. Instead, it marks the floundering studio's desperate attempt to move with the times by making a glossy, gory shocker with sacrilegious overtones, of the type that had begun to work so well for the major studios.

The movie was based on Dennis Wheatley's 1953 novel of the same name, but its execution is quintessential 1970s cynicism. The basic recipe for *To the Devil—a Daughter* is straightforward enough: combine one part *Rosemary's Baby* with one part *The Exorcist*, and tack on a (surprise!) seventies-style downbeat closer—the same formula that spawned the bloated and enormously successful movie *The Omen* in the same year. Despite its muddled exposition and a botched climax, *To the Devil—a Daughter* is, I think, a much better movie than *The Omen*, but since the latter film is a piece of tripe, this is damning with faint praise.

To the Devil—a Daughter begins promisingly enough, with an ornate excommunication ceremony. The guest of honor is defrocked priest Father Michael Rayner, who refuses to recant from what he insists is *"not a heresy."* Oh, yes it is: Rayner worships the Lord of the Flies, Astaroth, and founds a cult called "the Children of Our Lord" to serve his demonic deity. Twenty years later, a grayer Rayner and his acolytes are very near the culmination of their ultimate goal: the creation of an "avatar" of Astaroth, a demon in human form. Rayner's chosen vessel is a beautiful young girl, Catherine Beddows, who was pledged to the satanic cult from birth—enthusiastically by her mother, who died in a gory birth ritual, and more reluctantly by her drunken, fearful father. Since then, Catherine has been raised as a nun within the cult, which maintains Roman Catholic uniforms and trappings. Rayner and his disciples have succeeded in producing a froglike demon baby (which is really rather cute, in its rubbery way) and now intend to somehow fuse the thing with Catherine to bring about Astaroth's human manifestation.

Catherine's father, Henry Beddows, wants to prevent this, but is bound to the cult by a pact promising death by supernatural fire should he betray Rayner's secrets. Seeking help, he turns to John Verney, an American author of sensationalist novels about the occult (who seems modeled on Wheatley himself). Verney is intrigued by Beddows's story, which sounds like fine material for a new book. He manages to spirit Catherine away from her cultish handlers

NATASSIA KINSKI AS AN INNOCENT DISCIPLE OF ASTAROTH IN THE LAST HAMMER HORROR, *TO THE DEVIL—A DAUGHTER.*

and lodges her in his own London flat, and investigates the cult (learning much of what I've already told you), while Rayner makes increasingly nasty attempts to get her back. Finally, under the satanic priest's control, Catherine murders Verney's friend and agent, Anna (with a rat-tail comb through the ear!), and flees back into the arms of the cult.

At about this point, what was already a confusing movie begins to break down entirely. Hot on Catherine's trail, Verney and another friend, David, find the "pact"—actually a magical talisman—that bound Beddows to the cult; for no apparent reason, the firey curse claims David instead, burning him instantly to a crisp. Catherine, lying on the cult's altar, dreams that the demon-baby crawls up her legs and *roots* into her belly. At this point, the action culminates in what, for its general sense of anticlimax, must rate as one of the most disappointing endings ever. As Rayner sacrifices the demon-tot (why?), Verney sneaks up and clobbers one of his disciples with a baseball-sized rock. Rayner tempts Verney with a vision of a nude, seductive Catherine; Verney then beans Rayner with his rock, scoops up Catherine, and leaves(!). Rayner disappears, off-camera. At fadeout, Catherine's face takes on a decidedly evil expression, unseen by Verney, signalling the audience that he was too late; Astaroth apparently is *already* lodged within Catherine.

To the Devil—a Daughter originally was slated for production by Charlemagne, the short-lived production company created by Christopher Lee and frequent Hammer producer Anthony Nelson-Keys. Hammer picked up the rights to Wheatley's book when Charlemagne evaporated, then struggled for nearly two years to get the project before cameras. The company, nearly always undercapitalized, since the early seventies had relied almost exclusively on production and distribution deals made with British entertainment giant EMI. Now, however, EMI was becoming reluctant to bankroll Hammer's "small" horror movies, in the face of the rising tide of expensive sex-and-gore flicks from the major studios. EMI kicked in with part of the needed funds, however, and after considerable bowing and scraping, Hammer raised coproduction money from Terra Filmkunst, a German company. *To the Devil—a Daughter*'s $1 million price tag made it far and away the most expensive Hammer production ever, but the amount was still a pittance compared to what the majors were spending, even then—it's only a tenth of *The Exorcist*'s budget, for instance.

The money purchased some fairly handsome visuals, if little else. It's disconcerting but pleasant to see a Hammer film making extensive use of modern-day London scenery. As usual with Hammer, the movie also takes advantage of some spectacular stately home settings; the cult's English lair is at West Wycombe Park, a splendid Buckinghamshire mansion that once belonged to Sir Francis Dashwood of Hellfire Club infamy. However, director Peter Sykes demonstrates little ability to marshal these pretty pictures into an involving story. The basic tale is interesting, but it's told in an overly confusing manner, with pointless cross-cutting that makes it difficult to *sort out* the characters, much less become involved with them. Sykes probably wasn't helped in this effort by screenwriter Christopher Wicking, whose other films (such as *Blood from the Mummy's Tomb* and the baffling science-fiction-horror film *Scream and Scream Again*) display the same half-baked artsiness and irritating disinterest in their own stories.

The worst thing about *To the Devil—a Daughter*'s story is that zero of an ending, which apparently came about more or less by default. In an interview in *Shock Express*, Wicking claimed that the "bonk him with a rock" climax was Sykes's fault; Wicking had wanted to take a leaf from *The Devil's Bride* and close out with an actual appearance by Astaroth himself. Lee has said that alternate footage was shot for an ending in which he would be torn apart by invisible demons, but the effects work was probably never completed for this sequence. At any rate, EMI said "good enough" and shoved the thing out the door as is, turning down Hammer chief Michael Carreras's plea for funds to film a punchier conclusion.

To the Devil—a Daughter does offer a few moments of a genuinely spectral eeriness. In particular, there's a chilling flashback to Catherine's birth. Her mother dies horribly, a blood sacrifice, as her terrified father looks on; but then the woman's ghost appears and forces her erstwhile husband to swear loyalty to the Children of Our Lord. (This looks silly in print but actually plays rather well.) However, for each minor Gothic touch, the movie dishes up heaps of rather silly grue intended to shock—again, very much in the spirit of *The Omen* and its countless imitators; characters die in various gooey ways to prove their loyalty to the cult, and so forth. Most memorable is the birth of the demon-baby, which claws its way out of its host-mother's belly (a scene edited out of current United States video prints); in a particularly nasty touch, the woman's legs are tied together to prevent a more natural birth.

Natassja (now Natassia) Kinski was a completely unknown sixteen-year-old at this point; *Tess* was years in the future, and there's little to suggest the ability that she would later display. (She's dubbed throughout the picture, as Hammer so often did with foreign actresses.) Her talent for notoriety, however, is telegraphed by a nude scene that, in view of her age, is rather startling. The crucial role of Verney is thoroughly fumbled by a tired-looking and miscast Richard Widmark. Hammer sought a number of other actors for the role, including Cliff Robertson and, strangely, Richard Dreyfuss (that would have been interesting), but found them too pricey. Widmark reportedly felt the project was well beneath him, refusing to play some scenes and threatening to quit the production on a regular basis. His boredom and dissatisfaction shows through his thin performance all too clearly, and in any case he's entirely lacking in the kind of moral strength and sympathy called for in the part.

By contrast, costar Christopher Lee delivers the goods with his usual ability and an ear-to-ear leer. While it's not a part calling for any particular subtlety, it's really quite a good performance, if you're looking for straight-ahead villainy. His Rayner is a ghastly parody of priestly piety; Lee's eyes gleam with affection and concern as he urges a mangled disciple to die. He's *To the Devil—a Daughter*'s greatest redeeming feature, and its sole link to the Hammer tradition that ended—so far, at least—with this picture.

10

EPILOGUE:

The End of Horror?

By the end of the sixties, the horror boom was already on the wane in terms of quality, and the seeds of its economic failure were present as well, although continuing strength at the box office helped disguise that fact for awhile.

Of the major players, Roger Corman got out first, completing his significant horror work by 1964. His last two Poe films, *Masque of the Red Death* and *Tomb of Ligeia*, received his best critical notices ever but did indifferent business. Sam Arkoff thought the series had finally gotten too damned "artistic" to appeal to the teen audiences AIP depended on, and maybe he was right. Besides, Corman was tired of it, and bankrupt of

ideas; he'd probably taken Poe's limited oeuvre as far as it could go in film. AIP's post-Corman Poe efforts certainly ran into the ground quickly enough, and most of them are utterly forgettable today.

AIP and Corman simply moved on, to other fields ripe for exploitation. Their next project together was *The Wild Angels*, the highly successful prototype for all sixties biker flicks. Corman is still active at this writing, producing much the same sort of movies as ever. His *Jurassic Park* ripoff, for instance, was a bleak and witty little picture called *Carnosaur*, which had a lousy dinosaur and a much more interesting script than Spielberg's money machine. With drive-ins gone the way of velociraptors and independent theaters all but extinct, most of the

THE HORROR OF *ROSEMARY'S BABY*.

movies he backs these days are made for the increasingly lucrative direct-to-video market. After a break of nearly twenty years, Corman returned to directing to make *Roger Corman's Frankenstein Unbound* (1990) an underrated adaptation of a Brian Aldiss science fiction novel involving both Mary Shelley and her fictional creation in a complex time-travel plot. AIP's Jim Nicholson died in 1972, of brain cancer, and Sam Arkoff eventually sold American International to Filmways; but the movie-making itch hadn't left him, and he's been active in production in recent years as "Arkoff International Pictures"—so those famous three initials linger on awhile yet.

The end of Hammer was a more complex and rather sadder affair.

THE FALL OF THE HOUSE OF HAMMER

The breakup of Hammer Film Productions ultimately was prompted by cold economics, but family tensions played a part as well, giving the studio's end a tinge of tragedy.

Like a great many other charismatic leaders, Sir James Carreras appears to have been an aloof and fairly appalling father. Michael Carreras was raised almost entirely by his grandfather Enrique, and relations between father and son remained cool into adulthood. A major clash between the two occurred in 1960, when Jimmy Carreras personally cancelled an ambitious film project of Michael's. The following year, Michael left the company to form an independent production company, Capricorn Films, which continued to develop projects for Hammer. Sir James had no interest in the actual business of filmmaking, and was most useful in any case in his role as Hammer's salesman and ambassador; so Michael's departure forced Anthony Hinds to spend increasing amounts of time attending to the company's operations and finances from its London offices in Wardour Street, rather than at Bray Studios, in the creative role he most enjoyed.

By 1968, Hinds was fed up. In that year, he finished overseeing production of Hammer's first television series, "Journey into the Unknown," a half-hour show for Twentieth Century–Fox that ran a season on ABC in the United States. (A previous failed television pilot, "Tales of Frankenstein," had been made in America in 1958.) In this role, Hinds was forced to defer to an American producer, and reportedly he disliked the experience intensely. Tony Hinds was a very dissatisfied and very wealthy man. Upon his father Will's death in 1959, Anthony had inherited what amounted to a half-interest in Hammer, as well as substantial positions in literally dozens of other companies. Always retiring and temperamentally unsuited for show business, Hinds apparently decided it was time to get out. It's not hard to detect a note of exasperation in his 1969 sale to Sir James of his share of Hammer for the derisory sum of five thousand pounds. Hinds didn't formally resign from the company until 1970, but for all practical purposes he was gone a year earlier.

With both Hinds and Michael Carreras out of the company, Hammer was left without experienced in-house producers. From 1969 on, Sir James began dealing with independent producers for most of Hammer's product, such as Harry Fine and Michael Styles, who made the Carmilla trilogy. This fundamentally changed the nature of the company, making Hammer a releasing rather than a production business, not unlike AIP. Hammer's best movies had been made by a closely knit team that worked together in one location, on one production after another. By 1969, that era was over. Many of the old Hammer's technicians already had left or been fired, and in the year before, the company had abandoned its old home at Bray Studios (due in part to pressure exerted by Associated British Cinemas, Hammer's domestic distributor and the owner of rival Elstree Studios). At first, all these changes didn't matter much, because Hammer still had Sir James's fundraising magic; indeed, Hammer was virtually the only financially solvent movie company left in Britain. But the entire British film industry was sinking on a not-so-even keel.

For more than a decade, British filmmakers had become increasingly dependent on large infusions of American capital. United States companies had found United Kingdom film work to be competent and cheaper than its domestic equivalent, and the American tax code gave certain advantages to overseas operations. By the mid-1960s, all the United States majors had British subsidiaries, and American studios effectively controlled nine-tenths of the output of their British counterparts. Just a few years later, however, this trend was in full retreat. In 1968, the United States Congress eliminated the tax advantages previously available to overseas operations, and American studios began closing their British subsidiaries. Original British projects, meanwhile, were being slaughtered in United States markets, apparently because they were simply out of step with popular (which is to say American) tastes. Hammer had its share of disastrous flops, like its expensive and silly 1969 science fiction epic *Moon Zero Two*.

ONE OF LATE HAMMER'S FEW BRIGHT SPOTS: INGRID PITT IN THE STYLISH AND SEXY *THE VAMPIRE LOVERS*.

Also in 1969, Hammer lost its most influential friend in the American film industry, Eliot Hyman. Hyman, a close friend of Jimmy Carreras, had acted as a silent partner in some forty Hammer films, including *Curse of Frankenstein*, helping to arrange for funding and distribution in the United States market. Hyman realized a long-standing ambition by purchasing Warner Bros. in 1968, and the company immediately took over American distribution chores for Hammer. By the following year, however, Hyman had found that Warner Bros. was in desperate financial shape. The investor sold out to Kinney Corporation, effectively ending Hammer's easy entry to United States markets. Sir James attempted to recover by signing contracts with two of the biggest remaining British film companies, Associated British (later EMI) and the Rank Organization. These companies soon all but committed fiscal hara-kiri by attempting to force their way into the United States market, setting up their own American

distribution offices, and failing spectacularly.

In 1971, Michael Carreras rejoined a very different Hammer from the one he'd left a decade before. He returned at his father's request, to assume day-to-day responsibility for production. Predictably, however, Jimmy and Michael continued to clash. By mid-1972, Jimmy Carreras wanted out. He had the knighthood and a very comfortable lifestyle, which appear to have been his major goals. Sir James began negotiating with a major British conglomerate to buy Hammer, and neglected to tell his son, who only learned of the proposed sale during a production meeting, while his father was away on a cruise. Stung by the news, Michael approached the retirement fund of ICI, one of Britain's largest companies, and borrowed several hundred thousand pounds—enough to buy the company and begin financing a new series of productions—and literally met his father's boat at the dock with his counter-offer. Sir James accepted, and Michael became Hammer's sole proprietor.

Any triumph he felt must have been short-lived. The company he'd acquired was heavily in debt, and had never really been wealthy, due to its heavy reliance on the deep pockets to which Sir James had provided access. Michael Carreras later told *Little Shoppe of Horrors*: "Hammer in general did not take the risks; it used to put up the development money, yes, or persuade people to provide a screenplay, or do it in-house....But when pictures were made, Hammer was extremely reluctant to invest funds in the actual production." Consequently, Hammer essentially got relatively modest fees for the pictures they made, leaving most of the risks *and* the profits to its distributor-backers.

Carreras could take some comfort from the fact that the company still had a production contract with EMI. Moreover, rights to many of Hammer/Exclusive's productions had reverted to the company, and the resulting back catalog of movies could be sold to raise revenue. Could be sold, and *had* been, as it turned out. Only after his purchase did Michael learn that his father had already sold the rights to Hammer's older films. Another, equally serious blow soon followed, when EMI ended its arrangement with Hammer. In Carreras's telling, EMI said in so many words that their deal had been with his father, not him, which must have come as a shattering vote of no-confidence for the fledgling studio head. Michael was a very different personality than his father, just as bright and certainly more creative, but he lacked Sir James's uncanny knack for salesmanship, and would be dogged with financial problems for the remainder of his tenure with the company.

Ironically, as Hammer was dying, its critical discovery had just begun, spurred by one of the most influential books on genre film ever written, David Pirie's *A Heritage of Horror*, a 1973 overview of postwar British Gothic cinema that quickly becomes a sort of high-brow love letter to Hammer. Mr. Pirie is an *auteurist* of the psychoanalytic type, but he's also an extraordinarily intelligent and persuasive one. While some of his interpretations may sound dubious, he undoubtedly caught the attention of the mainstream critics and academics. As Kim Newman puts it in his relentlessly arch *Nightmare Movies:* "After years of being sneered at by British critics and film historians, Hammer Films were rehabilitated. Following David Pririe's seminal study…much interest was shown in a thriving tradition that was just about dead." Note the irony in that last sentence; the beginnings of intellectual respectability did nothing for the company's parlous finances.

The last Hammer horrors, such as *Legend of the Seven Golden Vampires*, continued to do well in world markets, but failed to receive any sort of decent release in the United States—the one market, in those days before the video revolution, that could make the difference between profit and loss. Hammer was dying in large part because the company simply could not compete against others in the niche genre markets it had

created for itself.

In the wake of the tremendous success of *The Exorcist*, major American studios—including the companies that once had acted as Hammer's partners—began crowding into the genre with big-budget scare shows of their own, including the Omen series, *The Sentinel*, and many others. These were mostly mindless, contemptible movies, but they had the stars and the special effects that Hammer couldn't provide. The last Hammer horror, *To the Devil—a Daughter*, 1976, was a naked and unsuccessful attempt to imitate the post-*Exorcist* wave. It was better than most of these films, but inevitably lacked the production values and promotional budget needed to survive in the brave new world of glossy, gory terror pictures. Hammer's final film production, an indifferent 1978 remake of Hitchcock's *The Lady Vanishes*, flopped badly, sinking any hopes of a financial recovery. The company's debt had climbed to £800,000. In April 1979, the bondholders responsible for Carreras's debt to the ICI retirement fund took the company away from him.

It's doubtful that Sir James himself could have kept the company afloat in the turbulent meltdown of the mid-seventies; his old friends at the big studios simply drove the company he'd built out of the market. Two of Hammer's British rivals in low-budget genre films, Tigon and Tyburn, stopped making features in the same period. Amicus broke up in 1975, amid bitter acrimony and accusations of thievery between Milton Subotsky and his partner, Max Rosenberg. Subotsky attempted to carry on as an independent producer for awhile, with little success; the man who had thought Hammer's movies coarse and undignified seemed utterly lost in the era of *The Driller Killer* and *Maniac*. At the decade's end, Margaret Thatcher's Conservatives removed the tax breaks and other incentives that were keeping what little remained of the United Kingdom film industry alive, and most of the British majors were forced out of business.

But Hammer still exists, technically, in a nebulous sort of corporate afterlife reminiscent of that enjoyed by RKO. After Carreras's ouster, Hammer's chief accountant and company secretary, Roy Skeggs and Brian Lawrence, purchased the rights to the Hammer name from the bondholders for £100,000 and used it for two more short-lived television series, "Hammer House of

Horrors" in 1980 and "Hammer House of Mystery and Suspense" in 1984 (the latter seen in America as "Fox Mystery Theater," on the USA cable network). Ironically, both series seemed to owe much more to Amicus's light-weight anthologies than to classic Hammer, and most Hammer fans have little enthusiasm for them. In 1985, Skeggs bought out Brian Lawrence, and little more was heard from Hammer's shadow kingdom for almost a decade.

Hammer diehards received a ray of hope in 1993, when Roy Skeggs signed a four-year agreement with Warner Bros. and director Richard Donner (best known for *Superman*) to remake a series of Hammer classics and to produce a new, forty-four-episode television series (to be called "The Haunted House of Hammer"). Something may yet come of this, but as I write this, at the end of 1994, there's been no word of any follow-through, and those who care are becoming skeptical.

But really, what difference does it make? Any such effort would be Hammer in name only. Like any other trend worth a moment's notice, the Gothic renaissance was the product of a unique combination of economic and cultural conditions and individual talents. The movie business is utterly different now, and most of the key talents involved in the 1957 wave either have retired or have joined the Really Silent Majority. Anthony Hinds is still living in quiet retirement, the sole survivor among Hammer's guiding spirits. Sir James Carreras lived until 1990, long enough to enjoy the well-connected gentleman's life he had wanted so badly. And 1994 brought the deaths of both Michael Carreras and Peter Cushing. Carreras died just two weeks after a dinner of "Old Hammeronians" held largely in his honor. Cushing's death, a few months later, prompted an outpouring of affection and respect from film fans equalled only by that for Vincent

Price, who had left us about a year before. Christopher Lee continues to act, the last of the century's horror icons.

Clearly, the parade has moved on, and any future Gothic revival will be accomplished by a new generation of filmmakers.

BUTCHER-KNIFE CINEMA AND BEYOND

As the Gothic renaissance dissipated, the dominant theme in scary entertainment became what one might call Grand Guignol, after the theater that offered prototypical gore thrills to Parisian audiences over the first half of this century, complete with simulated burnings, eye-gougings and mutilations. This theme can be traced through many, perhaps *most* modern "horror" films, as well as, God knows, any number of R-rated revenge fantasies ("They *kicked* his dog and *dented* his fender and now they'll *PAY!!!*").

I've already alluded to the satanic mini-boom of the early seventies, which ultimately can be traced to Roman Polanski's brilliant 1968 occult thriller, *Rosemary's Baby*. But this cold, rather cerebral film engendered little in the way of immediate imitators, becoming another of those large, isolated rocks in the sea I mentioned earlier in this book. Comes 1973 and *The Exorcist*, blood-hot and visceral, and the demonic floodgates opened, issuing forth a pack of glossy, stupid, high-dollar *Exorcist* wannabes. *The Exorcist* is a movie of considerable merit, with some thoughtful Gothic undercurrents that unfortunately are largely smothered by its gooey terror and suspense themes. Merit and thoughtfulness are qualities not commonly associated with *The Exorcist*'s fol-

PINHEAD, THE DEMONIC MONSTER OF CEREMONIES OF THE *HELLRAISER* SERIES.

lowers, most particularly the *Omen* series, which consists of little more than ridiculous killings, like gory Tex Avery cartoon gags, thinly strung together with a pompous pseudo-Catholicism. Cinematic demonology more or less went into eclipse by the early 1980s, but still surfaced occasionally thereafter, in vehicles like 1988's apocalyptic film *The Seventh Sign*.

The children of *The Exorcist*, though, thick on the ground as they were for awhile, pale into insignificance compared to the bazillion Crazy Guy with a Knife/Chainsaw/Power Tool/Dental Irrigator movies that graced our multiplex screens after the surprise success of John Carpenter's neat little 1978 killer thriller, *Halloween*. We're talking about the movie business, after all, where everyone wants to be first to be second. And just as *The Exorcist* begat *The Omen*, *Halloween* led inevitably to *Friday the 13th* parts I through XVII (to call the *Friday the 13th* series moronic is to insult morons everywhere), and reams of other drivel, all of it unaccountably dubbed "horror."

I don't propose to say much more about gore film here. There are plenty of resources available on these fine entertainments if you happen to enjoy them, as is certainly your constitutionally guaranteed and protected right (stay away from my daughter). Personally, I'd rather be boiled in owl urine than write about this stuff. The makers of gore movies, predictably, have wrapped themselves in the twin mantles of Art and Commerce, and deny any contributing responsibility for the violence, crassness, and sub-literate idiocy that are gradually eroding what we optimistically refer to as our culture. And their rationalizations are no more believable than those of the sleaziest gangsta rapper or Gucci-shod tobacco lobbyist.

By the end of the eighties, the blood-dimmed tide had receded a bit. The gore cycle finally seemed to burn itself out, not so much from PTA outrage as from sheer repetition and a complete lack of ideas and creativity. It was reminiscent of some urban walls you see, on which so much graffiti has been scrawled that the whole expanse finally blends down to an illegible and exhausted-looking grayish black. But the Grand Guignol sensibility lingers on in many, perhaps most alleged horror movies; when Dario Argento, a renowned maker of stylish if incomprehensible violence films, essayed Poe's "The Pit and the Pendulum" a few years back, it took

no brains whatever to predict not only that the deadly blade would sever its victim—naturally, a beautiful woman—but also that Dario would mount the camera on the pendulum and send it swooping through her ripped entrails. (Cool!)

At the risk of repetition, it seems appropriate to return to my opening point: most post-1976 "horror" isn't horror at all. At best, these are stories of terror and suspense. The emotions involved have nothing to do with the sort of impersonal wonder evoked by the best classic horror movies. Instead, they seem content to tickle that mammalian bio-survival circuit: *OhmyGod OhmyGod don't open that door don't open it RUN RUN AAIIIIEEE....* This is, by the way, the appropriate category for our modern "master of horror," the inescapable Stephen King, a storyteller of undeniable talent who can't seem to think of *anything* more frightening than being torn into little teeny pieces. Regardless of the increasingly outré nature of his baddies—whether they're goo-monsters, demon clowns, intelligent automobiles, aliens, or what have you—the bottom line is nearly always physical violence. And nothing more. There's more genuine horror in any four pages of M. R. James than in one of King's three-pounders.

A final point: many modern horror movies mix horror themes with Grand Guignol terrors; the Clive Barker-conceived *Hellraiser* trilogy, a "Dr. Strange meets Leatherface" saga, is a good example. I'm rather fond of this series, particularly its first two entries (the third trails off into gibberish). Barker's conception of a pocket universe inhabited by grotesquely sadistic spirits is genuinely eerie and compelling. But the terror elements constantly shatter the fragile horrific mood; it's hard to sustain a feeling of spectral horror while you're wincing over those gleaming hooks plowing through flesh. Movies like these continually pull us out of wonder, to worry, if vicariously, about our skins.

HORROR REBORN?

The years since 1976 have produced some attempts at "traditional" Gothic horror. Not a whole screaming lot of them, though. We live in a jokey, shallow era, and most modern movies are explicitly designed for teenaged boys—a group whose tastes run quite a bit more to violent action, and to wisecracking horror comedies such as *Evil Dead II*, *Re-Animator*, and their legion of less accomplished imitators. Your average Metallica-shirted mall dupe is about as likely to seek out and enjoy a Verdi opera as something like the *The Innocents*. (But Gregorian chant is back on the charts, so you never know....)

Pickings have been particularly slim for those of us who love ghost stories essayed in the classically creepy manner. (I've a sneaking suspicion that a perceived lack of sex appeal has something to do with their rarity.) The most noteworthy traditional ghost movie of the last fifteen years or so was probably Peter Medak's *The Changeling* (1979), a chilling and undeservedly obscure film concerning a composer who discovers his rented Seattle mansion is haunted by the spirit of a child murdered decades before by his father, a ruthless politician. Despite a few clunky aspects in its story construction, *The Changeling* is a first-rate Gothic gooseflesher, with excellent performances by George C. Scott and Melvyn Douglas; frustratingly, it has little of a following among most horror fans, apparently because the body count isn't high enough. Compared to *The Changeling*, a more recent and more highly praised ghost story in the classical mode, director Frank LaLoggia's *Lady in White* (1988), seems muddled and emotionally counterfeit.

Both films, though, are in every way superior to crashing disappointments like John Carpenter's terrible 1980 flick, *The Fog*, which can't come up with anything for its spooks to do except to stalk various cast members with pointy hooks. At least as bad was the 1981 John Irvin adaptation of Peter Straub's *Ghost Story*, which squanders a fine Gothic atmosphere on a lame string of "revenge from beyond the grave" killings. And of course, there's *Poltergeist* (1982), an entertaining but literally incredible Stephen Spielberg movie (allegedly) directed by Tobe

THE FRIGHTENING RESULT OF ONE OF SPECIAL EFFECTS ARTIST ROB BOTTIN'S INGENIOUS WEREWOLF TRANSFORMATIONS IN *THE HOWLING*.

Hooper. It's a fun roller-coaster ride with a nice central idea (though one blatantly stolen from Richard Matheson's unforgettable "Twilight Zone" episode, "Little Girl Lost"), but it abandons its "spectral" aspects pretty quickly in favor of a typically Spielbergian light show, which strains much too hard to wring wonder out of special effects. About *Poltergeist*'s sequels, the less said the better.

Of the traditional monsters, werewolves staged the most unexpected comeback of the eighties; as is so often the case, the first of this string, *The Howling* (1980), was also the best. *The Howling*'s director, Joe Dante, is a Boomer monster fan who worked every horror in-joke he could think of into the movie, including cameo appearances by *Famous Monsters of Filmland* creator Forry Ackerman and Roger Corman's fifties player Dick Miller; despite the constant pokes in the ribs, however, it's a tense and often frightening picture, with marvelous special effects by Rob Bottin that support rather than overwhelm a neatly horrific story. *The Howling* was followed by *way* too many inferior roman numeral sequels, as well as fitfully interesting titles like *An American Werewolf in London* (1981), Neil Jordan's surreal quasi-art film *The Company of Wolves*, and Stephen King's werewolf tale, *Silver Bullet* (both 1985)—none of which really generate horror. A better movie was 1981's *The Wolfen*. Dubbed by its director, Michael Wadleigh, as "a thinking man's horror film," *The Wolfen* is not quite as smart as it thinks it is, and is punctuated with more or less pointless violence. Its main conceit, though—an ancient race of intelligent and possibly supernatural wolves who lurk in the shadowy places of a modern city—is far-fetched (to say the least) but displays an imaginative intensity almost worthy of Lovecraft.

Speaking of Lovecraft, those of us who

love him are *still* waiting for an effective adaptation (my private dream is for a David Lynch black-and-white version of "The Dunwich Horror"). In fairness to the filmmaking community, it should be acknowledged that mind-boggling extradimensional horrors are by definition rather hard to translate into visual terms (and expensive, at that). Besides, Lovecraft's story poses other problems; they're often nearly as plotless and unpeopled as Poe's. The typical approach in recent years has been to co-opt Lovecraft's increasingly famous name and image, or a plot device such as his "cursed book," the *Necronomicon*, and weave them into a gooey movie that has little to do with his concepts.

The latter-day Lovecraftian cycle began with Sam Raimi's *The Evil Dead* (1983), which involve a Necronomicon-like book that summons up some intensely unpleasant demons; and Stuart Gordon's *Re-Animator* (1985), based faintly indeed on a minor 1922 tale of Lovecraft's. *Evil Dead* spawned two excellent sequels—the first of which, *Evil Dead II*, is a fabulously energetic horror comedy, one of the most entertaining genre works in years. Gordon's *Re-Animator* was almost as good as *Evil Dead II*, and in the same breathless mode—Guignol played for laughs as much as thrills; it was followed by a disappointing sequel. In the late eighties and early nineties, several more sort-of Lovecraftian films emerged, mostly on the direct-to-video market, such as *From Beyond*, *Unnameable*, and *Unnameable II*, *The Curse*, and *The Resurrected*; all pretty forgettable. Regardless of their merits, though, none of the recent movies really succeeds in evoking the doomladen "cosmic" atmosphere of Lovecraft's best work, and most didn't really even try. The most successful cosmic horror ever made owes nothing to the specifics of

ROBERT DENIRO'S BROODING CREATURE IN THE UNDERRATED *MARY SHELLEY'S FRANKENSTEIN* (1994).

Lovecraft; yet Peter Weir's *The Last Wave* (1978) comes closer than any other film so far to capturing Lovecraft's ineffable sense of brooding antiquity, and his profound pessimism for our species' destiny.

Frankenstein and his monster have gotten surprisingly little play in film since the end of Hammer's series—perhaps because (as some of my fellow monster-noodlers have speculated) the basic concept is now simply too close to humdrum medical reality to raise much of a ripple along modern spines. The only big-screen effort worth a look is Kenneth Branaugh's *Mary Shelley's Frankenstein* (1994), a movie that received rather cooler notices than I thought were warranted. It's certainly uneven, but it's a beautiful and audacious movie, done up in high *auteur*-ish style; Branaugh is one of the few overtly Wellesian filmmakers working today. In his film, you're always aware that you're watching an artifice, something that was *directed*, with dazzling, soaring camerawork and larger-than-life performances (and DeNiro as the monster was very close to brilliant). Yet it's also the most faithful rendition of Shelley's novel yet, barring an unfortunate "Bride of Frankenstein" subplot near the end that constitutes the movie's only major flaw. Indeed, the faithfulness of *Mary Shelley's Frankenstein* actually seemed to work against it, as the movie was criticized both for operatic excess and its tragic, downbeat tone—complaints that could be leveled with perfect accuracy against Shelley's novel as well (we tend to forget that *Frankenstein* was written by a teenager, and by all accounts a rather flighty one at that).

Unquestionably, though, the most popular and dependable Gothic denizens of the screen continue to be vampires. While the flow of vampire movies has abated somewhat from the flood of the early 1970s, it has never entirely ceased, particularly in the burgeoning world of direct-to-video releases, which has spawned everything from the moderately traditional and often interesting *Subspecies* series (1991 on) to the vampire cowboys of *Sundown* (1989; released in 1991). Other, somewhat higher-profile variants have included the funny and scary *Fright Night* (1985);

BACK-ROADS GOTHIC: A MOTLEY CREW OF ROAMING VAMPIRES FROM THE EXCELLENT *NEAR DARK*.

Joel Schumacher's overly slick but likeable *The Lost Boys* (1987), with its punk-teen vampires; the infinitely better *Near Dark*, also from 1987, which puts a backwoods, Faulknerian spin on Gothic with its straight-facedly ironic portait of the undead as serial-killing trailer trash; and director John Landis's failed 1993 attempt to co-opt *The Howling*'s distinctive brand of wry humor-horror, *Innocent Blood*.

One factor in the ongoing popularity of vampire cinema is the amazing resilience of the Dracula myth, which continues to attract and defeat filmmakers. As noted earlier, there've been four significant adaptations of Stoker's novel since 1976, if you count the reverent but somewhat dull 1978 BBC *Count Dracula* teleplay starring Louis Jordan; but all fall well short of Hammer's initial effort. Werner Herzog's *Nosferatu the Vampyre* (1979) was a glacial and ultimately boring remake of F. W. Murnau's 1922 version of the story. A few months later came John

Badham's 1979 version of *Dracula*, much hyped in its day and now all but forgotten (it was a financial disaster for Universal). The Badham *Dracula* is a lush, determinedly "romantic" adaptation of the hoary 1920s stage play by Hamilton Deane and John Balderston that originally made Bela Lugosi a star. The movie lurches uneasily between the play's antique camp and flashes of seventies-style gore; Frank Langella's vaguely Latinish, lounge lizard interpretation of the role completely misses the strength and danger embodied by Lee's count, while the indifferent script utterly squanders Laurence Olivier as its Van Helsing. It's a pretty movie, though, if that counts for anything.

Prettier still was Francis Ford Coppola's bizarre 1993 film *Bram Stoker's Dracula*, which weds beautiful, wildly Expressionist visuals with a hopelessly wrong-headed script that "borrows" all the wrong ideas from Dan Curtis's identically titled 1974 version. Coppola's version, which employs the same sort of restraint and understatement he brought to *Apocalypse Now*, is, at heart, Dracula-as-Harlequin Romance, meaning the title is a lie. *Bram Stoker's Dracula* gives us the embarassing sight of the count mooning over Mina like an undead teenager, and concludes with a *Return of the Jedi*-style happy ending death

LOUNGE LIZARD OF DARKNESS: FRANK LANGELLA'S LATIN-LOVER TAKE ON THE UNDEAD COUNT IN THE 1979 *DRACULA*.

for the love-redeemed vampire. Mind you, even on these terms, the movie could have been fun, but the script and performances are mostly lamentable. Gary Oldman's Dracula is quirky enough to be interesting, although his bizarre accent is occasionally indecipherable, but virtually the entire supporting cast is alarmingly vacuous. And what can you say about a movie that casts Anthony Hopkins, our greatest living actor, as Van Helsing and doesn't give him a single decent line?

It seems likely to me that Coppola's lovelorn approach to Dracula was in part an unfortunate byproduct of the most interesting development in Gothic fiction in decades, namely the Anne Rice phenomenon—which began, ironically, just as the last Gothic wave was crumbling, with the 1976 publication of her mega-selling *Interview with the Vampire*. Ms. Rice is several orders of magnitude more gifted than her fellow plutocrat, Stephen King (although her effulgent prose occasionally makes you feel trapped in an elevator with someone wearing too much perfume); her fortune was made largely by her decision to focus on the emotions and problems of her vampires, rather than their victims or pursuers. This use of the vampire's point of view was not an entirely new idea in horror fiction—one thinks immediately of P. Schuyler Miller's brilliant short story, "Over the River"—but certainly the theme had never been as fully developed as it would be in Rice's work.

Interview with the Vampire and its successors are all the more remarkable in view of the fact that their "fright" elements are rather weak. For the most part, Rice's humans aren't even victims but *props*; they're no one we see clearly or care about. Much of the violence in *Interview with the Vampire*—Lestat, for instance, kills several times a night, *every* night, without fail, and

GARY OLDMAN'S BIZARRE MAKEUP IN FRANCIS FORD COPPOLA'S OVERBLOWN *BRAM STOKER'S DRACULA* (1993).

apparently without generating the slightest suspicion or pursuit from human authorities—is therefore curiously unmoving and unconvincing. Her undead, moreover, have few interesting weaknesses beyond an aversion to sunlight. They are powerful almost to the point of silliness, as boringly invulnerable as Superman.

But Rice uses these fairly unpromising premises to achieve something altogether more interesting than a standard horror tale, which is a rich and increasingly detailed meditation on vampire psychology and mores. The much-ballyhooed homoerotic angle in her work doesn't amount to much, unless you're easily shocked. Her vampires, after all, stalk prey and drink blood, they don't have sex per se. But they *do* form emotional attachments among others of their breed, whatever the sex, because the Ricean vampire really only fears loneliness. The most appealing conceit in Rice's imaginative universe is the idea that these vampires are subject to death from a kind of existential despair. The company of their own kind is infrequent and untrustworthy. No longer human, they still feel attachments to man's works and pleasures, to cities, music, boulevard strolls, conversation; and yet, being immortal, they can only watch as the societies in which they feel at home pass away and are replaced by alien glass and steel. And then these troubled vampires know horror themselves, and despair, and sometimes die at last.

Anne Rice's "Vampire Chronicles" have helped inspire an entire school of modern Gothic tales by writers like George R. R. Martin and Chelsea Quinn Yarbro, and her legions of pallid, black-clad fans are heavily represented in a youthful new mini-movement that has adopted the Gothic label as its own, and finds itself highly attracted to the modern vampire esthetic of alienation and ambisexual decadence. It would certainly lend a neat and satisfying symmetry to this book if it could end by implying that Ricean Gothic represents the beginning of a new classic horror cycle, and that may be, but it's a dicey call at this point. The movement remains relatively small, and many of the "Gothic" teens and twenty-somethings one meets these days clearly are just another music-and-fashion tribe of the kind in which Western kids have banded together for some forty years now. (In a different circle of friends, one suspects, many of them could just as easily wind up head-banging to speed metal.)

TOM CRUISE AS LESTAT IN *INTERVIEW WITH THE VAMPIRE*.

There is, nonetheless, a nicely symmetrical note in the fact that, intentionally or not, Ms. Rice's books should be so redolent of Hammer's trademark sensuality and marble-and-velvet elegance—and that, after all the furor and hype, the long-delayed and awaited film version of *Interview with the Vampire* should seem so very much like a high-dollar Hammer movie. I can't honestly say that it was a *great* horror movie; for one thing, although it's largely an intelligent condensation of the novel, it packs too much in and consequently is sketchy at crucial moments. One of the key aspects of Rice's book, for instance, is the growing fascination between Louis, the reluctantly undead protagonist, and the wise but lonely French vampire Armand; but in the film this relationship comes and goes almost too quickly to register with persons not familar with the novel. And, after a largely enjoyable and faithful windup, the movie subjects you to a howlingly stupid "gotcha" ending designed to reassure the move-their-lips-while-reading set that Lestat will indeed be back in *Vampire Chronicles II*. (I wanted to remove this footage with garden shears.)

Yet there was much that was right with the film, after all. Director Neil Jordan pumps some welcome energy into Rice's somewhat slow and uneventful story, and—to get the tabloid controversy out of the way—yes, I thought Tom Cruise was *entirely* adequate as the charming and enthusiastically homicidal vampire Lestat. Brad Pitt's Louis is another matter, but it must be admitted that it's a fairly thankless role, since Louis has little to do beyond looking pensive for much of the story. Pitt accomplishes this, with an odd, half-hearted attempt at an accent and a few wooden line readings. Both actors are overshadowed by Kirsten Dunst's chilling turn as Claudia, the child-vampire whose mind grows cruel and subtle with the passing decades; it's certainly the best performance by a child in a horror film since Martin Stephens's work in *The Innocents*. In all, *Interview with the Vampire* is a satisfying and thoughtful horror tale that takes the traditional Gothic furniture, and a dash of the old Hammer verve, and for most of its length makes them seem fresh again. Which is, I think, as much as we can hope for at this point. We could do a lot worse than to see more of its kind, and given the film's box-office success, perhaps we will.

I told you early on that I wouldn't be concerning myself much with What It All Means, and I was only lying a little bit. But I realize that this book has said some fairly incendiary things about modern horror, and perhaps a few more words are justified. First of all: Yes, I *do* see an apparent contradiction in my position. I've chuckled at the moldy-fig critics of an earlier day who were so shocked, *shocked* by Hammer's sensual and sometimes brutal qualities; yet I've gone all maiden-auntish in a similar fashion over the modern taste for chop-'em-up movies. What gives?

Since I've probably alienated at least a portion of my readership, I'd like to be as clear and precise in my meaning as possible. For one thing, I'm not particularly squeamish. I consider George Romero's *Dawn of the Dead* one of the most interesting American films of the last few decades (although, no, I don't think it's a horror movie), and I even sort of enjoyed *Dead Alive*, a recent absurdist zombie comedy from New Zealand that gleefully billed itself as the goriest movie ever made (which claim, in terms of the sheer gallonage of obviously fake blood poured forth, may very well be accurate). Nor am I hiding any religious agenda, being no more devout than the typical golden retriever.

But I believe that ideas have consequences, and I do worry about the idea embodied both in gore-porn and a good many modern "horror" films. The underlying theme of Grand Guignol entertainment can be stated quite simply: You and I are pieces of meat, and all our interactions—anything we do to or for one another—are merely the random collisions of pieces of meat, without meaning or significance. This is a legitimate artistic position, and one developed with some brilliance by George Romero and others. It's also a tremendously popular idea in mass media. The handful of individuals who decide what appears on television and in our theaters, not being particularly altruistic by nature, must believe it's what you *want* to see.

The Gothic position, by contrast, is that good and evil do exist, and that men's actions carry a moral weight; that our choices count. And if our actions have some sort of importance, maybe we do, too. Maybe we're more than just the sum of our desires and hatreds.

That's an old-fashioned idea, I guess, and not one heard much today other than from televised Christians with amusing hair. But, true or not, and despite its silliness and secondhand nostalgia for a past that never existed, perhaps Gothic is still a useful fable for a world that may be entering a long night, and for a species that is (to paraphrase a favorite author) puzzled and lonely, but never quite defeated.

SELECTED BIBLIOGRAPHY

Arkoff, Sam, with Richard Trubo. *Flying Through Hollywood by the Seat of My Pants*. New York: Carol Publishing Group, 1992.

Beck, Calvin Thomas. *Heroes of the Horrors*. New York: Macmillan Publishing, 1975.

Beck, Calvin Thomas. *Scream Queens: Heroines of the Horrors*. New York: Macmillan Publishing, 1978.

Brosnan, John. *The Horror People*. New York: St. Martin's Press, Inc., 1976.

Butler, Ivan. *Horror in the Cinema*, third edition. New York: A. S. Barnes and Company, 1979.

Carter, Lin. *Lovecraft: A Look Behind the "Cthulhu Mythos."* New York: Ballantine Books, Inc., 1972.

Castle, William. *Step Right Up! I'm Gonna Scare the Pants Off America*. New York: G. P. Putnam's Sons, 1976.

De Camp, L. Sprague. *Lovecraft: A Biography*. Garden City, New York: Doubleday & Company, Inc., 1975.

Corman, Roger, with Jim Jerome. *How I Made a Hundred Movies in Hollywood and Never Lost a Dime*. New York: Dell Publishing, 1990.

Daniels, Les. *Living in Fear: A History of Horror in the Mass Media*. New York: Charles Scribner's Sons, 1975.

Del Vecchio, Deborah, and Tom Johnson. *Peter Cushing: The Gentle Man of Horror and His 91 Films*. Jefferson, North Carolina: McFarland & Company, Inc., 1992.

Derleth, August. *Some Notes on H. P. Lovecraft*. Sauk City, Wisconsin: Arkham House, 1959.

Dixon, Wheeler Winston. *The Charm of Evil: The Life and Films of Terence Fisher*. Metuchen, New Jersey: The Scarecrow Press, Inc., 1991.

Dixon, Wheeler Winston. *The Films of Freddie Francis*. Metuchen, New Jersey: The Scarecrow Press, Inc., 1991.

Eyles, Allen, Robert Adkinson, and Nicholas Fry, eds. *The House of Horror*. London: Lorrimer Publishing, 1973.

Fischer, Dennis. *Horror Film Directors, 1931–1990*. Jefferson, North Carolina: McFarland & Company, Inc., 1991.

Frank, Alan. *The Horror Film Handbook*. Totowa, New Jersey: Barnes & Noble Books, 1982.

Haining, Peter. *The Dracula Scrapbook*. London: Chancellor Press, 1992.

Halliwell, Leslie. *The Dead That Walk*. New York: Continuum Publishing Company, 1988.

Hanke, Ken. *A Critical Guide to Horror Film Series*. New York: Garland Publishing, Inc., 1991.

Hardy, Phil. *The Encyclopedia of Horror Movies*. New York: Harper & Row Publishers, 1986.

Hogan, David J. *Dark Romance: Sexuality in the Horror Film*. Jefferson, North Carolina: McFarland & Company, Inc., 1986.

Jancovich, Mark. *Horror*. London: B. T. Batsford Ltd., 1992.

Kendrick, Walter J. *The Thrill of Fear: 250 Years of Scary Entertainment*. New York: Grove Weidenfeld, 1991.

Knight, Damon. *In Search of Wonder*, 2nd edition. Chicago: Advent Publishers, Inc., 1967.

Lentz, III, Harris M. *Science Fiction, Horror & Fantasy Film and Television Credits*. Jefferson, North Carolina: McFarland & Company, Inc., 1983.

Marrero, Robert. *Horrors of Hammer*. Key West, Florida: RGM Publications, 1984. (Not recommended.)

McGee, Mark Thomas. *Fast and Furious: The Story of American International Pictures*. Jefferson, North Carolina: McFarland & Company, Inc., 1984.

McGee, Mark Thomas. *Roger Corman: The Best of the Cheap Acts*. Jefferson, North Carolina: McFarland & Company, Inc., 1988.

McNally, Raymond T., and Radu Florescu. *In Search of Dracula*. New York: Galahad Books, 1972.

Meikle, Denis. *A History of Horror: The Rise and Fall of the House of Hammer, 1947–1979*. Metuchen, New Jersey: The Scarecrow Press, Inc., 1995.

Morris, Gary. *Roger Corman*. Boston: Twayne Publishing, 1985.

Moskowitz, Sam. *Seekers of Tomorrow: Masters of Modern Science Fiction*. Westport, Connecticut: Hyperion Press, Inc., 1974.

Murphy, Michael J. *The Celluloid Vampires: A History*

and Filmography, 1897–1979. Ann Arbor, Michigan: The Pierian Press, 1979.

Naha, Ed. *The Films of Roger Corman: Brilliance on a Budget.* New York: Arco Publishing, Inc., 1982.

Newman, Kim. *Nightmare Movies.* New York: Harmony Books, 1988.

Nicholls, Peter, ed. *The Science Fiction Encyclopedia.* Garden City, New York: Doubleday & Company, Inc., 1975.

Pirie, David. *A Heritage of Horror: The English Gothic Cinema, 1946–1972.* New York: Avon Books, 1973.

Pirie, David. *The Vampire Cinema.* London: Hamlyn Publishing Group, 1977.

Pitts, Michael R. *Horror Film Stars*, second edition. Jefferson, North Carolina: McFarland & Company, Inc., 1991.

Pohle, Jr., Robert W., and Douglas C. Hart. *The Films of Christopher Lee.* Metuchen, New Jersey: The Scarecrow Press, Inc., 1983.

Skal, David J. *The Monster Show: A Cultural History of Horror.* New York: W. W. Norton & Company, 1993.

Ursini, James, and Alain Silver. *The Vampire Film.* New York: A. S. Barnes and Company, 1975.

Waller, Gregory A. *The Living and the Undead.* Urbana, Illinois: University of Illinois Press, 1986.

Warren, Bill. *Keep Watching the Skies!: American Science Fiction Movies of the Fifties.* Jefferson, North Carolina: McFarland & Company, Inc., 1982 and 1986.

Weaver, Tom. *Interviews with B Science Fiction and Horror Movie Makers.* Jefferson, North Carolina: McFarland & Company, Inc., 1988.

Weaver, Tom. *Science Fiction Stars and Horror Heroes.* Jefferson, North Carolina: McFarland & Company, Inc., 1991.

Wolf, Leonard. *A Dream of Dracula: In Search of the Living Dead.* New York: Little, Brown & Company, 1972.

Wolf, Leonard. *Horror: A Connoisseur's Guide to Literature and Film.* New York: Facts on File, 1989.

PERIODICALS

Castle of Frankenstein. North Bergen, New Jersey: Gothic Castle Publishing, 1962–1975.

No. 4, 1964: "*The Haunting,*" by Randolph Carter and Joseph Kaye; and "Curse of a Vampire," by Michel Parry.

No. 5, 1964: "*The Evil of Frankenstein,*" by

Nicholas Morgan.

No. 7, 1965: "A Visit to the Set of *Die, Monster, Die!*" and "Interview with Daniel Haller," by Michel Parry.

No. 8, 1966: "Roy Ashton: Monster Makeup Master of Hammer Films," by Michel Parry.

No. 19, 1972: "*Dracula A.D. 1972,*" by Nicholas Morgan; and "*Countess Dracula,*" "*Vampire Circus,*" "*Twins of Evil,*" and "*Blood from the Mummy's Tomb,*" by Cal T. Beck.

No. 22, 1974: "Peter Cushing on Frankenstein and Others," by Peter Cushing; and "*The Legend of Hell House,*" by Cal T. Beck *et al.*

No. 24, 1974: "The Many Faces of Boris Karloff," by Michel Parry and Harry Nadler.

Cinefantastique. Oak Park, Illinois: Frederick S. Clarke, 1970–present.

Vol. 2, No. 4, Summer 1973: "The Amicus Empire," by Chris Knight; "The Parallel Worlds of Jacques Tourneur," by John McCarty; "Tourneur Remembers," by Joel E. Siegel; "*Vampire Circus*" and "*Countess Dracula,*" by David Bartholomew; and "*Dracula A.D. 1972,*" by Lee M. Kaplan.

Vol. 3, No. 3, Fall 1974: "Castle: The Horror of Personality Directors," by Dan R. Scapperotti.

Vol. 3, No. 4, Winter 1974: "*Captain Kronos: Vampire Hunter,*" by Tim Lucas; and "*Frankenstein and the Monster from Hell,*" by John McCarty.

Vol. 4, No. 3, Fall 1975: "Terence Fisher: The Human Side" and "Terence Fisher: Underlining," by Harry Ringel.

Vol. 9, No. 1, Hall 1979: "*The Seven Brothers Meet Dracula,*" by Bill Kelley.

Vol. 13, No. 6/Vol. 14, No. 1 (double issue), September 1983: "Herk Harvey's *Carnival of Souls,*" by Jeffrey Frentzen.

Vol. 13, No. 5, June–July 1983: "Jack Clayton's *The Innocents,*" by Stephen Rebello.

Vol. 19, Nos. 1–2 (double issue), January 1989: "Vincent Price: Horror's Crown Prince," by

Steve Biodrowski and David Del Valle.

Vol. 20, No. 5, May 1990: "*Carnival of Souls*," by Daniel Schweiger.

Vol. 22, No. 1, August 1991: "Michael Reeves: Horror's James Dean," by Bill Kelley.

Filmfax. Evanston, Illinois: Michael Stein, 1986–present.

No. 7, June/July 1987: "*Curse of the Demon*," by Michael Dee; and "*The Haunting*," by Bill Schoell.

No. 14, March/April 1989: "Hammer Glamour," by Gary A. Smith; and "Veronica Carlson," by Mark A. Miller.

No. 15, May/June 1989: "An Interview with Ingrid Pitt," by Al Taylor.

No. 16, August 1989: "*Carnival of Souls*," by Michael Stein.

No. 19, March 1990: "The Diva of Dark Drama: Barbara Steele," by Mark A. Miller.

No. 20, May 1990: "Britain's Duchess of Dark Drama: Hazel Court," by Mark A. Miller.

No. 26, April/May 1991: "Call Me Sam (Arkoff, that is!)" by Mark Voger.

No. 37, February/March 1993: "Hinds Horrors: Forging the Fright Fantastic," by Randy Palmer.

No. 42, December 1993/January 1994: "The Art of Fright: Celebrating the Life of Vincent Price," by David J. Hogan; "And in the Beginning Was the Word: An Interview with Screenwriter Richard Matheson," by Matthew R. Brady; "Priceless," by Gregory J.M. Catsos; and "The Amicus Empire: An Interview with Milton Subotsky," by Dennis Fischer.

Little Shoppe of Horrors. Des Moines, Iowa: Richard Klemensen, 1972–present.

No. 4, April 1978: "Hammer: Yesterday, Today and Tomorrow," by Richard Klemensen *et al*.

No. 5, August 1980: "Anthony Hinds" and "Syd Pearson," uncredited interviews.

No. 6, July 1981: "Terry Fisher," by Bob Sheridan; and "The Evolution of the *Brides of Dracula*," by Oscar A. Martinez and Bob Sheridan.

No. 7, December 1982: "Barbara Shelley" and "*Captain Kronos: Vampire Hunter*," by Al Taylor.

No. 8, May 1984: "The Karnstein Trilogy," by Bruce G. Hallenbeck; and "Two Little Seen Hammers," by Dennis Fischer.

No. 9, March 1986: "The Story of Bray Studios," by Fred Humphreys; and "The Making of *Vampire Circus*," by Bruce G. Hallenbeck.

Nos. 10–11 (double issue), July 1990: "New Blood: Second Thoughts on Hammer," by David Schleicher; "The Making of *Kiss of the Vampire*," by Bruce G. Hallenbeck; "Andree Melly," by Oscar Martinez; and "John Carson," by Al Taylor.

No. 12, April 1994: "Dennis Wheatley at Hammer," by Bruce G. Hallenbeck; and "Sir James Carreras: The Man Who Would Be King," by Denis Meikle.

Scarlet Street. Teaneck, New Jersey.: R. H. Enterprises, Inc., 1991–present.

No. 9, Winter 1993: "Mornings with Peter Cushing," by Richard Valley; "Veronica Has Risen from the Grave," by Bruce G. Hallenbeck; and "The Cushing Collection," various authors.

No. 13, Winter 1994: Vincent Price As I Remember Him," by Roger Corman; and "Lovecraft on Screen," by Robert M. Price.

No. 14, Spring 1994: "Cat Girls, Gorgons, and Shakespeare: Barbara Shelley," by Bruce G. Hallenbeck.

No. 15, Summer 1994: "Hammer's Man of Many Parts: Michael Ripper," by Bruce G. Hallenbeck.

INDEX

NOTE: Page numbers in *italics* indicate illustrations/captions.

MAYWOOD PUBLIC LIBRARY
459 Maywood Ave.
Maywood, NJ 07607

791.43
WRI

1/00

Maywood Public Library
Maywood, NJ 07607

GAYLORD S